CHASING PROGRESS IN THE IRISH REPUBLIC
Ideology, democracy and dependent development

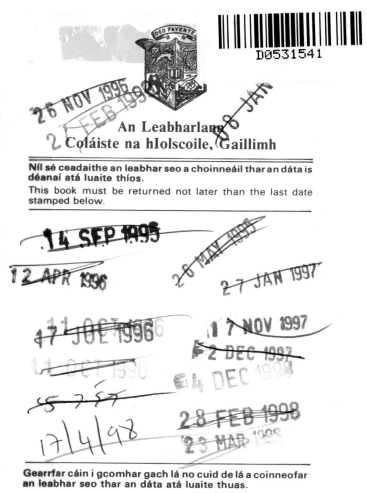

CHASING PROGRESS IN THE IRISH REPUBLIC

Ideology, democracy and dependent development

JOHN KURT JACOBSEN

Program in International Politics, Economics, and Security.
Department of Political Science University of Chicago

CAMBRIDGE
UNIVERSITY PRESS

Published by the Press Syndicate of the University of Cambridge
The Pitt Building, Trumpington Street Cambridge CB2 1RP
40 West 20th Street, New York, NY 10011-4211, USA
10 Stamford Road, Oakleigh, Melbourne 3166, Australia

First published 1994

Printed in Great Britain at the University Press, Cambridge

A catalogue record for this book is available from the British Library

Library of Congress cataloguing in publication data

Jacobsen, John Kurt
Chasing progress in the Irish Republic: ideology, democracy,
and dependent development / John Kurt Jacobsen.
p.   cm.
Originally presented as the author's thesis (Ph.D. – University of Chicago), 1982.
Includes bibliographical references.
ISBN 0 521 44078 5 (hc)
1. Ireland – Economic conditions. 2. Ireland – Industries – History.
3. Industry and state – Ireland. I. Title.
HC260.5.J33 1994
338.9417 – dc20   93–5649 CIP

ISBN 0 521 44078 5 hardback
ISBN 0 521 46620 2 paperback

To the memory of my mother
Helen Rose Jacobsen

Where are our twenty millions of Irish, should be here today instead of four, our lost Tribes? And our pottery and textiles, the finest in the whole world! And our wool that was sold in Rome in the time of Juvenal and our flax and our damask from the looms of Antrim and our Limerick lace, our tanneries and our white flint glass down there by Ballybough and our Huguenot poplin that we have since Jacquard de Lyon and our woven silk and our Foxford tweeds and ivory raised point from the Carmelite convent in New Ross, nothing like it in the whole wide world! Where are the Greek merchants that came through the pillars of Hercules, the Gibraltar now grabbed by the foe of all mankind, with gold and Tyrolian purple to sell in Wexford at the fair of Cormen. Read Tacitus and Ptolemy, even Giraldus Cambrensis. Wine, Peltries, Connemara marble, silver from Tipperary, second to none, our far-famed horses even today, the Irish hobbies, with King Philip of Spain offering to pay customs duties for the right to fish in our waters. What do the yellow-johns of Anglia owe us for our ruined trade and our ruined hearths? And the beds of the Barrow and the Shannon they won't deepen with millions of acres of marsh and bog to make us all die of consumption.

—As treeless as Portugal we'll be soon, says John Wyse, or Heligoland with its one tree if something is not done to reafforest the land. Larches, firs, all the trees of the conifer family are going fast. I was reading a report of lord Castletown's . . .

—Save them, says the citizen, the giant Ash of Galway and the chieftain elm of Kildare with forty-foot bole and an acre of foliage. Save the trees of Ireland for the future men of Ireland on the fair hills of Eire, O.

—Europe has its eyes on you, says Lenihan.

James Joyce, Ulysses

Contents

Acknowledgments

I must confess that this book is an outgrowth of a Ph.D. dissertation. Had I not on my first day as a University of Chicago graduate student encountered Lloyd Rudolph, who became my dissertation chairman, I would not have seriously considered an academic career. Lloyd demonstrated that a scholarly life can be a terribly worthwhile one. (I have since had plenty of misgivings but that's nothing to do with him.) I count myself fortunate to know him.

Philippe Schmitter was a superb guide into the realms of Western European politics and economic policy-making. Adam Pzreworski was highly influential in ways that may not be always apparent. Charles Lipson showed up at the university just in time to sharpen my knowledge of the field of international political economy.

I also benefited from contact with Ira Katznelson, Susanne Rudolph, Paul Ricoeur and David Greenstone. Later, as a research associate in the University of Chicago's Program on International Politics, Economics and Security (PIPES), I enjoyed the camerraderie and encouragement of Duncan Snidal, Daniel Verdier and especially Charles Lipson. All three made valuable suggestions on portions of this manuscript – some of which I even heeded.

I also profited from comments on parts or the whole of the manuscript by Jim Caporaso, Raymond Duvall, John Freeman, Jeff Friedan, Emmet Larkin, Brendan O'Leary, Kenny Thomas, Jim Wickham and three anonymous referees from Cambridge University Press. Joel Krieger deserves a special acknowledgment for aiding and abetting the entire enterprise. In Dublin, Basil Chubb gave valuable pointers to a novice researcher who had suddenly appeared at his doorstep. Patrick Lynch at UCD was flatteringly enthusiastic and helpful.

In Ireland I conducted dozens of interviews over several visits spanning ten years. Some interviewees are now gone. I especially want to thank Dr. Noel Browne, John Carroll, Basil Chubb, Anthony Coughlin, Garrett Fitzgerald, George Gilmore, Cathal Goulding, Dermot McAleese, Louden Ryan, Matt Merrigan, Kieran Kennedy, Michael J. Killeen, Patrick J. Lalor, Patrick Lynch, Dan McAuley, Charles McCarthy, Eugene McCarthy, Eoin O'Malley, Manus O'Riordan, Seamus Sheehy, Eamon Smullen, John Throne, Brian Trench, Paddy Whally, Jim Wickham, T. K. Whitaker and many more people I encountered formally and informally at the Industrial Development Authority and at the Department of Agriculture.

Skylla MacNamara maintained a tyrannical typing regimen, waiting impatiently to snatch each sheet of scrawlings from my hands, and thereafter pounced mercilessly upon miscreant sentences, incomplete references and whatnot. The manuscript is much the better for it. Skylla and Desmond MacNamara are dear friends and invaluable consultants on my voyages into Irish life and lore. Alba Alexander, keeper of winged wonder Ceres, spent a great deal of time lending a sympathetic ear – though I think we're even. I have to single out Dr. Noel Browne for being his inspiring, courageous and disputatious self. Thanks also for various reasons to Steven Bronner, Marie-Louise Colbert, Seamus De Burca, the late Peter Knauss, Manny and Ghisha Koenig, Billy Leahy, Robert Melville, Ruth Torrode, Brian Torrode, Mary and Hugh Schmuttenmayer and Jack and Nell Wendler.

I am grateful for the use of research facilities at Trinity College Dublin, University College Dublin, The National Library of Ireland, and the Industrial Development Authority of Ireland. In London I used the libraries at the University of London and the London School of Economics. In Chicago, of course, I toiled in Regenstein Library. A University of Chicago Travelling Scholarship funded my first Irish sojourn.

Parts of this work appeared in *Studies: An Irish Quarterly Review*, *Dissent*, *International Studies Quarterly* and *The International Political Economy Yearbook*. My deep thanks to Sheila McEnery for her astute copyediting. Finally, thanks to John Haslam at Cambridge University Press for shepherding the work through publication. As anyone acquainted with my stubbornness will appreciate, the usual disclaimer applies with special force.

Introduction

In a radio broadcast on Easter day 1943, Eamon DeValera, patriarchal Prime Minister of the Irish Free State, described his vision of a self-sufficient Gaelic nation replete with comely maidens, cosy homesteads and, presumably, a reunited Ulster. "The Ireland we dreamed of would be the home of a people who valued material wealth only as a basis of a right living," the Fianna Fail party leader intoned, "of a people who were satisfied with a frugal comfort and devoted their leisure to things of the spirit. It would, in a word, be the home of a people living the life that God desired men to live."[1] In 1958 the autarkic policies Fianna Fail had promoted since it first assumed political power a quarter century earlier were abandoned without fanfare or remorse. A "post-revolutionary" generation of self-proclaimed pragmatists steered their fraction of the island into Europe – by which they meant the common market – and the era of push button technology. God evidently desired that the Irish enjoy more prosperity.

Banishing the donkey-and-cart age to Tourist Board posters the Irish Republic industrialized by introducing economic planning – euphemized in the accurately timid term "programming" – and, more importantly, by converting itself into a haven for footloose capital. These two tactical strands interwove in a frayed way in the export-led development strategy by which policy-makers commenced "chasing progress."[2]

This "comparatively informed study" focuses on the interplay

---

[1] Oliver MacDonough, *Ireland: The Union and Its Aftermath* (2nd ed., London: George Allen and Unwin, 1977), p. 128.

[2] My title is plucked from the following quote referring to Sean Lemass, Irish Prime Minister 1959–66: "Lemass ... saw himself as a 'progress-chaser' ... he encouraged initiative, even unbridled initiative, and the spirit of competition among the new generation of young men

between policy-makers and domestic groups as they devise (or clash over) strategies for maneuvering within changing patterns of international trade and investment. The Irish Republic arguably occupies a fringe zone between advanced industrial states and the nations identified in the polite jargon of economists as "new industrializing" countries.[3] Ireland shares the Third World characteristics of a large (if shrinking) agricultural sector, high birth rates, underutilized resources (especially human resources) and a colonial heritage complete with a racist stereotyping that has not yet vanished in regions constituting the United Kingdom.[4] Hence, I draw upon Third World scholarship, particularly dependent development literature, to illuminate the Irish plight.[5] Unlike "vulgar" versions of *dependencia*, I will investigate how domestic actors influence policy response.

States are vital mediators of the impact of exogenous forces upon domestic groups whose political alliances, in turn, shape policy outcomes. This statement is now a truism in international political economy studies. But the prospects for success of any group's project depends not only on how congruent it is with the structure of opportunities offered by the global economy but also on the ability of a group to invoke the "conventional wisdoms" of economic policy so as to augment their project's desirability in the eyes of other social actors whose consent is needed to win political struggles over policy choices. This crucial ideological dimension requires analysis if we are to explain the dynamics and outcomes of policy conflict satisfactorily.

The first chapter spells out this argument in the context of debates over the analysis of policy choice, particularly in developing econo-

who had now reached office." In Basil Chubb, *Cabinet Government in Ireland* (Dublin: Institute of Public Administration, 1974), p. 36.

[3] The study intends to join "comparatively informed studies of critical cases" in which comparative assessment enters into the selection of the historical instance studied and speaks explicitly to the generalizability of the case study's findings. Peter Evans, Dietrich Rueschemeyer, and Theda Skocpol, "On The Road To A More Adequate Understanding of The State," in Evans, Rueschemeyer, and Skocpol, eds., *Bringing The State Back In* (Cambridge: Cambridge University Press, 1985), p. 349.

[4] On racist depictions of the Irish, which still pop up in the seamier English tabloids, see L. Perry Curtis, *Apes and Angels: The Irishman in Victorian Caricature* (Washington DC: Smithsonian Institution, 1971) and Richard Ned Lebow, *White Britain and Black Ireland: The Influence of Stereotypes On Colonial Policy* (Philadelphia: Institute for The Study of Human Issues, 1976).

[5] See Thomas Biersteker, *Multinationals, The State, and Control of The Nigerian Economy* (Princeton: Princeton University Press, 1987), pp. 11–51.

mies. Chapter 2 develops this analytical tack and specifies its useful-
ness in explaining policy-making in small open economies that must
manage tensions between domestic planning and foreign (and, for
that matter, local) investment. Chapter 3 supplies an historical
survey to enable readers to grasp the patterns of political and
economic development behind the evolution of policy patterns, that
conditioned the state's mediating role. This study strongly endorses
the view that "policy research should be based on *in-depth longitudinal
analysis* that views policy and change in policy as adaptation to
changing conditions and changing elite and mass perceptions, attitudes, and values" which requires "historical analysis of the circumstances surrounding the emergence of particular programs and
changes in programs, as well as a knowledge of the characteristic
development path or experience of particular countries."[6]

Chapter 4 investigates the "Irish miracle" period 1958–1973
when export-led industrial development generated genuine
economic gains and a virtual political consensus. Chapter 5 examines the influence exerted by "social partners" in quasi-corporatist
bodies such as the National Industrial Economic Council, and the
latter's impact on policy. Since 1970 the Industrial Development
Authority has been the central agency coordinating industrialization and so is scrutinized regarding its political and ideological
power and constraints. Chapter 6 examines responses by policy-
makers to adverse international conditions in the 1970s and to the
political exhaustion of the prevailing economic policy. Chapter 7
analyzes the subsequent struggle, easily won by groups championing
conservative diagnoses, to promote a successor project for development, to define the next "stage" or "phase." The work concludes
with the January 1993 election.

This study aims to provide a rigorous and provocative analysis of
modern Irish politics. Second, and more specifically, it contributes
an examination of the dynamics of policy-making within a small
open economy to the literature on international political economy.
Third, this work illustrates how ideas interact with material interests
to influence economic policy.

---

[6] Leon Lindberg, "General Introduction," in Leon Lindberg, et al., eds., *Stress and Contradiction in Modern Capitalism* (Lexington, MA: D.C. Heath, 1975), p. xii.

CHAPTER I

Reflex modernization:
state, ideology and dependent development

> The superior law of progress of the human spirit carries along
> and dominates everything, men are but its instruments.
>
> Saint-Simon

In a passage that an Irish audience might regard as a wickedly inaccurate jest, Karl Marx wrote that the "country that is more developed industrially only shows to the less developed the image of its future."[1] To be fair, Marx later in *Das Kapital* acerbically analyzed the plight of Ireland: "only an agricultural district of England, marked off by a wide channel from the country to which it yields corn, wool, cattle, industrial and military recruits."[2] But at that time colonies did not offer evidence of the fabled industrial tendencies "working with iron necessity toward inevitable results."[3] As deterministic as that phrase sounds, Marx was driven on occasion to admonish disciples who "absolutely must metamorphose my historical sketch of the genesis of capitalism into an historico-philosophic theory of the general path every people is fated to tread, whatever the historical circumstances in which it finds itself . . ."[4]

Ironically, a host of twentieth-century scholars hostile to Marxism identified progress with an image of lockstep industrial development. In his *Non-Communist Manifesto*, W. W. Rostow, for example, championed the Saint-Simonian notion of "stages of growth"

---

[1] Karl Marx, *Capital* (New York: International Publishers, 1958), vol. I, pp. 8–9.

[2] *Ibid.*, pp. 702–3.

[3] Baran and Sweezy observe that "Marx probably intended his message only for a group of independent and actually developing capitalist countries. 'De te fabula narratur' was specifically addressed to Germans who might think their country could escape the fate of Britain; and when he spoke of industrially less developed countries seeing the image of their future in the most developed, he probably had in mind countries which were developed by the standards of the time only less so than Britain." Paul Baran and Paul Sweezy, *Monopoly Capital: An Essay on The American Economic and Social Order* (London: Pelican, 1968), p. 25 fn.

[4] Quoted in Krishan Kumar, *Prophecy and Progress* (London: Penguin, 1978), pp. 61–62.

leading mankind linearly from the squalid pre-Newtonian world to one enjoying "the blessings and choices opened up by the march of compound interest."[5] In the late 1960s a scholar could still view the Faustian fray and conclude that historical experience "supports the notion of a single world historical development in which advanced nations advance further, and others follow their path to improvement."[6]

If religions were the opiate of the masses, the idea of progress was the opiate of elites. Science and technology, unhindered by yahoos and Luddites, would beget a new millennium – preferably a democratic and capitalist millennium. Political development consisted "in the elaboration of new and more complex forms of politics and government as societies restructure themselves so as to absorb progressively the stock and flow of modern technology."[7]

Industrialization denotes transformations in the productive apparatus of a society, but this occurs within a more encompassing process, termed "modernization." Landes defines modernization as "that combination of changes – in the mode of production and government, in the social and institutional order, in the corpus of knowledge and in attitudes and values – that makes it possible for a society to hold its own in the twentieth century; that is, to compete on even terms in the generation of material and cultural wealth, to sustain its independence, and to promote and to accommodate to further change."[8] Here appears urbanization, secularization, bureaucratization, the division of labor, individualization of conduct, reduction of birth rates, and mass education. "The one ingredient of modernization that is just about indispensable," Landes emphasizes, "is technological maturity and the industrialization that goes with it; otherwise one has the trappings without the substance, the pretence without the reality."[9] So every civilization

[5] W. W. Rostow, *The Stages of Economic Growth: A Non-Communist Manifesto* (London: Cambridge University Press, 1960), p. 6.

[6] Sidney Pollard, *The Idea of Progress: History and Society* (London: Pelican, 1968), p. 203.

[7] W. W. Rostow, *Politics and The Stages of Economic Growth* (London: Cambridge University Press, 1971), p. 3.

[8] David S. Landes, *The Unbound Prometheus: Technological Change and Industrial Development in Western Europe from 1750 To The Present* (London: Cambridge University Press, 1969), p. 6.

[9] *Ibid.*, p. 7. Reinhard Bendix distinguishes the terms "industrialization," "modernization," and "development" in the following way: "By *industrialization* I refer to *economic* changes brought about by a technology based on inanimate sources of power as well as on continuous development of applied scientific research. *Modernization* (sometimes called *social* and *political development*) refers to all those social and political changes that accompanied

can taxi along the Western-built runway for "take-off" into self-sustaining industrial growth. "The attribution of an inherent dynamism to the process of change is particularly evident in the use of '-ization' suffix words," Winner warns, "Here, perhaps, unintentionally, connotations of a self-generating, self-sustaining process frequently creep in."[10]

Modernization is variously described as the transition from folk society to urban (Redfield), *Gemeinschaft* to *Gesellschaft* (Tonnies), mechanical solidarity to organic (Durkheim), the sacred to the secular (Becker), familistic to contractual relationships (Sorokin), and patrimonial to legal-rational activity (Weber). In some self-caricaturing forms, modernization theories simulated the human maturation process. So the "icy waters of egotistical calculation" wash over puerile primitive cultures, transforming them into mature sophisticated societies. "Progress, if the concept were to sustain itself, could now only mean industrialization," Kumar writes, "And if, as in past ages, there was a dark side to the current phase, this was remediable phenomenon, necessary but temporary."[11]

Britain, the "workshop of the world," appeared far too difficult and idiosyncratic for other nations to imitate. Even in the heyday of English industrialism "the road to the free market was opened and kept open by an enormous increase in continuous, centrally organized and controlled interventionism."[12] Endowed with an unparalleled industrial base, an unchallenged navy, and a mobile and relatively skilled labor force, the British state need not intrude ostentatiously in the economic sphere. The leading industry, cotton

industrialization in many countries of Western civilization. Among these are urbanization, changes in occupational structure, social mobility, development of education – as well as political changes from absolutist institutions to responsible and representative governments, and from a *laissez-faire* to a modern welfare state. More simply, the two terms refer to the technical-economic and socio-political changes familiar to us from the recent history of Western Europe. The term *development* may be used where reference is made to related changes in both these spheres." Bendix, *Nation-Building and Citizenship: Studies of Our Changing Social Order* (2nd ed., Berkeley and Los Angeles: University of California Press, 1977), pp. 6–7.

[10] Langdon Winner, *Autonomous Technology: Technics-Out-Of-Control As A Theme in Political Thought* (Cambridge, MA: MIT Press, 1977), pp. 49–50.

[11] Kumar, *Prophecy and Progress*, p. 46.

[12] Karl Polanyi, *The Great Transformation: The Political and Economic Origins of Our Times* (Boston: Beacon Press, 1957), p. 140.

textiles, had been encouraged by tariffs; and historians since have cited a variety of state activities supporting industry.[13]

Where continental European states could not induce sufficient private investment, the state assumed these functions. Beside creating credit institutions, institutes for technical training, and public commercial enterprises, Landes writes that these states:[14]

provided technical advice and assistance, awarded subventions to inventors and immigrant entrepreneurs, bestowed gifts of machinery, allowed rebates and exemptions of duties on imports of industrial equipment. Some of this was simply a continuation of the past – a heritage of the strong tradition of direct state interest in economic development.

In his study of "latecomers," Gerschenkron identified the "basic propensity of a backward country to concentrate on areas of most recent technological progress, and thus to utilize the specific advantages of backwardness."[15] Germany, Italy, France, and Russia could purchase technologies, integrate them into their native "mix" of resources and selectively imitate the most relevant features of the British experience.

In the twentieth century new nations emerging from colonialism were eminently eligible to exploit the dubious advantages of backwardness. But Horowitz sourly cites disadvantages too: (1) intensification of features of modern labor that produce alienation; (2) the increasing gap between rural skills and industrial and commercial training; (3) the jarring effect of bureaucratized life; (4) a rise in competition between town (proletariat) and country (peasantry); and, not least, a "fantastically wide gap between' wealth and poverty as a function of the internationalization of class exploitation."[16]

If new nations had the aspirations, the West possessed the prescriptions for speeding economic growth and – sometimes simultaneously – maintaining political order. "To those primarily interested in buttressing a Western nation's political position in Africa or in

[13] Eric J. Hobsbawm, *Industry and Empire: An Economic History of Britain Since 1750* (London: Penguin Books, 1971), p. 21.

[14] Landes, *The Unbound Prometheus*, p. 151.

[15] Alexander Gerschenkron, *Economic Backwardness in Historical Perspective* (Cambridge, MA: Harvard University Press, 1962), p. 56. Also see the amended application of this analysis by James R. Kurth, "The Political Consequences of The Product Cycle: Industrial History and Political Outcomes, *International Organization*" 33, 1 (Winter 1979).

[16] Irving L. Horowitz, *Three Worlds of Development: The Theory and Practice of International Stratifications* (New York: Oxford University Press, 1972).

other spheres of 'primitive' or 'retarded' culture," Robert A. Nisbet pointedly writes, "the theory of social evolution was, of course, a marvellous justification for ascendency of the West," and for increasing economic interdependence and security ties.[17]

Industrial "prerequisites" were propounded, modified, resurrected. "Attribute checklists" were rife. The "logic of Industrialism" was evangelized. A Harvard psychologist accommodatingly told leaders of new nations all they wanted to know about entrepreneurship but were afraid to ask.[18] It was a matter of acknowledging the inevitable gracefully. Though they knew not quite where, Western societies had "arrived" and so too would the diligent latecomer.

Laden with the advantages of backwardness, new nations followed the "attribute checklist." Populating most lists were: a bureaucracy working in Weberian efficiency, a transport and communication infrastructure, a foreign exchange surplus, a light consumer-goods industrial base, and land reform undertaken to enhance agricultural productivity and to fill factories as the nation urbanizes. The state could hasten the industrialization process so long as it ultimately deferred to the needs of private entrepreneurs. When land reform was completed, the old oligarchy pacified, the middle class ascendant, income gaps diminished (though *greater* gaps were initially expected), social services expanded, the military subordinated, rural masses and urban working class politically integrated, a bourgeoisie generated, and industries were prospering, the creation of a self-sustaining economy guided by democratic practices would be well under way.

In a bygone era of cheap energy, dreams of Camelot, and not so Ugly Americans, technology was often pictured as a source of secular salvation, to be disseminated through the global community where levels of wealth would rise in line with supple adaptation of this machinery to the social structure. The dynamics of technology – benignly autonomous – would propel underdeveloped countries into

[17] Robert A. Nisbet, *Social Change and History: Aspects of The Western Theory of Development* (London: Oxford University Press, 1969), p.202.

[18] See David McLelland, *The Achieving Society* (Princeton: D. Van Norstrand, 1961). Albert Hirschman observes: "Whenever any theory was propounded that considered a given value system a *prerequisite* of development, it could usually be effectively contradicted on empirical grounds: development had actually taken place somewhere without benefit of the 'Prerequisite'." *The Strategy of Economic Development* (New Haven: Yale University Press, 1958), p. 4.

the promised land of computers, Cadillacs, and Corning ware. The road to mass consumption was paved with good and usually imported technologies. Skeptics were in short supply in the 1950s and early 1960s and few scholars questioned the viability of the notion that all nations should move toward a cornucopian and convergent destiny – which was supposed to replicate the life styles of prosperous American suburbs circa 1956.[19]

THE QUESTION OF DEPENDENCE

In 1972 Salvador Allende, his socialist experiment in Chile in grave danger, addressed the UN General Assembly on the drawbacks of what he saw as the perniciousness of the Western model of economic development. He decried a model of *"reflex modernization,* which, as technical studies and tragic realities demonstrate, excludes from the possibilities of progress, well being and social liberation more and more millions of people, destining them to a subhuman life."[20]

"Reflex" modernization was a doctor's term, conveying an image of thoughtless (or ill-thought) reaction to an external stimulus. *Dependencia* is another name for it. The concept of dependency denotes a conditioning situation "in which the economies of one group of countries are conditioned by the development and expansion of others . . ."[21]

Dominant countries are endowed with technological, commercial, capital and socio-political predominance over dependent countries – the form of this predominance varying according to the particular historical moment – and can therefore exploit them, and extract part of the locally produced surplus. Dependence, then, is based upon an international division of labor which allows industrial development to take place in some countries while restricting it in others, whose growth is conditioned by and subjected to the power centres of the world.

---

[19] An early exception to this analytical trend is Lloyd and Susanne Rudolph, *The Modernity of Tradition: Political Development in India* (Chicago: University of Chicago Press, 1967).

[20] Allende's speech, delivered 4 December 1972, is reprinted in Hugo Radice, ed., *International Firms and Modern Imperialism* (London: Penguin, 1975), pp. 233–47.

[21] Theotonio Dos Santos, "The Crisis of Development Theory and the Problem of Dependence in Latin America" in Henry Bernstein, ed., *Underdevelopment and Development in The Third World* (London: Penguin, 1973), p. 76. Also see the appraisal of various approaches in Thomas J. Biersteker, *Multinationals, The State, and Control of The Nigerian Economy* (Princeton: Princeton University Press, 1987), pp. 11–51.

Briefly stated: "In the dependent countries imported factors of
production (e.g., capital and technology) have become the central
determinants of economic development and sociopolitical life."[22]
According to crude versions of *dependencia*, the colonized periphery is
compelled to distort its productive base to supply the metropole with
raw materials in exchange for manufactured goods. Indigenous
technological capacity is curbed or suppressed, and these nations
become inequitably integrated into the world economic system.
They experience minimal economic development because "their
capital goods production sectors are not strong enough to ensure
continuous advance of the system, in financial as well as in technological and organizational terms."[23] In extreme and easily refutable
formulations *dependencia* theory denies that any development can
occur in a dependent country.[24]

PERIPHERAL POSTINDUSTRIALIZATION

Contrary to bleak *dependencia* prophecies, the new industrializing
countries (NICs) achieved impressive growth rates, hikes in
exported manufactures, diversified industrial structures, and a mul-
tiplication of trade outlets.[25] The developing countries' share of
global value-added edged up 3 percent between 1965 and 1980, but
ten NICs recorded almost 75 percent of the gain.[26] Seven NICs –
Hong Kong, Taiwan, Singapore, South Korea, Argentina, Mexico,
and Brazil – are sources of more than 60 percent of the South's
manufactured exports. The industrial virtuosity of the NICs is

[22] Susanne Jonas, "Dependency and Imperialism: The Roots of Latin American Underdevelopment," in Ira Katznelson, Philip Brenner, David Gordon, eds., *The Politics and Society
Reader* (New York: David McKay, 1976).

[23] Fernando Cardoso and Enzo Faletto, *Dependency and Development in Latin America* (Berkeley:
University of California Press, 1979), p. xxi.

[24] For refutation of simplistic formulations of dependency, see Robert R. Kaufman, Daniel S.
Geller, and Harry I. Chernotsky, "A Preliminary Test of The Theory of Dependence,"
Comparative Politics 7, 3 (April 1975).

[25] "Countries commonly given 'newly industrialized' status include Argentina, Brazil,
Greece, Hong Kong, Republic of Korea, Mexico, Portugal, Singapore, Spain, Taiwan,
and Yugoslavia," according to John P. Lewis, "Overview" in Lewis and Valeriana Kalleb,
eds., *U.S. Foreign Policy and The Third World: Agenda 1983* (New York: Praeger-ODC, 1983).
Lists of NICs vary, depending on the criteria applied. Some rankings exclude OECD
nations by virtue of that affiliation with the "rich man's club." In others, Israel is
occasionally cited, and I include the Irish Republic. In any case, the list here is not
exhaustive or indisputable.

[26] *I.D.S. Bulletin*, Institute of Development Studies, Sussex, 13, 2 (1982), p. 2.

exhibited not only in steel, textile, shipbuilding and other "mature" industries but also in high-tech sectors such as electronics, in which the Asian "Gang of Four" (Hong Kong, South Korea, Taiwan, and Singapore) boosted their share of the South's exports from 60 percent in 1967 to 80 percent by 1980.[27]

Although beset by Northern protectionism, foreign debt, authoritarian regimes (or precarious transitions from them), the NICs demonstrated that "late-comers" are not condemned by an iron law to perform as hewers of wood, drawers of water, and assemblers of final-stage products in peripheral enclaves regressively linked to the world economy. Brazil, Mexico, South Korea and India – endowed with requisite natural, human and organizational resources – developed capital goods industries, and are shifting (as are smaller NICs) into "more skill- and technology-intensive areas of production."[28]

In a volume surveying outward-oriented development policies, Ruggie contends that liberal economists and *dependentistas* alike "overstate the determining impact of the international division of labor on national welfare."[29] Liberals "tend to ignore the critical importance of, and *dependencia* discounts the generative potential in, domestic political structures." Worse are neo-Marxists who allegedly ignore "the opportunities in developing countries created by new institutional arrangements for indigenous entrepreneurs, the state, and the process of local accumulation."[30]

These charges appear quite peculiar in light of the Marxists' virtual obsession with the role of the state; and all the more peculiar if one troubles to scan the caustic critiques exchanged between *dependistas*, and neo-Marxists.[31] Cardoso, for instance, long ago spurned "overly static, mechanistic views of the relationship between the polity and the economy," urging scholars to focus upon political forces and policy possibilities unfolding within dependent developers – a task requiring the "formulation of concepts linked to

27 Jeremy Clarke and Vincent Gable, "The Asian Electronics Industry Looks To The Future," in *ibid.*, p. 24.
28 Quoted in John Gerard Ruggie, ed., *The Antinomies of Interdependence* (New York: Columbia University Press, 1983), p. 9.
29 *Ibid.*, p. 39.
30 *Ibid.*, p. 481. Also see Tony Smith, *The Pattern of Imperialism* (Cambridge: Cambridge University Press, 1981).
31 For Marxist critiques of dependency literature, see Bill Warren, *Imperialism: Pioneer of Capitalism* (London: New Left Books, 1982), Anthony Brewer, *Marxist Theories of Imperialism* (London: Routledge and Kegan Paul, 1982), and Ronaldo Munck, *Politics and Dependence in The Third World* (London: Zed Press, 1984).

the effort to explain how internal and external processes of domination relate to one another."[32] Cardoso and Faletto cite the dynamic development role, class composition, institutional structure, and the internal and external sensitivity of states that have achieved wider "margins of maneuver" within the changing international division of labor.[33]

Dismissive appraisals of dependency literature too often confine themselves to ritualistic scorn for the stagnationist theses of Paul Baran and of Andre Gunder Frank.[34] Nonetheless, critics of dependency (and world-systems) analyses have made welcome efforts "to contextualize the economism of the debate in larger institutional terms and frameworks."[35] Analysis focuses on local factors and social forces which promote or hinder adjustment to patterns of global production and trade. The prescriptive implication is that peripheral polities – instead of prattling on about imperialism, repressed alternatives, and quixotic aspirations for national autarky – more prudently ought to put their own houses in order so as to maximize the benefits that the capitalist world-economy offers to the adept. Thus, research agendas evolved that strive to explain the differential impact of exogenous events upon local producer groups, sectors and branches, institutional structures and networks, state strategies, and their implications for coalition formation.

But political and social elites, when undertaking adjustment, will try to guide the manner and limit the extent to which socio-organizational changes required to upgrade the economy occur so that policy measures designed to increase accumulation will not upset the internal distribution of power. Specifying conditions in which these trade-offs occur between economic adjustment and power-

---

[32] F. Cardoso, "Associated-Dependent Development: Theoretical and Practical Implications," in Alfred Stepan, ed., *Authoritarian Brazil* (New Haven: Yale University Press, 1973), p. 143; and Cardoso and Faletto, *Dependency and Development in Latin America*, p. xviii. They continue: "*Strictu Sensu*, the capacity for action of various Latin American States, has increased. In this sense, one might consider that they are 'less dependent.' Our concern, however, is not to measure degrees of dependency in these terms – which fail to ask, 'less for whom?' for which classes and groups?" p. 210.

[33] Cardoso and Faletto, *Dependency and Development in Latin America*.

[34] Paul Baran, *The Political Economy of Growth* (New York: Monthly Review Press, 1957) and Andre Gunder Frank, *Capitalism and Underdevelopment in Latin America* (New York: Monthly Review Press, 1969). The thrashing continues. See Henry Bernstein and Howard Nichols, "Pessimism of The Intellect, Pessimism of The Will: A Response to Gunder Frank," and Andre Gunder Frank's reply, "What Is To Be Done With Straw Men?" in *Development and Change* 14, 4 (October 1983).

[35] Ruggie, *Antinomies of Interdependence*, p. vii.

retention, and their consequences, has been the special concern of the literature on bureaucratic authoritarianism.[36] *An implicit or insufficiently explicit premise in studies of the political dynamics of adjustment is that economic shifts rarely are presented to the state in the form of an unambiguous "stimulus," demanding an invariant policy "response."* Rather, these events, in effect, are appropriated through the interpretive (ideological) capacities of domestic actors to reinforce their dominance, or else to weaken that of rivals. Global shifts *signal* the need for internal adjustment, but these signals are converted by ideological mediation into programmatic *messages* to the citizenry as to the desired form the policy response should take. Cardoso and Faletto adumbrate this thesis in depicting the state not only as an agent but also as a crucial field of contest for groups and classes with competing "projects" whose success will be determined "by how international conditions are used in the internal power game, rather than by the particular economic conditions themselves."[37]

In the ensuing study of the determinants of policy response to market forces by a democratic developing nation I elaborate means by which the role of ideological activity can be incorporated into explanations of choice in the politics of adjustment. A related concern is the consequences of these ideological struggles (in which development "projects" are cast in the most persuasive terms so as to gain the consent of groups who are crucial to the outcome of policy debate) for the limits of state autonomy. I argue that the Irish case exemplifies a syndrome of wider significance, "peripheral postindustrialization."[38]

Peripheral postindustrialization denotes: (1) the policy-induced diffusion of high technology industries within peripheral nations; (2) a truncated form of development (minus linkages and a local technology-generating capacity), wherein developing states latch onto the more labor-intensive phases of industries with a "postindustrial" vocation (electronics, pharmaceuticals, etc.); and (3) an *ideological* strategy for extending hegemonic developmental schemes against

---

[36] See e.g. Guillermo O'Donnell, *Modernization and Bureaucratic Authoritarianism: Studies in South American Politics* (Institute of International Studies, University of California, Berkeley, 1973); and "Reflections on The Patterns of Change in the Bureaucratic Authoritarian State," *Latin American Research Review* 12, 2 (Winter 1978).

[37] Cordoso and Faletto, *Dependency and Development in Latin America*, p. 175.

[38] A preliminary formulation of this argument is J. K. Jacobsen, "Peripheral Postindustrialism: Ideology, High Technology, and Development," in James A. Caporaso, ed., *A Changing International Division of Labor* (London: Frances Pinter Press, 1987).

challenges presented by global economic trends and from local
counter-elites. The Irish Republic is an intriguing case because it is
an ex-colonial nation with uncharacteristically durable democratic
institutions. It embarked on export-led industrialization in the late
1950s and since 1975 has selected electronics as the basis for pion-
eering a new structure of "complex-factor cost industries" that,
ideally, will maximize the competitive advantage of skilled labor
against lower-wage export platforms vying for markets and investment.[39] The Irish experience, like that of other European "interme-
diaries," should shed light "on the predicaments facing both the
large, advanced industrial states" and the "less-developed countries."[40]

STATE–SOCIETY RELATIONS AND POLICY CHOICE

Dependistas and *non-dependistas* agree that the state is a pivotal actor
with interests and resources of its own, but differ in depictions of
state–society relations.[41] Non-*dependistas* favor a "statist approach,"
which posits that strong states like South Korea, Taiwan, Mexico,
and Brazil can and do shape the preferences of societal groups so as
to serve state-defined ends. The stronger a state is, the more
autonomously it acts, and so the more likely are the preferences of
societal groups to be overruled when these conflict with the pragmatic course plotted by policy-makers.[42] These states may appear to

[39] The term "postindustrial" refers to science-based, research-intensive industries. A "postindustrialization" strategy uses such industries as the cornerstone of intended economic
development. This analysis and usage in no way subscribes to the particular claims and
argument of Daniel Bell's forecasting venture, *The Coming of Post-Industrial Society* (London:
Penguin, 1973).

[40] Peter J. Katzenstein, "The Small European States in The International Economy: Economic Dependence and Corporatist Politics," in Ruggie, *Antinomies of Interdependence*, p. 95,
and his *Small States In The World Economy* (Ithaca: Cornell University Press, 1986).

[41] Aidan Foster-Carter, "From Rostow to Gunder Frank: Conflicting Paradigms in The
Analysis of Underdevelopment," *World Development* 4, 3 (March 1976); Theodore H.
Moran, "Multinational Corporations and Dependency: A Dialogue for Dependentistas
and Nondependentistas," *International Organization* 32, 1 (Winter 1978); and Thomas J.
Biersteker, *Distortion or Development? Contending Perspectives on the Multinational Corporation*
(Cambridge, MA: MIT Press, 1979).

[42] The most comprehensive argument advanced for the statist approach is Stephen Krasner,
Defending The National Interest (Princeton: Princeton University Press, 1978). A critique is
presented in John K. Jacobsen and Claus Hofhansel, "Safeguards and Profits: Civilian
Nuclear Exports, Neo-Marxism, and The Statist Approach," *International Studies Quarterly*
28, 2 (June 1984). For a pluralist response, see Gabriel Almond, "The Return To The
State," *American Political Science Review* 82, 3 (September 1988).

act as autonomously as Frankenstein's creature, but studies usually yield more ambiguous findings.

In a "statist" analysis of South Korea, Haggard and Moon note that the state "relied heavily on domestic entrepreneurs to perform the miracles" and, more tellingly, "the business–State alliance has proscribed thoroughgoing liberalization" politically as well as economically.[43] Duvall and Freeman find "state entrepreneurship" occurs where the private sector is unable or unwilling to undertake developmental tasks or may "generate some substantially undesirable patterns of development."[44] New public assets are deployed to complement private activity and profitable public assets may be sold off. Some *dependistas* argue the state ultimately aims at creating a bourgeoisie, a "reinvented" bourgeoisie that gradually acquires control over the state itself.[45]

Dependistas tend to explain this "bias of statism" in terms of structural Marxist models.[46] The reproduction of capitalist relations requires a relatively autonomous state apparatus whose managers attend to the often divergent tasks of promoting *accumulation, legitimation,* and *security.* The weight policy-makers attach to each "function" depends on the balance of class forces and the intensity of class struggle (penetrating all branches of the state). An important implication is that state managers can act not only against the short-term interests of "particular capitals," but also, under certain sets of conditions or "conjunctures," adopt programs which actually endanger capitalist dominance. So the state is a curious entity (a "material condensation" of class conflicts but not *reducible* to them) capable of playing or buying off class-based organizations, class fractions, or interest groups in order to achieve goals designated according to the policy-makers' own calculus. But even when situational factors augment state autonomy, managers do not do just as they please because at least tacit alliances are needed to assure

---

[43] Stephen Haggard and Chung-In Moon, "The South Korean State in The International Economy: Liberal, Dependent, or Mercantile?" in Ruggie, *Antinomies of Interdependence,* p. 161.

[44] Raymond Duvall and John Freeman, "International Economic Relations and The Entrepreneurial State," *Economic Development and Cultural Change* 32, 2 (1984), p. 375.

[45] The literature is vast. For overviews see Martin Carnoy, *The State and Political Theory* (Princeton: Princeton University Press, 1984) and Bob Jessop, *State Theory: Putting Capitalist States in Their Place* (Oxford: Polity Press, 1990).

[46] See Peter Evans, "Reinventing the Bourgeoisie," in Michael Burawoy and Theda Skocpol, eds., *Marxist Inquiries* (Chicago: University of Chicago Press, 1982).

compliance with policy. So analysts must attend to the class origins, positional interests, and ideological stances of policy-makers. Obviously, the state's resource base constricts the range of responses to global market changes but the level of resources policy-makers can summon depends on the degree of cooperation they can elicit. The *quality* of cooperation – from consent to coercion – is itself a resource. In short, politics really matter.

In principle *accumulation* is realizable via *several* strategies, each posing different distributions of the benefits and burdens of development among social classes. The form of the policy response will be guided according to the *legitimation* scheme of state managers (who may be impelled by social resistance to reappraise whose ox they gore). Autonomy reaches its pragmatic zenith when state managers, motivated by economic exigencies, support policy packages, based on new coalitional formations, which challenge the immediate interests of dominant groups. "Pragmatism" is a term evocative of the blending of political entrepreneurship with brokerage that portends policy change; capitalist states, with vile historical exceptions, are not purely "autonomous.")[47] What remains is to identify conditions that precipitate "pragmatic" state action, and to examine *how* one is linked to the other.

Among these conditions are debt crises, the exhaustion of industrialization phases (e.g. import-substitution), mismatches between production structure and international marketing patterns, and other forms of severe pressure to adjust in costly ways. International influences will be tested, as Cardoso and Faletto urge, as "endogenous variables," whose local expression enables us to understand and anticipate the content of policy responses by nations on the weak side of asymmetries. Perhaps one useful means for invigorating the flagging "dialogue" between *dependista* and non-*dependista* is for the latter to apply the "sensitivity-vulnerability" distinction to intrastate relations (between and among components of the state "apparatus," which interact with societal groups) as well as to interstate affairs, and proceed to inquire how changes in "sensitivities" affect policy formulation, economic performance, and the distribution of power and wealth.[48] But even this enterprise is likely

---

[47] On political entrepreneurship see John Mollenkopf, *The Contested City* (Princeton: Princeton University Press, 1983).
[48] The distinction is drawn from Robert Keohane and Joseph Nye, *Power and Interdependence* (Boston, MA: Little, Brown and Co., 1977).

to neglect crucial determinants that do not lend themselves easily to transcription into statistical tables. The most resistant is ideology.

INTERESTS, IDEOLOGY, AND POLICY STRUGGLES

Odell's study of US international monetary policy argues that a cognitive perspective (which claims reigning ideas exert an "independent effect on policy content") ought to be considered in a multiple explanatory framework, including four other perspectives: security, market, domestic structure, and bureaucratic politics. He traces ways in which explanatory foci interpenetrate and cites conditions under which their relative importance changes.[49] A cognitive perspective is least significant for explaining policy response by states under extreme market or other "situational" pressure; it is most useful when studying states blessed with structural power and domestic tranquility that allow a "breathing space" where ideas play a major role in shaping decisions. The scope of choice is conditioned not only by global impacts and domestic forces but by the pool of policy "ideas" that are intellectually available, economically viable, and politically permissible. I say *conditioned* rather than *constrained* because critical conjunctures can draw authoritative attention to "ideas," which enlarge the pool of choices.

Given the esoteric nature of monetary issues, Odell restricts his analysis of cognitive factors to the "circulation of policy ideas in Washington." His approach is less useful when dealing with issues where a wider public audience readily recognizes the stakes they have in policy outcomes. More clues for investigating how these explanatory foci interrelate are contained in the work of Antonio Gramsci, whose writings on hegemony are gaining currency among non-Marxian students of political economy.[50] Hegemony occurs in a socio-organizational "phase in which ideologies, which were germinated earlier, become 'party' and enter into struggle until one (or a combination) of them"

tends to predominate, to impose itself, to propagate itself throughout the whole social sphere, causing, in addition to singleness of economic and political purpose, an intellectual and moral unity as well, placing all

[49] John Odell, *U.S. International Monetary Policy* (Princeton: Princeton University Press, 1982).

[50] See Robert Keohane, *After Hegemony: Cooperation and Discord in The World Political Economy* (Princeton: Princeton University Press, 1984), p. 84, and Walter Dean Burnham, *The Current Crisis in American Politics* (New York: Oxford University Press, 1984), p. 266.

questions around which the struggle rages not on a corporative, but a
"universal" plane and creating in this way the hegemony of a fundamental
social group . . . the ruling group is cordinated concretely with the general
interests of the subordinate groups and State life is conceived as a continual
formation of unstable equilibriums (unstable within the ambit of the law)
. . . equilibriums in which the interests of the ruling group predominate but
only up to a certain point, e.g., not as far as their mean economic
corporative interests would like.[51]

The state is ideologically an "educator" and, in the economic field,
an "instrument of rationalization."[52] Gramsci argued that counter-
hegemonic parties should engage in a wide-ranging "war of position" to garner support and, in effect, surround, as well as penetrate,
the state because economic crises do not, and the assumption of state
power cannot, guarantee "transformative" or socially progressive
results.[53] He notes "the fact that international relations are inter-
laced with these internal relations of a nation-state, creating new,
original and historically concrete combinations," which present
opportunities. Gramsci emphasizes both the systemic sources and
conflictual undercurrents because "it is at the level of ideologies that
men become conscious of conflicts in the world of the economy."

For analysis of short-term, non-transformative situations ("second-
stage" struggles inside the "fundamental existing framework"),
more suitable concepts are needed. Albert Hirschman has contributed the notion of "propensity to defer" to "economic exigencies."[54] Taken a step further, societal actors will have differing
"propensities to defer" to global market conditions, and to state
policy. Where the term "deference" appears I refer to the propensity of a group to defer to the prevailing policy prescriptions.

Why do actors defer? The reasons are interrelated: rewards,
coercion, organizational impotence, lack of persuasive alternatives,
costs and risks of opposition, apathy, "poor" information, and
simple approval. The latter depends on ideological predispositions
that enter into the calculus of self-interests. Hence, one witnesses the
resonance of the phrase, "Stay the course," even among those most
mauled by the "magic of the market-place." While state managers

---

[51] Antonio Gramsci, *Prison Notebooks* (New York: International Publishers, 1971), pp.
181–82.
[52] *Ibid.*, p. 247.   [53] *Ibid.*, p. 182.
[54] Albert Hirschman, "The Turn to Authoritarianism in Latin America and The Search For
Its Determinants," in D. Collier, ed., *The New Authoritarianism in Latin America* (Princeton:
Princeton University Press, 1979), p. 65.

and dominant coalition members may differ in their attachment to the mixed product of their negotiations, I will focus on subordinate groups, and *the "propensity to defer" should be understood as being imbued with Gramsci's acute sense of the material underpinnings of prevailing ideology.* This depiction is not exclusively Marxist. Schumpeter's remarks on the manipulation of ideas and of public opinion are familiar.[55] Lindblom examines the institutional sources of "constrained volition" in polyarchal systems that produce a "lopsided competition of ideas," and Burnham discusses the "politics of excluded alternatives."[56] We should be astonished, as Barrington Moore observed, if social systems did not propagate core beliefs favorable to elites insofar as these beliefs preserve the "absence of a demand for change."[57] A *high* propensity to defer is defined by this "absence" because a dominant coalition needs acquiescence, not love. A low propensity is indicated by usual measures of dissent: strikes, demonstrations, rapid rises in support for opposition and fringe parties, and any knitting together of these elements of resistance. Dispersed or inchoate protest is no challenge: organization is the key.

Policy-makers are spared a test of their skills if there is high public confidence in the state's ability to cope efficiently and (more or less) equitably with economic setbacks or transitions. If this public confidence (or propensity to defer) is low at the start or falls rapidly after the onset of adversities, the state will undergo a "policy crisis" whose outcome will be shaped by the severity and duration of adjustment, the strength of the state, the capacity of dominant groups to repress or appease opposition, and the capability of counter-elites to mobilize support for alternative programs. If policy crises are acute and protracted (and conflict sharpens within the dominant coalition), state managers have the opportunity to exercise political entrepreneurship to the extent that new alliances are formed with formerly subordinate groups promoting alternative schemes.[58] This pragmatic scenario is less likely to unfold where a "triple alliance" reigns, more likely to occur in corporatist

[55] Joseph Schumpeter, *Capitalism, Socialism, and Democracy* (3rd ed., New York: Harper and Row, 1975).
[56] See Charles Lindblom, *Politics and Markets* (New York: Basic Books, 1977) and Burnham, *The Current Crisis in American Politics*.
[57] Barrington Moore, Jr., *Reflections On The Causes of Human Misery* (Boston: Beacon Press, 1972), p. 144.
[58] For an application to the issue area of nuclear power and fuel policy, see Jacobsen and Hofhansel, "Safeguards and Profits."

frameworks where the alliance is "quadrupled" (i.e., includes an independent and assertive labor representation).

The Irish case fits Evans' definition of dependent development as a "special case of dependency," characterized by "capital accumulation at the local level accompanied by increasing differentiation" of industrial structure.[59] But Evans, and the bureaucratic-authoritarian literature, focus on repressive renditions where "ambivalent alliances" of the local bourgeoisie, multinationals, and the state rule. The Irish Republic resembles the European corporatist polities where consent must be managed through democratic institutions. When "hard choices" appear on the horizon, elites will resort to material concessions and ideological appeals long before bayonets are considered. If the elite's policy choice is portrayed successfully as the wisest choice or else the only one, then "the openness of an economy provides the means to combat the demands of the working class for higher wages and for economic and political reforms."[60] But even when "the logic of economic vulnerability prevails over the logic of worker militancy," democratic structures can provide incentives for bargaining on non-wage bases (e.g., investment controls over "wages foregone").[61] Of course, policy crises, untended, can flare into systemic crises that no prudent elite desires.

To reiterate: international market forces signal the need to adjust, but the precise *form* of adjustment will depend on how such signals are converted by social contestants and institutions into programmatic messages to the citizenry. One should not suppose *a priori* that these (diagnostic and prescriptive) messages reflect only the narrow interests of elites. Nor should one suppose that the state will obey elite preferences (even when unambiguous), especially if these preferences are hotly contested and, in system-maintenance terms, differ marginally from other programs. Further, we must not assume that counter-programs are less congruent with international economic shifts or are inferior to the adjustment schemes championed by

[59] Peter Evans, *Dependent Development* (Princeton: Princeton University Press, 1979), p. ii. Evans further stipulates that the term is applicable in cases where "capital accumulation and diversified industrialization are not only occurring ... but are dominating the transformation of the economy and social structure," p. 32.

[60] Fred L. Block, *The Origins of International Economic Disorder* (Berkeley: University of California Press, 1977), p. 3.

[61] Peter Lange, "Unions, Workers and Wage Regulation," in John Goldthorpe, ed., *Order and Conflict in Contemporary Capitalism: Studies in the Political Economy of Western European Nations* (Oxford: Oxford University Press, 1984).

dominant groups. The reverse may well be the case. If so, and the opposition is strongly organized (and crafty), a policy crisis ensues that will pose an interesting trial for the pragmatic capabilities of state managers.

TOWARD COMPLEX DEPENDENCY

An investigator of the Peruvian case argues that a "new bourgeoisie" may arise as a "hegemonic candidate" in developing nations.[62] Especially in countries endowed with "bonanza" resources (having high volume, value, and demand), domestic industrialists' suspicion regarding state activity will diminish in proportion to: the transformation of industrial entrepreneurs from an individualist to an organization-based class; the restructuring of the state along technical-managerial lines and the infusion of a managerial ideology; and the continuing growth of the "bonanza," which will enable industrialists to enjoy the advantages of a strong state at a low cost. In an "expanding sum" game, industrialization encourages cooperative industrial relations in particular, and democratic trends in general.

Even if unblessed by a resource "bonanza," a mature "developmentalist" bourgeoisie can engineer the integration of the working class into the capitalist order by relying on the spread of high-productivity enterprises which collectively can afford to pay rising wages.[63] Industrialists enjoy stability and profits; workers get higher living standards; the state reaps more revenue to fund infrastructural and welfare requirements. However, the widespread phenomenon of wage "givebacks," work rule erosion and union-busting so evident lately in advanced industrial states attests to the contingent nature of the "maturity" of private enterprises when opportunities to "roll back" labor arise. Whether a "rollback" occurs in specific cases will hinge not on how enlightened management is but foremost upon the relative strength of contestants and their success in enlisting the support of the state.

High sensitivity to international market conditions induce corporatist-style bargaining (e.g., wage controls in exchange for job

---

[62] David G. Becker, *The New Bourgeoisie and The Limits of Dependency* (Princeton: Princeton University Press, 1983), p. 239.
[63] *Ibid.*, p. 278.

guarantees, public employment expansion, tax reforms, and monitoring of investment) only if (1) the requisite conditions of centralization and concentration among the bargaining groups obtain; (2) propensity to defer (to an interest-based depiction of economic "exigencies") is diminishing; and (3) improved organization enables a counter-elite (seeking, where possible, allies) to promote credible alternatives. The political exhaustion of an economic policy course then impels policy-makers to search out new coalitional arrangements.

Gourevitch, too, argues that crises "render politics more plastic," emphasizing how the "international situation" shapes internal group behavior according to sectoral locations in the global division of labor.[64] The conditions for the cohesion of a dominant coalition give way, opening up possibilities for new coalitional configurations (a process which "political entrepreneurs" may guide, depending on the resources they can summon, or to which they are *forced* to resort). My argument is that just how "plastic" politics becomes during crises will be retarded or accelerated by ideological interpretations of the response "demanded" by economic exigencies. This is a vital supplement to the sociological approach of Gourevitch, who writes:

A given policy preference is not necessarily in the "interest" of the actor. On the contrary, it is possible to posit a calculus or frame of reference that could make a range of conflicting policies reasonable from the standpoint of different strategies ... The way out of this interpretive trap is to be sociological, to ask what sorts of strategy various groups actually did prefer.[65]

The "interpretive trap" had sprung on the *actors* before the crisis; the "way out" is confined by the prevailing frame of reference; and the latter may be upset by international market forces so that the "calculi" of various groups become confounded. A critical moment occurs in which the governing coalition loses adhesion, becomes porous *vis-à-vis* subordinate group demands, incorporates new and/ or sheds old components, and in which the preferences of coalition members (and their weighting) change with obvious implications for the design of adjustment strategy.[66]

---

[64] Peter Gourevitch, "Breaking With Orthodoxy: The Politics of Economic Responses To The Depression of The 1930s," *International Organization* 38, 1 (1984), and his *Politics in Hard Times* (Ithaca: Cornell University Press, 1986).

[65] Gourevitch, "Breaking With Orthodoxy," p. 99.

[66] See Jacobsen and Hofhansel, "Safeguards and Profits."

A high "propensity to defer" is *ideologically induced vulnerability* that serves the interests of coalition but also is based on diffusion of real material benefits to other groups. Waning deferentiality is by no means irreversible, nor are counter-elites always poised to exploit it. The British miners' strike of 1984–85, a defensive struggle, failed because they offered no program by which to galvanize wider support, and because they faced a well-prepared Tory government (deploying superior resources) that proved adept at promoting its own "definition of the situation."[67] In the Irish case, recent economic adversities sparked massive demonstrations for tax reform, worker sit-ins in factories, attacks on the Labour Party by trade unions for "anti-working-class measures," while in coalition government, and in 1987 a Labour Party pull-out from, and the collapse of, the coalition government.[68] But these expressions of a declining deference still amount to sporadic grumbling.

THE IRISH CASE

Ireland shares the characteristics that Poulantzas identified with "externally-centred" industrialization in Portugal, Spain, and Greece: a spectacular increase of the urban working class, depopulation of the countryside, a massive increase in white-collar employment, high rates of unemployment, high emigration, foreign investment as a central determinant and dynamic of growth, and (less so) an accompanying rise in political conflict/class struggle.[69] Overlooking Ireland, Poulantzas states that the lures offered to foreign capital by the southern European regimes resulted in an "absence of any real control" over foreign investment "without any parallel in the other European countries."[70]

The distinctions between Irish circumstances and those in Third World nations are illuminated by an Irish economist who in the

---

[67] Geoffrey Goodman, *The Miners Strike* (London: Pluto Press, 1985) and Mark Hollingsworth, *The Press and Political Dissent* (London: Pluto Press, 1986), pp. 242–85.

[68] *Sunday Tribune*, 15 December 1985, and J. K. Jacobsen, "Ireland's Right Wing Rut," *The New Leader*, 15 June 1987.

[69] Nicos Poulantzas, *The Crisis of The Dictatorships* (London: New Left Books, 1976), pp. 88–89.

[70] *Ibid.*, p. 20. Also see Roy Hudson and Jim Lewis, eds., *Uneven Development In Southern Europe: Studies of Accumulation, Class, Migration and The State* (London: Methuen, 1985) and Costis Hadjimichalis, *Uneven Development and Regionalism: State, Territory and Class in Southern Europe* (London: Croom Helm, 1987).

1970s shrewdly cited reasons for the apparent harmony between foreign investors and the natives.[71] First, the composition of foreign ownership was diverse (33 percent British, 29 percent American, 19 percent German by number of projects over the 1970–75 period), so that the political animosities aroused in instances of domination such as by United Fruit in Central America or Firestone in Liberia do not flare in Ireland. Secondly, tax evasion via transfer pricing and other bookkeeping techniques are not a source of tension because the state did not tax manufacturing exports. Thirdly, resentment over foreign firms' high profit rates is muted because Ireland does not compel disclosure of these rates. (But the US Department of Commerce disclosed that Ireland is the most profitable location in Europe with an average real profit rate of over 25 percent recorded by US firms in the early 1980s versus a 14.3 percent rate in the EEC as a whole.)

The Irish case fits the definition of "dependent development" as "capital accumulation and diversified industrialization of a more than superficial sort are not only occurring in a peripheral country but are dominating the transformation of its economy and social structure."[72] While Cardoso and Faletto, and Evans, provide insightful guidance into dependent development, supplementary analyses are needed in order to understand the politics of policy choices. Static statistical evidence cannot prove that a state is "imprisoned" in dependency or that it is merely a passive adaptor to exogenous economic events or the instrument of an *entreguista* bourgeosie. Even if policy decisions are predicated on the "fact" of dependence, there remains an active element in this compliance that requires explanation. Neither the recent dependency writers nor neo-Marxists deny this.

CONCLUSION

It is indeed important, as Theda Skocpol and her "bringing the state back in" cohort argue, to "take states seriously as actors and structures."[73] Yet it is all too tempting to err in the opposite extreme. Apart

---

[71] Dermot McAleese, "Capital Inflow and Foreign Direct Investment in Ireland 1952–70," *Journal of The Statistical and Social Inquiry Society*, 22, 4 (1970–71).

[72] Evans, *Dependent Development*, p. 32. Also see Gary Gereffi, *The Pharmaceutical Industry and Dependency in the Third World* (Princeton: Princeton University Press, 1983).

[73] Margaret Weir and Theda Skocpol, "State Structures and The Possibilities for 'Keynesian' Responses To The Great Depression in Sweden, Britain and The United States," in

from the question of whether the state was ever "out" anywhere but in certain precincts of American social science during the 1950s and 1960s, the most common pitfall is to fetishize the state as "autonomous." While it is perfectly legitimate, for example, to characterize the state as "a set of rules and institutions having peculiar drives, compulsions, and aims distinct from the interests of any particular groups," this definition should not imply that these criteria are sufficient for a state to operate autonomously.[74] In the analysis of policy outcomes state strategy certainly can be a causal variable but only under conditions which need to be specified.

State-centric analysts embrace the refrain that politics is mediated by an "institutional setting," which Marxists presumably ignore because this factor ruins simplistic class analysis. In reply Cammack makes a strong case against state-centric analysts, particularly Skocpol and her many collaborators, who distort Marxist and neo-Marxist analysis by creating a "false contrast between the 'society-centred' perspective of classical Marxism, and the state-centred perspective she [Skocpol] endorses and affects to find in neo-Marxist writing."[75] Hence, they move "from a genuinely Marxist perspective in which state and social classes are seen as interrelated to one in which 'the state' confronts civil society" so that the idea that the "state is differentially penetrated by conflicting classes, and incorporates, reflects and affects the struggle between these, becomes literally unthinkable."[76]

The objective is to deny in practice the presence of classes and class struggle within the state. Further, "these inconsistencies and distortions are not casual," Cammack contends, "as they make it possible to present as damaging to a Marxist or neo-Marxist analysis of the state and its relations to social classes material which in fact strongly confirms the validity of such an analysis."[77]

But Cammack targets only American scholars when one need hardly cross the Atlantic to find examples. An Oxford author, for instance, declares herself "diametrically opposed" to the Marxist tradition so as to seize the high ground of common sense and

Peter Evans, Dietrich Rueschemeyer, and Theda Skocpol, eds., *Bringing The State Back in* (Cambridge: Cambridge University Press, 1985), p.118.

[74] Krasner, *Defending The National Interest*, p. 12.

[75] Paul Cammack, "Bringing The State Back In?" *British Journal of Political Science* 19, 2 (April 1989), p. 289.

[76] *Ibid.*, pp. 282, 289.   [77] *Ibid.*, p. 262.

scholarly acumen.[78] In a study of corporatism in Ireland, this author argues that "contrary to Marxist" critics, "it may be to the advantage of organized labour to participate in bargained agreements of a concertative sort" – which would be a more compelling point if she had not based this insight on the work of authors who hail from the very Marxist tradition for which she expresses contempt.[79]

In the 1990s books on international political economy continue to appear which routinely claim to recognize variables that dependency writing has ignored; for example, "the role of macro-economic shocks, country size, and the political influence wielded by great powers."[80] Typically, the author then goes on to cite approvingly vital features of the indicted literature.[81] So authors are Marxists or *dependistas* or pariahs of some other sort when it suits one's purposes, and something else entirely when one acknowledges culling concepts from their work.

We certainly "need theories of how domestic political factors intervene between external constraints and policy choice."[82] The ensuing analysis attempts this feat and is indebted to Marxist and neo-Marxist writing even though these practitioners would probably reject it as Marxist analysis because of a lack of explicit links of political phenomena to "modes of production." When and how and to what extent state aims shape policy outcomes is a question that demands a fine-grained focus on the internal socio-political coordinates in specific cases. That is the task undertaken here.

[78] Niamh Hardiman, *Pay, Politics and Economic Performance in Ireland 1970–1987* (Oxford: Oxford University Press, 1988), p. 23.

[79] *Ibid.*, p. 13. She quotes the work of Adam Przeworski and Michael Wallerstein.

[80] Stephen Haggard, *Pathways From The Periphery: The Politics of Growth in Newly Industrializing Countries* (Ithaca: Cornell University Press, 1990), p. 3.

[81] *Ibid.*, p. 26. Citing Cardoso and Faletto.   [82] *Ibid.*, p. 9.

CHAPTER 2

Perils of planning: foreign capital, domestic policy, and the problem of state "strength"

> The large private corporation fits oddly into democratic theory
> and vision. Indeed, it does not fit.
>
> Charles Lindblom, *Politics and Markets*

During a visit to Dublin in the late 1970s John Kenneth Galbraith
paused in his analysis of the "two-tiered economic system" and
critcisms of free market lore to reassure an audience of financial
executives that "the multinational corporation is not multi-
nationally wicked."[1] Asked to appraise the Irish industrialization
strategy of export-led growth via injections of foreign direct investment, he replied soothingly that "the notion of outside control
should not be too alarming. While multinationals are a menace to
weakly governed countries, they present no threat to those strongly
governed."

Yet apprehensiveness was justifiable. In contrast to Galbraith's
upbeat assessment, one could find at that time an Irish prime
minister promoting his nation's industrial advantages in a *Fortune*
magazine advertisement. "The main thing," he emphatically
explains, "is that we impose as few conditions as possible."[2] In this
courteous and hospitable English-speaking milieu, prospective
investors may rest assured that "policies never change" in the
transition from one government to another and also that "Irish
products are politically acceptable everywhere" in a fitting finish to
an elegant plea.

In the wake of a recital of impeccable investment criteria, the
managing director of the Industrial Development Authority in 1975
noted finally that "we have not experienced the luxury of turning
away viable industrial projects because they could not use native
raw materials or because their potential linkages were not fully to

---

[1] *Irish Times*, 10 May 1977, p. 1.   [2] *Fortune* 92, 3 (March 1975), p. 89.

our liking ... we cannot afford to shut out any source which is currently supplying viable industries."[3]

The bargaining position of Irish governments *vis-à-vis* foreign investors was bluntly expressed in the National Economic and Social Council's report, *Prelude to Planning*:[4]

if private foreign investment is needed to provide the new jobs that are required in Ireland and if it is not permitted or if it is discouraged, Irish people will still have to work with capital that is not owned by Irishmen – but they will be working with it outside Ireland rather than at home.

These instructive examples do not bespeak the strong government Galbraith imagined to preside over the Republic of Ireland. While the Irish state capably fulfills civil functions in a manner most Third World nations might envy, since the policy shift from protectionism to free trade in 1958 it could not be too indulgent to foreign capital. Of course, the capacity of a regime to create internal order tells us no more about its capacity to control private capital than about the justice and equity of the order created.[5]

An incomplete list of incentives offered to lure foreign firms into locating in Ireland includes export tax holidays; cash grants on a percentage basis varying with the region; duty-free import of capital equipment; high depreciation allowances; training grants; guaranteed loans and subsidization of interest; provision of ready-made factories in industrial parks; research and development grants; re-equipment grants; and after-care services.[6] A hard-core capitalist might imagine an agonized Adam Smith twirling under his tombstone during this recitation of entrepreneurial aids.

Though labor costs cannot match the minimal wages of Singapore or Taiwan, they are appetizingly low relative to the United States and to much of continental Europe. There are no restrictions on repatriation of profits, share ownership in native firms, and mergers

[3] Michael J. Killeen, "Industrial Development and Full Employment" (Dublin: Industrial Development Authority, 1976), p. 11.
[4] NESC Report No. 26, *Prelude To Planning* (Dublin: Stationery Office, October 1976), p. 20.
[5] See Noam Chomsky's "Objectivity and Liberal Scholarship," in James Peck, ed., *The Chomsky Reader* (New York: Pantheon, 1987).
[6] According to a plant location survey of Common Market incentives in the 1970s, the Irish Republic ranked first in attractiveness for "minor capital intensive industries," as runner-up in "labor intensive" and "medium capital intensive" industries, and limping across the finish line regarding "high capital intensive" industries. See Plant Location International, "A Comparative Study of Incentives Offered to Industry Within Common Market Countries" (Plant Location International, Independent Consultants, 1975).

and take-overs. Procuring investment is a competitive business but it may ultimately be a destabilizing and detrimental one for the Republic – however beneficial the short-term gains. "The perfect investment climate," observes one investigator of foreign firm-host country relations "may well be a politically unstable one that must at some stage collapse."[7] Ireland's heavily baited "open door" policy is provocatively reminiscent of Chile's *Nuevo Trato* (New Deal) experiment in the fifties: "The country opened its doors to capital and so it flowed away elsewhere," summarizes a researcher.[8] In the 1980s the Irish experienced the opening of a "black hole" through which funds flowed from the economy.[9] The onset of this and other drawbacks of the industrialization strategy raise hard questions regarding the capacity of the Irish state to evolve into a stronger bargaining stance in order to extract better terms from investors.[10]

In the Irish case "national planning acknowledges the country's dependence on foreign capital by leaving capital inflows as the residual in the planning process."[11] If anything, that residual increased since the inauguration of planning by the government in 1958 and has exceeded what life there was in the plans themselves – the last "program" lapsing in 1972. Although bargaining studies indicate that host governments, in the long run, are likely to obtain beneficial agreements with multinational firms, this happy outcome is not evident in the case of "export processing platforms" like Ireland.

Not only is the export manufacturing activity extraordinarily "footloose", dependent as it is on neither local resources nor local markets, but it is also likely to bind the host country both to sources of inputs and to market outlets over which it has an absolute minimum of control. Bargaining strength is likely to be considerably less for a country manufacturing

[7] Louis Turner, *Multinationals and The Third World* (London: Croom Helm, 1974), p. 75.

[8] Theodore H. Moran, *Multinational Corporations and The Politics of Dependence: Copper in Chile* (Princeton: Princeton University Press, 1974), p. 109.

[9] See James Stewart, "Aspects of The Financial Behaviour of Multinational Companies in Ireland," in Jim Fitzpatrick and John Kelly, eds., *Perspectives on Irish Industry* (Dublin: Irish Management Institute, 1986). Also Maev-Ann Wren, "A Residual 'Black Hole,'" *Irish Times*, 1 August 1987.

[10] An earlier treatment is J. K. Jacobsen, "Changing Utterly?: Irish Development and The Problem of Dependence," *Studies*, 268, 67 (Winter 1978).

[11] Robin Murray, "The Internationalization of Capital and The Nation-State," *New Left Review* 67 (May–June 1971), p. 108.

components or undertaking middle-stage processing than it is even for a raw materials exporter.[12]

As carriers of coveted packages of capital, technologies, marketing expertise and connections, and managerial expertise, multinational corporations are useful yet unwieldy "instruments" for host state policy-makers to invite and deploy. The policy question is not whether foreign direct investors should be encouraged but rather how stringently they will be monitored and controlled, in what areas and with what degree of coercion or guidance they will be integrated into the wider developmental scheme.[13] (In the current climate of a disintegrating and investment-hungry Eastern bloc and of deeply indebted Third World nations, the issue of control is very low on most host state agendas.) The potential for abusive influence that multinationals exert depends on the policy environment that governments set around these entities; the shape of that policy environment depends upon the outcomes of struggles among interests inside the state. In studying the interplay of foreign investment with the Irish planning experience – the former an integral if not integrated feature of the latter – one can trace a developmental tendency toward deepening dependence wherein domestic goals are trimmed to suit the designs of multinational firms and their local allies. Planning presumes a modicum of state autonomy, so an initial premise explored here is that state planning and foreign investment are contradictory processes.

COPING WITH MULTINATIONALS: POLICY RESPONSES

Galbraith argues that "the impairment of sovereignty – the accommodation of the state to the needs and purposes of the corporate technostructure, is the very essence of the operations of the planning system," and that the interpenetration of the public and private sectors culminates in a "bureaucratic symbiosis," which is a decisive feature of a "weak" state.[14] Political theory does not account for the legitimacy of the influence of private corporations

---

[12] G. K. Helleiner, quoted in Hugo Radice, ed., *International Firms and Modern Imperialism* (London: Pelican, 1972), p. 100.

[13] Joseph LaPalombara and Stephen Black, *Multinational Corporations in Comparative Perspective* (New York: McGraw Hill, 1977), p. 7.

[14] John Kenneth Galbraith, *Economics and The Public Purpose* (New York: Houghton Mifflin, 1973), p. 143.

upon public policy.[15] Inasmuch as 200 firms command two-thirds of US manufacturing assets the neo-classical model hardly offers a full account of competitive activity. General Motors, whose output exceeds that of Austria or Denmark, ought to be considered, Dahl insists, "both a *political system* and a *social enterprise*."[16] Indeed, there are signs that citizen groups are beginning to view large firms in these terms.[17]

Planning in the private sector became imperative as the nineteenth-century factory system evolved into the multidivisional corporation and then developed into multinational corporations (defined by possession of six or more subsidiaries in as many countries). International ventures are nothing new but their scale and sophistication is.[18] From 1950 to 1970 US foreign direct investment grew at a 10 percent per annum pace. By 1971 the US accounted for 52 percent of foreign direct investment, trailed by Britain's 14.5 percent, France's 5.8 percent, West Germany's 4.4 percent, and Japan's 2.7 percent. Between 1960 and 1972 American investment abroad tripled, with two-thirds pouring into developed nations. The aggregate profits of American investors rose from 8.6 percent in 1957 to 26.9 percent of total earnings in 1974, and eight of the top ten corporations obtained at least 40 percent and as much as 87 percent earnings abroad. In the mid-1970s a fifth of corporate profits and a quarter of new investment took place abroad. The "second American economy" overseas became the fourth largest on the planet. In the mid-1970s 80 percent of foreign sales of US multinationals consisted of interaffiliate trade. An estimated 20 percent of American exports were sold by parent firms to their affiliates.

The "American challenge" reached a crest in the 1970s. By 1981 US foreign investment (while rising in absolute terms) fell to

---

[15] David Vogel, "The Corporation As Government: Challenges and Dilemmas," *Polity* 8, 1 (Fall 1975).

[16] Robert A. Dahl, "On Removing Certain Impediments To Democracy in the United States," *Dissent* 25, 3 (Summer 1978) and his *Dilemmas of Pluralist Democracy* (New Haven: Yale University Press, 1982).

[17] See Barry Bluestone and Bennett Harrison, *The Great U-Turn: The Restructuring of Industry and The Polarizing of America* (New York: Basic Books, 1989).

[18] Statistics cited are, unless otherwise noted, drawn from C. Fred Bergsten, Thomas Horst, and Theodore H. Moran, *American Multinationals and American Interests* (New York: Brookings Institution, 1978).

42 percent of the world total as the Japanese, especially, increased overseas manufacturing activity.[19] In 1983 American investment underwent its first decline since the Second World War. "Foreign spending plans of U.S. Companies again declined sharply in 1986, after an increase in 1984 and 1985," Kolko writes. "Most investment in affiliates was reinvestment of earnings" although subcontracting and purchases from independent local producers for distribution grew as well.[20] In the "new multinationalism" characterizing the 1980s Gilpin notes that the American shift in investment preferences from "wholly owned subsidiaries abroad to joint ventures and other forms of intercorporate alliances" had been motivated by frequent host state demands that a domestic partner be found, the need to spread the risk in times of rapid technological change, and the decline of American technological leadership in many areas.[21] Third World nations generated their own multinational firms (33 of the top 500 outside the US by 1980) for which some OECD national development agencies competed. But whatever the flag they flew at headquarters all multinationals engage in planning their webs of production, distribution, and research and development. These schemes rarely coincide with the preferences of host nation governments so problems of compliance arise: who will adjust to whom?

Stephen Hymer long ago posed the promise of national public planning systems against the backdrop of those international private "planning systems" we call multinational firms. Instead of private institutions organizing industries across nations, he highlighted the advantages of organizing industries on a regional basis through developed and coordinated institutions:

The advantage of national planning is its ability to remove the wastes of oligopolistic anarchy, e.g., meaningless product differentiation and an imbalance between different industries within a geographical area. It concentrates all levels of decision-making in one locale and thus provides each region with a full complement of skills and occupations. This opens up new horizons for local development by making possible the social and political control of economic decision-making.[22]

---

[19] Robert Gilpin, *The Political Economy of International Relations* (Princeton: Princeton University Press, 1987), p. 246 and Joyce Kolko, *Restructuring The World Economy* (New York: Pantheon, 1988), p. 81.

[20] Kolko, *Restructuring The World Economy*, p. 83.

[21] Gilpin, *The Political Economy of International Relations*, p. 254.

[22] Stephen Hymer, "The Multinational Corporation and The Law of Uneven Development," in H. Radice, ed., *International Firms and Modern Imperialism*, p. 52.

Nowhere has such a regionalized planning scheme appeared. Instead, West European states favored indicative over imperative, technocratic over democratic, and centralized administrative over decentralized forms of planning. (Curiously, many European states, including Ireland, were first spurred into planning exercises by American requirements for local allocative programs accounting for use of Marshall Plan funds.)[23] The French model of indicative planning – replete with a planning commission, concertative practices, input–output iterative tables – proved most compatible with capitalist market mechanisms in the late 1950s and early 1960s.[24] The British and the Irish adopted what they judged were suitable features of the French experience. In effect, French-style planners were to behave like "Leninists of the bourgeoisie," a vanguard guiding economic elites toward schemes of enlightened self-interest. As Shonfield argued, the "bleak and squalid system" of pre-war capitalism gave way to a modern capitalism characterized by full employment, high productivity, generous social welfare, and an assortment of "conspiracies in the public interest."[25]

Primarily a market research device, the French model of planning did deploy influential policy instruments, at least in its early stages. "We prefer to get results not by commanding what must be done," a British emulator of the French model explained in the 1960s, "but by putting out a piece of cheese and trusting that some particular mouse will go after it."[26] Planners pursued discriminatory strategies by supplying cheap capital (especially effective in the post-war reconstruction), accelerated depreciation, tax relief, and a variety of grants to compliant firms.[27] Business quickly discovered that "the

[23] Joseph J. Lee, *Ireland 1912–1985: Politics and Society* (Cambridge: Cambridge University Press, 1989), p. 305.

[24] For an institutional approach and account see Peter Hall, *Governing The Economy* (New York: Oxford University Press, 1981) and his "Patterns of Economic Policy: an Organizational Approach," in Stephen Bornstein, David Held, and Joel Krieger, eds., *The State in Capitalist Europe: A Casebook* (Cambridge, MA: Harvard University Press, 1984).

[25] Andrew Shonfield, *Modern Capitalism: The Changing Balance of Public and Private Power* (London: Oxford University Press, 1965), pp. 63, 130. Also see the critical treatments in Jack Hayward and Michael Watson, eds., *Planning, Politics and Public Policy: The British, French and Italian Experiences* (London: Cambridge University Press, 1975).

[26] Samuel H. Beer, *British Politics in The Collectivist Age* (New York: Vintage, 1969), p. 323.

[27] An instructive theme emerging in a recent survey of economic policy (and, by extension, indicative planning) is that these devices were most successfully implemented in societies where business elites viewed them as the lesser of two evils (versus more intrusive options). See Peter A. Hall, ed., *The Political Power of Economic Ideas: Keynesianism Across Nations* (Princeton: Princeton University Press, 1989).

French planning process was designed to accommodate itself to the existing environment of private decentralized decision-making and to the existing power-structure within the State bureaucracy."[28] French planning essentially was a self-liquidating venture: the stronger the private firms grew the less they needed to resort to state resources.[29]

The growth of "the relative importance of foreign trade and investment runs counter to a basic premise that underlay most national planning," even if, as Zysman notes in the French case, planners managed to manipulate foreign competition to generate pressure for internal industrial upgrading.[30] British planning ended with the 1966 deflationary crisis and the French Sixth Plan (1970–75) was scuttled by adverse international trends.[31] Prior to the Single European Act, aimed at razing non-tariff barriers, Community regulations had eliminated tariff reduction as a policy instrument, impeded use of counter-cyclical instruments, and reduced controls over balance-of-payments.[32] EC members encountered the dilemma that imposing strict controls on foreign investors might drive them to a congenial member state and where they then export into the "difficult" state.

Multinational firms avail of the Eurodollar market, engage in transfer pricing, and in instances have interfered with internal politics in host countries.[33] Yet they also create jobs, produce better products, enhance competition, upgrade management skills, increase value-added, develop neglected resources, widen the tax base, improve balance-of-payments, and encourage economic inte-

---

[28] Stephen S. Cohen, *Modern Capitalist Planning: The French Model* (Berkeley: University of California Press, 1977), p. 4. If international relations scholars had been attentive to comparative politics studies such as Cohen's, less credence would have been granted to simplistic "strong state – weak state" characterizations and there would be less need to bother debunking "strong state" images that, elsewhere in the discipline, already had been found flawed.

[29] See *ibid.*

[30] John Zysman, *Governments, Markets, and Growth: Financial Systems and the Politics of Industrial Change* (Ithaca: Cornell University Press, 1983), p. 145.

[31] See David Coates, *Labour in Power?* (New York: Longman, 1980) and Joel Krieger, *Reagan, Thatcher and The Politics of Decline* (New York: Oxford University Press, 1986). See also the recent detailed account in Clive Ponting, *Breach of Promise: Labour in Power 1964–1970* (London: Penguin, 1990), pp. 167–314.

[32] Stuart Holland, *Uncommon Market: Capital, Class and Power in the European Community* (London: Macmillan, 1980).

[33] See the "inventories" of costs and benefits assembled in Thomas Biersteker's *Distortion or Development?*

gration. If multinationals are pirates the jolly roger is saluted everywhere. Lipson notes that even "most expropriations and forced sales are really state efforts to restructure the transnational network and redistribute their economic benefits, not to shut them out entirely."[34]

But, according to the "obsolescing bargain," a host state dissatisfied with the initial terms of investment will enjoy at a later stage the bargaining advantage over "sunk" foreign capital. The state can increase local content requirements, export quotas, joint ventures and so on.[35] The "product cycle" model envisions a profusion of products and processes of multinational firms being absorbed by avid local imitators so that in the long run all foreign investors are dead. But investigators have noted how high-technology-oriented manufacturers have proven to be exceptions to the hand-me-down dynamics of the product cycle. Through rapid renewal of science-intensive components, multinationals literally can innovate the evil day away. Recent inquiries disclose a leap-frog process whereby multinationals move production facilities before standardization of product is reached. Production of components may occur in Third World countries while final assembly goes on in advanced nations (though administrative, financial, and R & D control also remain).[36] Even in the realm of high technology industries inquiries into Third World states – especially India and Brazil – cite partial successes by states promoting domestic manufacture of minicomputers and microcomputers in the face of opposition by foreign firms.[37] The key actor – or enabler – is the state, viewed both as the

---

34 Charles H. Lipson, *Standing Guard: The Protection of U.S. Foreign Investment* (Berkeley: University of California Press, 1985), p. 180.

35 Gilpin, *The Political Economy of International Relations*, p. 255, Edmund Scibberas, *Multinational Electronics Companies and National Economic Policies* (Greenwich, CT: JAI Press, 1977), pp. 19–23. Also Biersteker, *Multinationals, The State, and Control of the Nigerian Economy*, p. 292.

36 On the "product cycle" see Raymond Vernon, *Sovereignty at Bay* (New York: Basic Books, 1971). Among critiques see Barbara Jenkins, "Reexamining The Obsolescing Bargin; A Case Study of Canada's National Energy Policy," *International Organization* 40, 1 (Winter 1986).

37 Studies of these partial successes include Joseph Grieco, *Between Dependency and Autonomy: India's Experience With The International Computer Industry* (Berkeley: University of California Press, 1984) and Emanuel Adler, "Ideological 'Guerrillas' and The Quest For Technological Autonomy: Brazil's Domestic Computer Industry," *International Organization* 40, 3 (Summer 1986), pp. 673–705. Both studies reinvigorate the product cycle model via state intervention strategies (in alliance with local entrepreneurs) more than they manage to refute a fanciful theoretical creature which Adler calls "classic Marxist structural dependency theory."

legal order and public bureaucracy, and the set of personnel who occupy positions of formal authority, and, as indicated in chapter 1, as the "pact of domination" within the institutional boundaries of which coalitions of class forces formed.[38] It is almost axiomatic to say the state is the crucial mediator between the domestic order and external economic agents (multinational firms and banks, international institutions, other states' agencies) amid global shifts and shocks. However, understanding causes and motives behind state policy responses in the international arena requires that we attend not only to administrative arrangements, intellectual exchange, and policy "legacies" but also that we examine carefully the concepts of state *autonomy, capacity,* and *strength.*[39]

STATE STRENGTH: IRONY OR CONTRADICTION?

In characterizing situational bargaining strength between host countries and multinational investors, Alfred Stepan provides an instructive four cell table (see Table 1).[40] Few states aspire to cell I (uncommitted capital – high FDI priority) status, because of lack of technological, financial, or material resources. In the twentieth century autarky for its own sake rarely beguiled national elites. An ambitious developmental state may invite foreign investment and nonetheless intend to achieve the status of cell II or cell III where bargaining leverage improves. But why must a state convert improved resources into actual bargaining power? Although many studies imply that states maximize sovereignty at every opportunity, there is nothing obvious or empirically compelling about this assumption. Migdal notes the "bizarre paradox" that many state leaders "persistently and consciously undermined their own state agencies – the very tools by which they could increase their capabilities and effect their policy agendas."[41] Skocpol, who defines state

---

[38] On dual aspects of the definition of the state see Stephen Krasner, "Approaches To The State: Alternative Conceptions and Historical Dynamics," *Comparative Politics* 16, 2 (January 1984) and Roger Benjamin and Raymond Duvall, "The Capitalist State in Context," in Roger Benjamin and Stephen Elkin, eds., *The Democratic State* (Lawrence: University of Kansas, 1985).

[39] Theda Skocpol, "Bringing The State Back In: Strategies of Analysis in Current Research," in Evans et al., *Bringing The State Back In.*

[40] Alfred Stepan, *The State and Society: Peru in Comparative Perspective* (Princeton: Princeton University Press, 1978).

[41] Joel Migdal, *Strong Societies and Weak States: State-Society Relations and State Capabilities in The Third World* (Princeton: Princeton University Press, 1988), p. xv.

Table 1. *Importance to state of attracting foreign investment in particular sector*

	Low priority	High priority
Uncommitted	**I** State can bar entry of foreign capital at almost no economic or political cost.	**IV** State has to offer incentives to attract foreign capital.
"Sunken"	**II** State can control or even eliminate foreign capital but at some economic and political cost.	**III** State cannot eliminate foreign capital but has some capacity to impose greater controls and exact greater rents.

Scale of state potential to control foreign capital
I = Highest IV = Lowest
Source: Alfred Stepan, *The State and Society: Peru in Comparative Perspective* (Princeton, NJ: Princeton University Press, 1978), p. 244.

strength "in terms of the state's autonomy from social groups or in terms of its capacities to intervene on its own or others' behalf," joins Migdal, Evans, and other scholars in observing that economic intervention can result in "a diminution of state autonomy and to a reduction of any capacities the state may have for coherent action."[42] Private groups counter-mobilize to penetrate and/or frustrate the state, which is not so very "bizarre". So the supreme irony of state strength is that the state loses it by using it.[43]

Stepan elaborates a six-variable chart depicting host country power potential *vis-à-vis* foreign investors in national savings/investment capacity, technological prowess, marketing links, domestic market size (and growth rate), scarce valuable resources, and "sunken" versus "uncommitted" capital as a political variable. Finally, he focuses on the internal characteristics of a given state: the state elites' strength and commitment to control corporate guests, technical and evaluative skills, and the political and administrative capacity to monitor foreign capital and to "use the power of the

[42] Evans, Rueschemeyer, and Skocpol, "On The Road To A More Adequate Understanding of The State," in *Bringing the State Back In*, pp. 354, 355.
[43] For a slightly different slant see John Ikenberry, "The Irony of State Strength: Comparative Responses To The Oil Shocks in The 1970s," *International Organization* 40, 2 (Spring 1986).

Table 2. *State's potential sectorial power* vis-à-vis *foreign capital for six variables*

Variables	High potential state power in sector	Low potential state power in sector
I State/National Savings and investment capacity	State can fully finance with internal state/national resources all new planned investment in the sector.	State cannot generate internal public or private capital to carry out planned projects and thus needs to go to international capital market.
II Technological capacity	State and national entrepreneurs dominate existing technology and have capacity to generate new technology as required.	State and national entrepreneurs do not have adequate knowledge to make or access to the techniques and social organization they need.
III Marketing capacity	State-national exporters have internal capital and external marketing outlets and customers.	State-national potential exporters must rely on international marketing firms to get domestic products on world markets and to find buyers.
IV Domestic market size	A sufficiently large, valuable and growing market that foreign capitalists do not want to lose to competition and will be willing to submit to stringent regulations as price of entry.	Actual and potential market so small that there is little competition to enter and in fact the state has to offer package of incentives to attract foreign investment.
V Value and quality of export items	State controls large quantities of valuable scarce resources.	State does not control any known large quantity of valuable scarce resources.
VI "Sunken" versus "Uncommitted" foreign investment in high priority and low priority investment sectors.	Because of I and v, the state attaches a very low priority to attracting or retaining foreign investment to sector; state can block new investment. If "sunken," state can extract much better terms by credible threats.	Because of I and v, the state can only develop if it attracts foreign investment. The combination of high state foreign investment priority plus uncommitted foreign investment places state in the weakest of the four positions.

Source: Stepan, *The State and Society*, p. 259.

state apparatus to structure outcomes."[44] The key question is, what would motivate the state elite to impose its preferences in spite of foreign (or local) investors?

In the oil industry, as in manufacturing, the "cycle of growing national assertiveness" is modified by technological change and by ideology (see Table 2).[45] Inadequate technical prowess (Stepan's variable II) retards assertiveness. A strong nationalist ideology can accelerate assertiveness (though not assure success) despite a "laggard" technology. Likewise, a nation enjoying augmented technological capacity can be deterred from exploiting its productive potential due to ideological commitments. In the Zambian case Sklar describes an emergent "doctrine of domicile" implying

both the corporation and the foreign state in which the parent company resides will yield to the state in which the subsidiary is domiciled in matters of local policy . . . this interpretive formulation justifies corporate expansion while it legitimates large-scale foreign investment . . . It is a proposition about interests and values which says nothing about the actual division of power.[46]

A highly probable outcome for an export-led developing country is that the policy momentum of an ideologically linked coalition of interests continues carrying it along the original developmental path even as alternatives become viable and desirable, until the economic strategy loses legitimacy and becomes politically exhausted. In short, the end ("self-sustaining growth") is consumed by the means (repeated injections of foreign investment). Naturally, this trend will be dismissed so long as local interests are satisfied with the distribution of gains.

Small states invariably are advised in the neo-classical literature to sacrifice a modicum of autonomy (defined as "the ability to frame and carry out objectives of domestic economic policy that diverge broadly from other countries") in order to benefit from global trade.[47] But interdependence also "is a strenuous form of existence"

[44] Stepan, "State Power and The Strength of Civil Society in The Southern Cone of Latin America," in *Bringing The State Back In*, p. 330.

[45] Michael Moran, "The Politics of International Business," *British Journal of Political Science* 8, 2 (April 1978), p. 229.

[46] Richard Sklar, *Corporate Power In An African State: The Political Impact of Multinational Mining Companies in Zambia* (Berkeley: University of California Press, 1975), p. 186. Also David G. Becker, Jeff Frieden, Sayre P. Schatz, and Richard Sklar, eds., *Postimperialism: International Capitalism and Development In The Twentieth Century* (Boulder: Lynn Rienner, 1987).

[47] A classic statement is Richard N. Cooper, *The Economics of Interdependence* (New York: McGraw Hill, 1966), p. 4.

and its unruly consequences become "a prime argument for national planning."[48] These pressures are especially acute in a small state pursuing a "peripheral postindustrialization" route.

DEPENDENT STATES AND HIGH TECH STRATEGIES

The OECD Inter-Futures Report enthusiastically portrayed micro-electronic technology as a "decisive qualitative leap" such that "the electronics complex during the next quarter of a century will be the main pole around which the productive structures of the advanced industrial countries will be reorganized."[49] Among so-called post-industrial industries are computers and software, semiconductors, lasers and fiber optics, electronic consumer goods, biotechnology, and ancillary activities. Although research and development (R & D) and other sophisticated functions are metropole-centred, the strategic fragmenting of standardizable aspects of production has brought the heady taste of the "micro millennium" to poorer climes.[50] Envisaging silicon valleys, glens and enterprise zones, several NICs and peripheral European states (the Irish Republic, Scotland, Spain, Portugal, and Greece) selected the electronics sector as the cornerstone of development or else have figured it prominently among their industrial aims. The stirring success of the "East Asia edge" during the 1970s was widely noted; the rush was on to share the bounty.[51] The South Korean and Taiwanese states actively direct their economies so as to attain an R & D based

[48] Michael Kidron, *Western Capitalism Since The War* (London: Penguin, 1971), p. 79.

[49] OECD, *Interfutures: Facing The Future* (Paris: Organization for Economic Cooperation and Development, 1979), p. 336.

[50] On the issue of metropole control of technology see Lynn Krieger Mytelka, "Knowledge-Intensive Production and The Changing Internationalization Strategies of Multinational Firms," in James A. Caporaso, ed., *A Changing International Division of Labor* (London: Frances Pinter, 1987); Jeffrey James, *The Economics of New Technology in Developing Countries* (London: Frances Pinter, 1982); and Helge Hveem, "Selective Dissociation in The Technology Sector," in Ruggie, *Antinomies of Interdependence*.

[51] Roy Hofheinz and Kent Calder provide a Kiplingesque tribute to the productive proper-ties of non-democratic "deference." Noting how sparse democratic activity is (or was) in regions "where East Asian Officials form a caste of oligarchs vying with one another to exercise authority over a deferential and productive society," they observe that "citizens of East Asia, especially the business-men, are comfortable knowing their governments do not change." *The East Asia Edge* (New York: Basic Books, 1983). See the critical treatment in Bruce Cumings, "The Origins of The Northeast Asian Political Economy: Industrial Sectors, Product Cycles, and Political Consequences," *International Organization* 38, 1 (Winter 1984) and the essays in *I.D.S. Bulletin* (Developmental States in East Asia) edited by Robert Wade and Gordon White, 15, 2 (1984).

competitive structure. Ireland and Scotland are "enablers" in approach, attracting foreign industries whose cumulative implantation on native soil not only will form an integrated network but will prod local entrepreneurs to complement them.[52] An "enabling" mode of intervention is ineffective if local entrepreneurial elements are weak (because of high risk, uncertainty, higher rates of return elsewhere, etc.), but states strike different balances among intermingling modes over time.[53] These societies are not content to await the expiration of product-cycles. Job creation and investment may be the immediate goals; the ultimate aim is to create a base of "postindustrial" industries and endow them with R & D that give their products a "cutting edge" in the market. This ambition is consonant with the assumption that as a state's "capacity for action" grows (administrative skills improve, industry diversifies, entrepreneurship improves, saving and investment rates rise), so too is the state more motivated to pursue the goal of "alleviating dependence on foreign capital and technology."[54]

Liberal economists score points in questioning the welfare-enhancing wisdom of too zealous a pursuit of this aim. States do trade off a degree of autonomy to reap the benefits of interdependence. But there are distinctly domestic reasons why autonomy cannot be consistently pursued, and these reasons can be characterized in the form of two "satisficing" bargains, *elite* and *consensual*.[55] What is "satisficed" in these bargains is the goal of

---

[52] States are "enablers" if they rely on indirect incentives and market mechanisms to guide the choices of private economic agents. They are "complementary" when engaged in substantial public commercial activity more or less in tandem with private capital (and indeed abetting the latter), and are "entrepreneurial" if the state undertakes directive planning, public–private coordination, and commercial activity in a manner superordinate to the private sector. A genuinely "entrepreneurial" state is a risk-taker in a dual sense: with respect to international marketplace challenges, and with regard to challenges from internal economic elites. On the ambiguous relation between state and capital in "state entrepreneurship" see Peter Evans, "Declining Hegemony and Assertive Industrialization: U.S.–Brazil Conflicts in The Computer Industry," *International Organization* 43, 2 (Spring 1989), pp. 207–30.

[53] John R. Freeman, "State Entrepreneurship and Dependent Development," *American Journal of Political Science* 26, 2 (1983).

[54] Raymond Duvall and John Freeman, "International Economic Relations and The Entrepreneurial State," *Economic Development and Cultural Change* 32, 2 (January 1984), p. 375.

[55] Herbert Simon first developed the theory of "satisficing," which "asserts that people do not seek the best alternative in a feasible set [of choices] but limit themselves to what seems to be 'good enough' or satisfactory." Jon Elster, *Rational Choice* (New York: New York University Press, 1986), p. 25.

autonomy. A consensual bargain is endorsed because autonomy goals are really a *means to other ends* (full employment, rising living standards, economic opportunities) that may be achieved by embracing interdependence. In an elite bargain "triple alliance," comprador coalitions, state corporatism, and some forms of societal corporatism), dominant groups resist any policy shifts that portend erosion of their shares of power and wealth. Thus, ideologically linked societal interests (or the "pact of domination") seek to impose policies that not only reject autonomy goals but also injure non-elites by sacrificing their salient concerns (jobs, living standards, social services) which otherwise, if improving, induce consent.[56] Non-elites may be better served by promoting autonomy (e.g., enhancing indigenous R & D, sacking more state regulation and coordination in commercial arenas, shading the developmental emphasis toward local resource bases). Freeman and Duval argue that "there is no reason to believe that the state's activities are an effective means of achieving control over industrialization and of alleviating dependence on foreign capital and technology."[57] Empirically sound, this verdict founders on the premise of high "propensities to defer" by subordinate strata whatever their organizational capabilities, whatever the feasibility of alternatives, whatever the level and form of socio-economic conflict, whatever the strength of the state at a given juncture. Of course, situational factors may press so powerfully that no alternative course is possible; even so, the analytical tack here requires consideration of counterfactual alternatives which serve to sharpen an interpretation. These theoretical concerns are to be fleshed out in the following analysis.

CONCLUSION

Neither capacity nor autonomy – even if virtually infinite – yield useful clues as to how a state will behave in the international arena. Nor is the degree of autonomy necessarily related to changes in capacity. Conflating the two concepts results in misplaced attri-

---

[56] A similar formulation applied to advanced states is Andrew Martin, "Political Constraints on Economic Strategies in Advanced Industrial Societies," *Comparative Political Studies* 7, 4 (October 1977).

[57] Raymond Duvall and John Freeman, "The Techno-bureaucratic Elite and the Entrepreneurial State in Dependent Industrialization," *American Political Science Review* 77, 3 (1983), p. 391.

butions of intent.[58] For example, a study utilizing this line of analysis found the Irish state was "monumentally unsuccessful either in ensuring sustained economic growth or in moderating inegalitarian tendencies in the class system," which presumes the state (or "pact of domination") actually attempted the latter accomplishment because it possessed a capacity to do so.[59]

The task of explaining the relation between state strength and policy content begins by examining the dominant coalition members and the economic model they champion, which guides their diagnoses. Only crises can detach coalition members from the reigning model and from one another. What the international economic arena does is "strengthen or weaken certain arguments and the resources of those advancing them."[60] I argue that the ascendence of a "certain argument" in the policy realm owes more to the resources of proponents than to an objective congruence between circumstances and a particular option, and that the domestic diagnosis of a crisis is itself a political process.

"Ireland is a fringe country," Chubb writes, "geographically on the fringes of Europe, socially and economically on the fringes of the 'British Isles' and, for long, a fringe province of the United Kingdom."[61] The Irish Republic also is a very *small* country, roughly the size of Austria or the state of Alabama, with one-twentieth of the population of the largest Common Market members and with a third of the citizenry crowded into the capital city. In so compact a society it is possible within political, business, and academic circles for everyone to know everyone else.[62] Whatever familiarity breeds, this is a significant factor inasmuch as culture affects the perception

---

[58] The editors of *Bringing The State Back In* do warn readers that it is not "helpful to assume a single dimension of 'state strength' that conflates different features of state organization and resources or, worse, confounds the matter of state autonomy with issues of the capacities a state has for performing certain kinds of tasks" (p. 355).

[59] Richard Breen, Damian F. Hannan, David B. Rottman, and Christopher T. Whelan, *Understanding Contemporary Ireland: State, Class and Development in The Republic of Ireland* (Dublin: Gill and Macmillan, 1990), p. 209.

[60] Peter Gourevitch, "Keynesian Politics: The Political Sources of Economic Policy Choices," in Peter A. Hall, ed., *The Political Power of Economic Ideas* (Princeton, Princeton University Press, 1989), p. 102.

[61] Basil Chubb, *The Government and Politics of Ireland* (Stanford: Stanford University Press, 1970), p. 50.

[62] On the role of "personalism" in Irish politics see David E. Schmitt, *The Irony of Irish Democracy* (Lexington, MA: D.C. Heath, 1973).

of issues, conduct within institutions processing policy issues, and the policy outcomes.[63]

If Britain or France have been vexed by powerful corporations and banks, a semi-peripheral nation faces a particularly daunting task. To analyze national policies under conditions of complex interdependence (or "complex dependence") Keohane and Nye ask what range of choice is available and what factors determine the response chosen. A cogent answer "would require close comparative analysis of the domestic structures and political processes of particular states."[64]

Chapter 3 provides a compact account of the vicissitudes of development of the economy, political institutions, and class formation within Ireland through 1958, the year of the "great break" from a shabby autarky to a commitment to free trade. This chapter will elucidate the politics that lay behind the evolution of policy, and that conditioned the state's mediating role in the local and the international marketplaces.

[63] J. P. O'Carroll, "Strokes, Cute Hoors and Sneaking Regarders: The Influence of Local Culture on Irish Political Style," *Irish Political Studies* 2, 1 (1987).

[64] Robert Keohane and Joseph Nye, *Power and Interdependence* (Boston, Little Brown, 1977), p. 224.

CHAPTER 3

The pale replica

We are the most conservative revolutionaries in history.
Kevin O'Higgins, Minister of Justice, 1924

Although Irish scholars are correcting a traditional inclination to blame all woes on perfidious Albion, the impact of colonial domination – for better and for worse – was powerful.[1] As England's first colony Ireland in the seventeenth century was coercively integrated into the core economy.[2] The rebellious natives were dispossessed by post-Reformation (Protestant) English authorities so that by 1703 only 14 percent of the land was in native (Catholic) hands. In this period of colonial consolidation "a grim pattern was established, lasting into the twentieth century, whereby the density of the Irish rural population was in inverse proportion to the quality of the land on which it was settled."[3]

English rule was no unalloyed boon for the subject economy. The Cattle Acts of 1666 prohibited export of cattle to England, and were repealed when English interests changed. The Navigation Acts of 1679 forbade Irish trade with other colonies except via English merchant ships – which helps explain their otherwise odd lack of a maritime tradition. The English parliament banned Irish woollens

[1] See Ronan Fanning, "The Great Enchantment: Uses and Abuses of Modern Irish History," in James A. Dooge, ed., *Ireland in The Contemporary World* (Dublin: Gill and Macmillan, 1986) and Roy F. Foster, ed., *The Oxford History of Ireland* (Oxford: Oxford University Press, 1992). That this revisionist trend can also err is a worthwhile point made in David Johnson and Liam Kennedy "Nationalist Historiography and the Decline of the Irish Economy," in Sean Hutton and Paul Stewart, eds., *Ireland's Histories: Aspects of State, Society and Ideology* (London: Routledge, 1991).

[2] Eric Strauss, *Irish Nationalism and British Democracy* (London: Methuen, 1953), p. 15. See details of the draconian developmental scheme advanced in the seventeenth century by Sir William Petty in his "Treatise on Ireland," in C. H. Hull, ed., *Economic Writings of Sir William Petty* (Cambridge: Cambridge University Press, 1899).

[3] Erhard Rumpf and A. C. Hepburn, *Nationalism and Socialism in Twentieth Century Ireland* (New York: Barnes and Noble, 1977), p. 3.

exports in 1699. Irish breweries were forbidden in 1710 to import hops except from England, and glass manufacturing was crippled by legislation in 1746. Linen manufacture did not compete directly with English goods, and was encouraged in the Northeast. It was Ireland's misfortune to rival England in many economic areas. British policy reinforced Irish dependence on land by discouraging virtually every promising manufacturing scheme. Although recent scholarship claims that "trade was not greatly hampered by colonial restrictions," much depends on how one calculates the "not greatly."[4] Minor increments often make all the difference in trade.

Industrial initiatives and agricultural upgrading were stymied except in the North where a loyal Protestant ascendancy held sway, and where the "Ulster Custom" may have afforded a modest security for the largely non-Anglican Protestant farmers (who also, to a much lesser degree, were affected adversely by anti-Catholic Penal Codes).[5] Industrialization in Ulster "had little impact on the agricultural South beyond offering employment in Belfast as an alternative to emigration."[6]

After the 1798 rebellion Ireland was forcibly united to the core state and the result was "a colony – not of the classical English form, but rather of the style of Algeria, nominally part of the United Kingdom, but in practice governed on different principles."[7] Ulster apart, Ireland was excluded from the industrial revolution and compelled to rely on the exchange of primary products for manufactured imports. Nonetheless Hechter argues:

Sovereignty might have facilitated and encouraged economic diversification in the Celtic territories. On the eve of the Union (1801) the development prospects of the Irish economy appeared very favorable. Prices for agricultural products were rising, but there also were strong signs

---

[4] Foster, "Ascendency and Union," p. 143. J. C. Beckett, *The Making of Modern Ireland, 1603–1923* (New York: Alfred A. Knopf, 1966), p. 168. Also see L. M. Cullen, *An Economic History of Ireland Since 1600* (London: B.T. Batsford, 1972).

[5] On the "Ulster Custom" see Edith Mary Johnston, *Ireland in The Eighteenth Century* (Dublin: Gill and Macmillan, 1974), pp. 27–30. The Penal Code, enacted between 1697 and 1727, made the native Irish Catholic a legally extinct creature, shorn of virtually all rights. One should perhaps say the "supposed" Ulster Custom, as historians these days dispute whether it had any effect or conferred any distinct advantage on Ulster agriculture. See Foster, "Ascendency and Union," p. 169, and Kennedy, "The Rural Economy," in Liam Kennedy and Philip Ollerenshaw, eds., *An Economic History of Ulster* (Manchester: University of Manchester Press, 1985).

[6] Belinda Probert, *Beyond Orange and Green: The Political Economy of the Northern Ireland Crisis* (London: Zed Press, 1978), p. 33.

[7] Desmond Greaves, *The Irish Crisis* (New York: International Publishers, 1974), p. 36.

of industrial diversification. The linen industry was booming. In fact, Ireland's industrial development was so promising that manufacturing interests in Britain violently opposed the establishment of free trade between the islands in 1785.[8]

Cullen argues that these advantages were fleeting, and soon eroded by cheapening transport costs, falling prices, and other factors, nonetheless the capacity to resort to protective trade barriers *might* have sustained embryonic industrialization.[9] In a sovereign state industrial expansion could have been propelled by rapid growth in population and the domestic market (rising from 4.7 million in 1791 to 8 million by 1841, or half England's population). Lack of resources posed no insuperable barrier since coal "was as cheap as in many parts of England outside the mining centers, and in Belfast it was a little cheaper than elsewhere."[10] In retrospect what appears to have been most damaging were the problems incurred by so suddenly competing with structurally superior English rivals, which were a damaging and, many argue, lasting legacy of English rule in this pre-Union period.[11] Ireland instead became a supplier of food – and capital – to the industrializing "mainland."

Scholars citing the beneficial aspects of imperialism point to many administrative accomplishments and to the investment of English capital in infrastructural projects especially. But English capital customarily was available to complement and fortify previous English investment, not meet Irish needs.[12] Irish capital proved, unsurprisingly, no more adventurous or "patriotic." Because harsh discriminatory laws were difficult to enforce, a Catholic middle class of merchants, small proprietors, and professionals did arise in the "lowly" but highly taxable commercial sector. Ample capital was available in nineteenth-century Ireland, but neither the will nor the

---

[8] Michael Hechter, *Internal Colonialism: The Celtic Fringe in British National Development* (Berkeley: University of California Press, 1977), p. 92.

[9] Cullen, "The Irish Economy in The Eighteenth Century," in L. M. Cullen, ed., *The Formation of The Irish Economy* (Cork: Mercier Press, 1968), p. 20.

[10] Hechter, *Internal Colonialism*, p. 93 on population, and Cullen, "Irish Economic History: Fact and Myth," in *The Formation of The Irish Economy*, p. 123 on fuel resources.

[11] See especially Eoin O'Malley, "The Decline of Irish Industry in The Nineteenth Century," *Economic and Social Review* 12, 1 (October 1981). These barriers include economies of scale, learning curve improvements, technological capacity, and specialized skills and marketing acumen and power, which a late starter must confront in its established rivals.

[12] See Joseph Lee, *The Modernisation of Irish Society, 1848–1918* (Dublin: Gill and Macmillan, 1973), chapter 1, and Hechter, *Internal Colonialism*, p. 88.

economic incentives to risk it productively at home.[13] "The public interest required an extensive industrialisation drive," Lee writes, observing that banking dividends at this time often exceeded 10 percent. "The private interest of the commercial sector – importers and exporters, wholesalers, assemblers – the typical cross-section of an enclave economy, simply required to be left in quiet possession of their modest patrimony."[14] Substantial sums were wastefully applied within Ireland or else transferred to the more remunerative money markets of London.

Protestant landlords dominated the economy, but were varied in their fortunes, and overall they were undergoing an historical decline in the nineteenth century. It would likewise be a mistake to characterize tenants as a uniformly destitute group with common interests. A system of thirty-one-year leases developed so that tenant farmers, in their exploitative turn, employed a class of cheap-wage laborers as well as renting parcels of land to cottiers. Many tenant (Catholic) farmers thus became Lilliputian landlords. This serial exploitative network would not ease with the release of the absentee landlord's grip later in the nineteenth century under various land reform and land purchase acts.[15] "On the contrary, once Irish agriculture settled into the pattern of the small farm, run by a single family, with the succession and the revenue jealously guarded," Lyons notes, "the gulf between the farmer and the landless man came to mirror all too faithfully the gulf that had formerly existed between landlord and tenant."[16]

With markets restricted through the eighteenth century and industries inhibited by a "late start" in the early nineteenth century, the Irish economy responded strictly to the English market. A singularly adverse affect on Irish development was the fourfold rise in cattle prices relative to grain since George III's reign:

The expanding Irish cattle-exporting industry, by supplanting other agricultural enterprises with a high output/acre, caused a decline in demand

---

[13] Lee, "Capital in the Irish Economy" in Cullen, *The Formation of the Irish Economy*. Foster argues that the idea that Ireland was drained of investible funds by rack-renting absentee landlords "does not stand up." R. F. Foster, *Modern Ireland, 1600–1972* (London: Penguin, 1989), p. 374.

[14] *Ibid.*, p. 30.

[15] K. Theodore Hoppen, *Ireland Since 1800* (New York: Longman, 1989), p. 5. See especially Raymond Crotty, *Irish Agricultural Production: Its Structure and Output* (Cork: Cork University Press, 1966).

[16] F. S. L. Lyons, *Ireland Since The Famine* (London: Fontana Books, 1973), pp. 26–27.

from the land-intensive export sector. Simultaneously, competing exports were depressing nonexport industries. The combined effect was greatly to reduce total demand, scale of operations, and hence overall efficiency in labour and capital-intensive industry in Ireland.[17]

As unit production costs rose due to declining scale, the "remedy" of wage reduction aggravated the fall in local demand.[18] Meanwhile, the expanding cattle trade ("on the hoof" for mainland value-adding) was displacing small farmers and tenants, crowded onto ever smaller parcels of land. The stage was set for a gruesome display of "propensity to defer" – the great famine of 1845–49. A Malthusian tragedy aggravated by Manchester liberals, the famine made emigration a fatalistic substitute for radicalism, an invaluable "prop" for the social order.[19] Population fell from 8.5 million in 1845 to less than 5 million at the turn of the century. Still, struggles for land reform intertwined with the Home Rule movement several decades later. Incremental concessions culminated with the 1903 Wyndham Act which created a new class of peasant proprietors who, like large "ranchers," undertook a socially conservative existence. Home Rule was frustrated by a league of English and Ulster Tories (supported vigorously, indeed virulently, by Protestant under-classes), and a minor insurrection in 1916 eventuated in the Anglo-Irish War of 1919–21.

In the 1923–23 civil war, the new Free State defeated rebels who opposed partition, and had also beaten wage levels below those during the infamous 1913 Dublin lockout.[20] Bereft of the industrial Northeast (containing 40 percent of taxable capacity, 30 percent of population, and a third of port trading), the new regime presided over a primary commodity-exporting economy. Irish labor organizers were confronted with "a potential proletarian movement which was bedeviled by its internal class divisions, engulfed in a largely conservative agricultural society, divided by denomination but condemned by bourgeois religious orthodoxy, and distracted by

[17] Crotty, "Capitalist Colonialism and Peripheralisation: The Irish Case," in Dudley Seers, ed., *Underdeveloped Europe* (Atlantic Highlands, NJ: Humanities Press, 1979), p. 227.
[18] See also R. B. McDowell, "Ireland On The Eve Of The Famine," in Owen Dudley Edwards and T. Desmond Williams, eds., *The Great Hunger* (New York: New York University Press, 1973).
[19] See Cecil Woodham-Smith, *The Great Famine* (New York: Signet, 1962).
[20] Desmond Greaves, *The Irish Transport and General Workers Union: The Formative Years 1909–1923* (Dublin: Gill and Macmillan, 1982), pp. 315–23.

the primacy of the national question."[21] Further, the Irish Labour Party had committed a massive strategic error – according to Lipset-Rokkan design – by withdrawing from the general election of 1918 so as to provide the national question with a clear field for electoral decision.[22] The Irish electorate had expanded from 701,475 in 1910 to 1,936,673 in 1918; so two of every three voters were on their first visit to the polls.

In the 1922–23 civil war, large farmers, professionals, and commercial classes supported the pro-treaty forces while anti-treaty Republican forces were notably filled with small farmers and laborers who had abstained from the Anglo-Irish war. An estimated 130,000 unemployed people in Ireland were dismayed to find they had fought the English for what one Northern Ireland minister sardonically called their "civil right to emigrate." By May 1923, when hostilities ceased, Ireland's leadership was decimated and the dream of an *Eire Nua* had disintegrated. The treaty cleavage inflicted a most profound influence on party formation and participation patterns in the twenty-six county Free State.[23] The dominant agricultural and petit bourgeois were content with the inherited scheme of things. Those who couldn't afford to love Ireland left it, or were driven out.

IMPERIAL STANDARDS, REPUBLICAN INCOMES

Technically a dominion, the new state was a recreation of British institutions and economic ideology. The civil service was a "Whitehall, writ small."[24] The legal system became more British

[21] J. Bowyer Bell, *The Secret Army: A History of The IRA 1916–70* (London: Sphere Books, 1972).

[22] Seymour Martin Lipset and Stein Rokkan, "Cleavage Structures, Party Systems, and Voter Alignments," in Lipset and Rokkan, eds., *Party Systems and Voter Alignments* (New York: Free Press, 1967); John A. Murphy, *Ireland in The Twentieth Century* (Dublin: Gill and Macmillan, 1975), p. 5.

[23] Peter Mair cogently makes the case that although party cleavages were a persisting product of the 1918 election, there were ample opportunities in subsequent decades for realignments to take place, and that, overall, Irish political behaviour "should not be dismissed as simply bizarre" in comparison to other West European cases. See his *The Changing Irish Party System: Organisation, Ideology, and Electoral Competition* (London: Frances Pinter Press, 1987), p. 11. On the origins of the Irish state, see Brian Farrell, *The Founding of Dail Eireann: Parliament and Nation-Building* (Dublin: Gill and Macmillan, 1973), Bruce Logan, "The Irish Parliamentary Tradition" (Ph.D. Dissertation, University of Chicago, 1975), and Jeffrey Prager, *Building Democracy in Ireland: Political Order and Cultural Integration in a Newly Independent Nation* (Cambridge: Cambridge University Press, 1986).

[24] Patrick K. Lynch, "The Economic Scene," in Owen Dudley Edwards, ed., *Conor Cruise O'Brien Introduces Ireland* (Dublin: Gill and Macmillan, 1969), p. 24. The sub-title "Imperial Standards, Republican Incomes" in this chapter was coined by Patrick Lynch.

than the system the British themselves retained, and the tax system was adopted with only minor modifications.[25] Dail Eireann was a hibernicized House of Commons; Seanad Eireann a feebler counterpart to the House of Lords. The flags were Irish, but the flagpoles probably were manufactured in Britain. The Catholic Church, a source of solace and identity in plainer colonial days, guarded the gates against Bolshevik demons and bawdy authors, while emigrants poured out.

While anti-treaty deputies refused to recognize the Dail, the pro-treaty party Cumann na nGaedheal (League of Gaels) shouldered the tasks of reconstruction. The army – not without a precarious moment – was subjected to civilian control, and law and order reestablished. Irish administrators began to balance their very own budgets, and the machinery of government was tested.[26] The Labour Party and the Farmers Party obligingly played the role of "loyal opposition." (The 1923 election yielded 63 pro-treaty seats, 44 anti-treaty, 15 Farmers Party and 14 Labour.)

Designating agriculture as the motor for the growth of secondary industries, the first government "aimed at the reduction of all costs of production in order to enable exporters to compete successfully abroad; this entailed low taxation and low expenditures."[27] "Abroad" meant Britain, and "exporters" meant the cattle ranchers. "Low taxation" meant low direct taxes only, and "low expenditures" meant misery, migration, and self-prescribed "low stateness."

In 1926, 57% of the male working population were employed in agriculture and in 1929 33% of the national income was earned by this sector. In the same year, 88.99% of exports by value were agricultural and 42.08% came from the main export to Britain, mainly cattle; 92.3% of exports went to the United Kingdom ... 58% of imports by value were manufactured goods and 78% of imports came from the United Kingdom.[28]

25 Rumpf and Hepburn, *Nationalism and Socialism in Twentieth Century Ireland*, p. 127, and Josephine Corrigan, *Business and Sales Taxation in the Republic of Ireland* (New York: Praeger, 1971).
26 On finance, see Ronan Fanning, *The Irish Department of Finance 1922–1958* (Dublin: Institute of Public Management, 1978).
27 Anthony W. Orridge, "The Blueshirts and The 'Economic War': A Study of Ireland in The Context of Dependency Theory," *Political Studies* 31, 3 (September 1983), p. 353. Also see the general survey, James Meenan, *The Irish Economy Since 1922* (Liverpool: Liverpool University Press, 1972).
28 Orridge, "Blueshirts," p. 354.

There was enormous variation in the productivity, profit, and capitalization of agricultural holdings. Large farmers (50 acres plus) out-prosper small neighbours because of scale benefits. Under the livestock breeding system disproportionate costs were borne by small farms that transferred young cattle to the "fattening regions."[29] Small farmers were not enamored with the Free State government.

The government slashed income taxes by 40 percent, and keeping Irish taxation beneath British rates became an implicit policy. The revenue was made up by cutting public expenditure and by hiking indirect taxes. In one thrifty year, old age pensions were reduced by a shilling. The biblical edict of Cumann na nGaedheal was not "To him that hath shall be given" so much as "From him that hath shall not be taken." Until 1927 electoral reprisal was impossible because of the obstinate wandering of De Valera's party in the abstentionist wilderness. Industrialists, however, were content with Free State free trade policies because they feared that protectionist measures would invite retaliation driving up raw material prices as well as restricting access to markets overseas.

Despite emigration, unemployment never dipped below 6 percent. By 1930 Irish investment in British assets was twice that of the reverse flow.[30] An ardently *anti-dirigiste* government was impelled to create "state-sponsored bodies" to fill the entrepreneurial gaps in the economy – utilities, credit, transport, and, later, commercial public enterprises.[31] But the "great spurt" of industrial development under organized direction, noted elsewhere by Gerschenkron, only occurred in sporadic dribbles in Ireland. Why?

The "advantages of backwardness" were superseded, in part, by the "advantages of dependence" for particular strata. Dominant

29 Meenan, *The Irish Economy Since 1922*, p. 111.
30 D. R. O'Connor Lysaght, "British Imperialism in Ireland," in Austen Morgan and Bob Purdie, eds., *Ireland: Divided Nation, Divided Class* (London: Ink Links Press, 1980), p.24. This is an estimate. In any case, Cullen agrees that there was a substantial outflow, the "credit surplus between 1914 and 1921 amounted to £76.6 million. To this sum should be added an unknown sum in respect of net invisible earnings (interest on existing investments, pensions, emigrant remittances, earnings in HM's forces)." Cullen, *Economic History of Ireland*, p. 172.
31 Lyons, *Ireland Since The Famine, p. 608*. On these curiously defined public bodies, see Garret Fitzgerald, *State Sponsored Bodies* (Dublin: Institute of Public Administration, 1963), Sean Lemass, "The Role of State Sponsored Bodies in The Economy," in Basil Chubb and Patrick K. Lynch, eds., *Economic Development and Planning* (Dublin: Institute of Public

rural and petit bourgeois interests shunned Sinn Fein party's reveries of national self-sufficiency, and were better served by free trade. Liberal economic orthodoxies were embedded in institutions inherited from Britain. The "island behind an island" felt no pressing military threat that might motivate state-directed development and, as a marginally privileged member of the "Celtic periphery," Ireland was *insufficiently* backward because of earlier British infrastructural investments (albeit to facilitate particular patterns of trade and traffic) and political reforms. Partition, of course, played an imponderable and ceaselessly pondered role.

As in Latin America the 1930 depression made a necessity of the Sinn Fein virtue of import-substituting industrialization (ISI), which a newly elected populist government (Fianna Fail) intended to pursue in 1932. The most ardent protectionist was Sean Lemass who was "to find it easier to persuade his governmental colleagues to adopt protectionism than to take specific actions on employment and development policies."[32] In the late 1920s Fianna Fail called for (1) the reunification of the country; (2) a cultural revival and restoration of the language; (3) the placing of the wealth and resources of the nation at the service of the "whole population"; (4) economic self-sufficiency as far as possible; (5) as many families as possible settled on the land; and (6) an intensive rural industrialization scheme.[33] The party promised to promote a merchant fleet, a fishing industry, afforestation, and to erect tariff walls within which industry could incubate safely and, they presumed, robustly. Fianna Fail exhibited interest as well in housing and social welfare in this its "radical reformist phase."[34] Meanwhile Labour Party fortunes fell, their twenty-two seats shrinking in the 1927 election. As one exasperated union leader explained, "the workers expected Fianna Fail to fulfill all their wishes."[35]

In the 1920s and early 30s, Bowyer Bell explains "people were uneasy and despairing but socialist language and ideas did not speak clearly to the countryside where the horror of the parish priest at the

Administration, 1969) and, latterly, Paul Sweeney, *The Politics of Public Enterprise and Privatisation* (Dublin: Tomar Press, 1990).

[32] Brian Farrell, *Sean Lemass* (Dublin: Gill and Macmillan, 1983), p.34.

[33] Rumpf and Hepburn, *Nationalism and Socialism in Twentieth Century Ireland*, p. 102.

[34] See Tom Garvin, *The Evolution of Irish Nationalism* (Dublin: Gill and Macmillan, 1981); also Mair, *The Changing Irish Party System*, chapter 1.

[35] Quoted in Rumpf and Hepburn, *Nationalism and Socialism*, p. 107.

Table 3. Distribution of Dail seats, index of legislative fractionalization, and turnover of seats, 1948–1987

Elections	1948		1951		1954		1957		1961		1965		1969	
	N	%	N	%	N	%	N	%	N	%	N	%	N	%
Parties														
Fianna Fail	68	46.3	69	46.9	65	44.2	78	53.1	70	48.6	72	50.0	75	52.1
Fine Gael	31	21.1	40	27.2	50	34.0	40	27.2	47	32.6	47	32.6	50	34.7
Labour	14	9.5	16	10.9	19	12.9	12	8.2	16	11.1	22	15.3	18	12.5
National Labour	5	3.4	–	–	–	–	–	–	–	–	–	–	–	–
Progressive Democrats	–	–	–	–	–	–	–	–	–	–	–	–	–	–
Clann na Poblachta[a]	10	6.8	2	1.4	3	2.0	1	0.7	1	0.7	1	0.7	–	–
Clann na Talmhan	7	4.8	6	4.1	5	3.4	3	2.0	2	1.4	–	–	–	–
National Progressive Democrats	–	–	–	–	–	–	–	–	2	1.4	–	–	–	–
Sinn Fein[a]	–	–	–	–	–	–	4	2.7	0	0	–	–	–	–
Workers' Party[b]	–	–	–	–	–	–	–	–	–	–	–	–	–	–
Others	12	8.2	14	9.5	5	3.4	9	6.1	6	4.2	2	1.4	1	0.7
Total	147	100	147	100	147	100	147	100	144	100	144	100	144	100
Index of fractionalisation[e]	0.717		0.683		0.670		0.632		0.643		0.620		0.592	
Turnover of seats[d] (%)	27.9		21.1		19.7		22.4		25.2		22.4		30.6	

Elections	1973		1977		1981		1982 Feb.		1982 Nov.		1987	
	N	%	N	%	N	%	N	%	N	%	N	%
Parties												
Fianna Fail	69	47.9	84	56.8	75	45.2	81	48.8	75	45.2	81	48.5
Fine Gael	54	37.5	43	29.1	65	39.2	63	38.0	70	42.2	51	30.7
Labour	19	13.2	17	11.5	15	9.0	15	9.0	16	9.6	12	7.2
National Labour	–		–		–		–		–		–	
Progressive Democrats	–		–		–		–		–		14	8.4
Clann na Poblachta	–		–		–		–		–		–	
Clann na Talmhan	–		–		–		–		–		–	
National Progressive Democrats	–		–		–		–		–		–	
Sinn Fein[a]	–		–		2	1.2	0	0	–		–	
Workers Party[b]	0	0	0	0	1	0.6	3	1.8	2	1.2	0	0
Others	2	1/4	4	2/7	5	3/0	4	2.4	3	1.8	4	2.4
Total	144	100	148	100	166	100	166	100	166	100	166	100
Index of fractionalisation[c]	0.614		0.578		0.633		0.608		0.608		0.654	
Turnover of seats[d] (%)	19.4		31.8		33.7		17.5		15.7		25.3	

[a] Refers to anti H-Block Committee candidates in 1981
[b] In 1973 Official Sinn Fein
[c] Based on the formula in Rae (1971)
[d] Percentage of TDs who were not members of the outgoing Dail
Source: Mair, *The Changing Irish Party System.*

audacity of the Reds and the traditional Republicanism of De
Valera seemed more relevant."[36] On the crest of surging economic
and social discontent, Fianna Fail took office in March 1932 with
Labour Party support, and in 1933 secured a majority in a snap
election. The party's aims were:

1. To remove the Article of the Constitution which makes the signing of
   the Oath of Allegiance obligatory on members entering the Dail ...
2. To retain the Land Annuities in the State Treasury ... With two of the
   three million pounds involved the farmers can be relieved completely of
   the rates on their holdings. Another million is available for the relief of
   taxation, or for such purposes as the Dail may determine.
3. To submit to counsel for their opinion the question of the obligation to
   make other annual payments to Britain, including the pensions of the
   former Royal Irish Constabulary ...
4. To organize systematically the establishment of the industries required
   to meet the needs of the community in manufactured goods ... Suitable
   fiscal laws would be passed to give the protection necessary against
   unfair foreign competition.
5. To preserve the home market for our farmers and to encourage the
   production by them of our food requirements to the greater extent
   possible.
6. To negotiate trade agreements that would secure for our products
   preferences in foreign markets ... Machinery and other capital equipment for our industries will have to be purchased from abroad. We can
   in these purchases accord a preference to Britain in return for a preference in her markets for our agricultural produce.[37]

THE IRISH STATE AND ECONOMIC "SELF-SUFFICIENCY"

In 1933 on a Dublin visit John Maynard Keynes conferred a
guarded blessing on Fianna Fail's program, wondering aloud
whether Ireland possessed a diverse and ample enough resource
base "for more than a very modest measure of national self-
sufficiency to be possible without a disastrous reduction in a standard of life which is already none too high."[38] But in response to the
great depression beggar-thy-neighbor became the standard course.
Britain had erected tariffs and protected its agriculture. The Irish
Free State, ironically, only followed suit.

---

[36] Bell, *The Secret Army*, p. 111.
[37] Frank Munger, *The Legitimacy of Opposition* (New York: Sage, 1974), pp. 15–16.
[38] John Maynard Keynes, "National Self-Sufficiency," *Studies* 86, 2 (June 1933), pp. 177–93.

But Irish exponents of Friedrich List's gospel of protected industrialization had not imagined that infant firms would thrive during a steep contraction in trade and agricultural production, as occurred in the 1932–38 "economic war" with Britain over the new government's retention of payments for land purchase funded by British government stock. Britain retaliated by imposing punitive duties on Irish cattle exports whose volume and value fell by a third (with no alternative outlet found).[39] The new Fianna Fail government was at the same time waging an internal war with the social bases of Cumann na nGhaedhael, especially large ranchers who despite shrinking incomes managed to survive and to resist state plans to increase tillage. Fianna Fail, however, had tapped an aggressive populist nationalism, mobilizing social support (small farmers, rural laborers, urban workers, and small native home-market enterprise) to counter powerful "pro-metropolitan" interests, and so enhanced state autonomy with respect to the rural and urban bourgeoisies so long as they remained aligned with the opposition. The latter flirted in the early 1930s with a flourishing but fleeting fascist-inspired movement of "Blueshirts." ("The very poor, of course, could not afford a blue shirt," a scholar dryly observes.)[40] By 1936 the fascist threat had disintegrated, undone by a blend of state bans, a left-leaning IRA, and a host of internal contradictions in addition to very clumsy leadership.[41] Those who resisted the Blueshirts attest this outcome was by no means foreordained.[42] In the costly course of the tariff war with the UK and the domestic struggle with aspiring fascists, the Irish state gained autonomy almost paradoxically by exerting a decidedly negative capacity – displacing rather than "shaping" the preferences of key societal interests.

During the economic war Irish exports plummeted while the standard of living *vis-à-vis* Britain fell from 61 percent in 1931 to a mere 49 percent by 1938. Still, Fianna Fail emerged from the 1938 election with a clear majority. While the world economy foundered and emigration outlets were clogged, Fianna Fail took advantage of

---

[39] Orridge, "Blueshirts," p. 361.   [40] Bell, *The Secret Army*, p. 147.
[41] See Maurice Manning, *The Blueshirts* (Dublin: Gill and Macmillan, 1972), which is dismissive of the threat. Also see the discussion of the Blueshirts in Paul Bew, Ellen Hazelkorn, Henry Patterson, *The Dynamics of Irish Politics* (London: Lawrence and Wishart 1989), pp. 41–88.
[42] Interview with George Gilmore.

the structural opportunity and the necessary mass support to upset traditional elite preferences for free trade (with Britain at least) in order to implement autarkic policies and to mount an industrial-ization drive. The most vigorous promoter of industrialization-by-insulation within Fianna Fail was founding party member and new Minister of Industry and Commerce, Sean Lemass, the self-described "progress-chaser."[43]

Lemass derived his policy objectives from Arthur Griffith, founder of Sinn Fein, who in the late nineteenth century had reasoned that a "mere agricultural nation can never develop to any extent a home or a foreign commerce, with inland means of transport and foreign navigation, increase its population in the due proportion to their well-being, or make notable progress in its moral, intellectual, social, and political development" and "will never acquire impor-tant political power or be placed in a position to influence the cultivation and progress of less advanced nations and to form colo-nies of its own."[44]

The imperialist urge within Griffith's prose is almost touching. Equally touching is his assumption that unbridled Irish capitalism would suffice to sever dependence on Britain, without resort to state assistance. But Lemass, like Griffith, viewed protectionism as an expeditious and short-term device by which local entrepreneurs and a manufacturing base were to be created. Lemass, who introduced industrial efficiency bills in 1932 and 1937, always rejected the notion of retaining high tariffs and quotas for their own sake or for the sake of making "fortunes for dishonest manufacturers who had no need of protection."[45] But the Fianna Fail party would not prove to be so immune to the blandishments of a new and grateful group of import-substituting industrialists.

Under ISI industrial employment rose from 100,589 in 1931 to 166,513 by 1938 while industrial output increased by 40 percent and then skidded quickly with the exhaustion of "easy" opportunities. In the absence of exchange controls and specific policies to induce use of indigenous raw materials or to direct linkage patterns, price levels rose in a complacent industrial climate.[46] Tariffs and low

[43] Basil Chubb, *Cabinet Government in Ireland* (Dublin: Institute of Public Administration, 1974), p. 36.
[44] Quoted in Lyons, *Ireland Since The Famine*, p. 254.
[45] Quoted in T. K. Whitaker, "From Protection To Free Trade," *Administration* 24, 1 (1976).
[46] Farrell, *Sean Lemass*, p. 36.

taxation pleased both small scale industries and agricultural exporters. (British investors were undaunted by a porous Control of Manufacturers Act which decreed that firms must be Irish-owned.)[47]
While creating public enterprise in peat production, sugar, chemicals, airlines, and food processing, the party's deputy leader asserted
that "private enterprise should be supported by the state until it
matured and that private enterprise, if strong and willing, should be
permitted to take over public enterprise."[48] Despite Lemass'
cabinet-level agitation the state did not impose a "scale-down" tariff
design to improve efficiency nor was there an effort to rationalize
firms or coordinate relations between private and public sectors in
order to enhance economies of scale and factor utilization. The
development of a capital goods industry was not on the agenda, and
so producer goods imports and the overall ratio of imports to
national income increased in the Sinn Fein haven through the 1950s.

Import substitution opportunities were quickly exploited and
exhausted in footwear, bricks, glass, leather, clothing, confectionery,
paper, and other items. By 1951 11 percent of labor worked in
manufacturing, 18 percent in industry "broadly defined" but only
16 percent of output was exported and only 6 percent, excluding
food, alcohol, and tobacco.[49] The disinclination of an economically
orthodox (and socially conservative) state to coordinate the mixed
economy, as Patrick Lynch observed, bred conflict between the
public and private sectors that continued "to inhibit the performance of both." In effect, the state encouraged the import of raw
materials over (cheaper) finished goods, and induced British direct
investment. Capital goods imports brought heavy pressure on the
balance-of-payments, and the remedy customarily was deflation.

THE POLITICAL EXHAUSTION OF ECONOMIC NATIONALISM

By the mid-1940s Fianna Fail's "radical populist phase" was spent:
it had become a classic "catch-all" party.[50] Industry and large

---

[47] Meenan, *The Irish Economy Since 1922*, p. 151, fn 36.
[48] Quoted in P. K. Lynch, "The Economic Scene," in *Conor Cruise O'Brien Introduces Ireland*,
Owen Dudley Edwards, ed. (Dublin: Gill and Macmillan, 1969), p. 24.
[49] John Blackwell and Eoin O'Malley, "The Impact of EEC Membership on Irish Industry,"
in P. J. Drudy and Dermot McAleese, eds., *Ireland and The Economic Community* (Cambridge:
Cambridge University Press, 1984), p. 109.
[50] Rumpf and Hepburn, *Nationalism and Socialism in Twentieth Century Ireland*, Paul Sacks, *The
Donegal Mafia: Machine Politics In The Irish Republic* (New Haven: Yale University Press,
1976), p. 3. Also Tom Garvin, *The Evolution of Irish Nationalism*.

landowners appeared "to have a veto over progress sanctioned by a party system in which neither political group felt it electorally possible to attack" and rectify the shortcomings of laggard economic sectors.[51] An exception is Minister of Industry and Commerce, Lemass, a no-holds-barred pragmatist and economic nationalist, who usually was thwarted. In 1947 Lemass again introduced an industrial efficiency bill that would compel firms to modernize. He fought futilely in cabinet for a role for the state in planning, sought friendlier and more cooperative relations with a trade union movement he tried to streamline, and bitterly criticized Irish banks for their anemic and even adverse role in domestic development.[52] Lemass was outflanked and outnumbered, and overruled, though he did oversee the creation of more compensatory state-sponsored bodies in transport (1945), peat production (1946), and steel (1947).

Over 1946–51 industry generated one job for every thirty job seekers. In fact despite massive emigration total employment had risen a single percentage point since 1926. In a saturated home market industrial production (and volume of agricultural exports) was static from 1953 to 1958. Further development of Irish industry was hampered by small-scale production, low technical capacities, weak links between raw materials suppliers and industry, Dickensian managerial styles, and contentment with home market hegemony.

The 1948–51 inter-party coalition government ejected Fianna Fail, resurrected the electoral fortunes of Fine Gael (Cumann na nGaedheal, formerly) and began to open the economy. The government established a Land Rehabilitation project; an Industrial Development Authority (1949) to promote Irish industry; a Grants Board to fund industry in underdeveloped areas (1952); a Board (Coras Trachtala) to promote trade; the "first explicit expression of Keynes in an Irish budget"; and, complying with Marshall Plan requirements, devised a White Paper that was a precursor of later programming efforts.[53] The government also undertook a housing

---

[51] Paul Bew and Henry Patterson, *Sean Lemass and The Making of Modern Ireland* (Dublin: Gill and Macmillan, 1982), p. 41.

[52] *Ibid.* Also Farrell, *Sean Lemass*, pp. 77–79.

[53] Lynch, "The Irish Economy Since The War," p. 187. According to Farrell, *Sean Lemass*, and Lee, *Ireland: Politics and Society*, the first earnest cabinet debates over planning occur in 1942 with the stimulus of the war.

Table 4. *Data on general elections, 1937–1951 (Dail), seats won*

	1937	1938	1943	1944	1948	1951
Fine Gael	48	45	32	30	31	40
Fianna Fail	69	77	67	76	68	69
Labour	13	9	17	8	14	16
National Labour	–	–	–	4	5	
Clann na Poblachca	–	–	–	–	10	2
Clann na Talmhan	–	–	14	10	7	6
Others	8	7	8	9	12	14
Total deputies elected	138	138	138	138	147	147
Total turnout %	76.2	79.0	74.2	67.7	74.2	75.3

Source: Chubb, *Government and Politics of Ireland*, pp. 332–34.

Table 5. *Emigration and unemployment, 1953–1958*

Year	Emigration (thousands)	Unemployment (thousands)	Unemployment (percentage)
1953	37	65	5.3
1954	48	65	5.2
1955	49	62	5.1
1956	44	63	5.3
1957	60	78	6.7
1958	34	73	6.3

Source: National Industrial Economic Council, *Report on Full Employment*, no. 18, pr. 9188 (1967); National Social and Economic Council, *Population and Employment Projections 1986: A Reassessment*, no. 35, pr. 6340 (1978).

and hospital building program, and wiped out the scourge of tuberculosis.[54]

In fact, Finance was hesitant to accept Marshall Plan loans on the grounds that prodigal politicians would be sure to waste it.[55] The "Finance attitude" was unrelievedly negative, and the mission of the senior civil servants there was to prevent the state from acquiring interventionist capabilities, to protect private property and their

[54] Murphy, *Ireland In The Twentieth Century*, p. 124. Also see Fanning, *The Irish Department of Finance*.
[55] Lee, *Ireland: Politics and Society*, p. 303.

Table 6. *Sectoral shares in total product and in employment, various years (percent)*

Sector	1926	1938	1949	1961	1971
(i) Employment					
Agriculture	53.5	48.0	42.9	36.0	25.9
Industry	13.3	17.8	21.5	24.4	30.6
Services	33.2	34.2	35.6	39.5	43.5
(ii) GDP at current factor prices					
Agriculture	31.9	27.9	29.5	24.2	16.2
Industry	18.1	24.1	25.7	30.6	33.8
Services	50.0	49.0	44.7	45.2	48.2

Source: Kieran Kennedy and Richard Bruton, *The Irish Economy* (Brussels: Comm. of the European Communities, 1975), p. 11.

Table 7. *Employment and investment of state-owned trading and industrial enterprises in some European countries, 1957 (percent)*

Country	% of active population employed	% of total fixed investment
Austria	8	27
Belgium	4	10
France	7 (1956)	25
Ireland	5	23
Italy	na	27
Netherlands	na	13
Sweden	7	15
United Kingdom	14	32

Source: Chubb, *Government and Politics of Ireland*, p. 251.

own free-market orthodoxy from incursions. The civil service hailed particularly from the lower middle class and rigorously stultifying education, and tended to package their class bigotry in the ill-disguised (yet virtually unchallenged) form of "objective" economic analysis consisting mostly of a parade of prejudices rather shockingly shorn of evidence.[56] The degree of "deference" which Finance ministers and secretaries alike blithely demanded of unlucky citizens

[56] Ibid., pp. 310–28, where Lee provides an excoriating critique.

knew no bounds. A Fine Gael Finance minister, observed Dr. Noel Browne, Minister of Health in the 1948–51 inter-party government, two decades earlier had

offered the widows of Ireland the bleak prospect that 'when there were only limited funds at the government's disposal, people might have to die in the country, and die of starvation.' This speech was delivered at a time when a widow with five children had been found dead of starvation. It was just from such an Ireland that so many of us had fled.[57]

Finance resisted creation of the Industrial Development Authority, relenting when assured it would be part of no "crackpot socialist" scheme.[58] Finance subjected the state-sponsored bodies to extremely tight monitoring. By 1951 these organizations "controlled 25% of investments, and employed 5% of all employed workers at a wage 40% higher than average," Ellis finds.[59] Even if public pay levels were only 4 percent above average there was ample potential for friction between the "profligate" state-sponsored bodies and small business, as well as with the cohort of doctrinaire conservatives populating all government and administrative ranks. In view of the lethargic performance of the sheltered private firms these state-sponsored enterprises were a potentially embarrassing and, where commercially successful, even subversive presence.[60]

Through the mid-1950s Finance conducted a "deflationary crusade," exacerbating economic downturns. As Lee reconstructs events, department secretary McElligot "needed a crisis to purge the economy of inter-party promiscuity."[61] The Finance case involved exaggerations of balance-of-payments deficits and the succeeding Fianna Fail government (1951–54) accordingly cut domestic demand in an ideologically dictated "stop-go" fashion.[62] Stagnation set in.

What is remarkable is that no opposition party picked apart

---

[57] Noel C. Browne, *Against The Tide* (Dublin: Gill and Macmillan, 1986), p. 197.

[58] Lee, *Ireland: Politics and Society*, p. 310.

[59] P. Beresford Ellis, *A History Of The Irish Working Class* (London: Gollancz, 1972). Even so, Ellis cites evidence that Irish elites were doing quite nicely: of the total population "10% owned 66.7% of land and capital in 1953" (p. 259).

[60] This is the program (public sector commercial expansion) of the Workers Party since the late 1970s. See *The Irish Industrial Revolution* (Dublin: Repsol, 1977). On the origins of state-sponsored entities see Fitzgerald, *State Sponsored Bodies*. For a comparative analysis and appraisal see John R. Freeman, *Democracy and Markets: The Politics of Mixed Economies* (Ithica: Cornell University Press, 1989).

[61] Lee, *Ireland: Politics and Society*, p. 324.   [62] *Ibid.*

either the faulty data or the logic behind the diagnosis. Fianna Fail and Fine Gael differed marginally at most over economic issues, and the Labour Party was already suffering the price of compromise as the perennial weak partner in a coalition government with a seven seat loss in 1951. Both the Labour Party and the labor movement underwent formal schisms in the 1940s. So there was no cohesive, coherent organizational base within which to devise and propagate policy alternatives.

The performance of Fianna Fail in 1951–54 and of a Second Coalition in 1954–57 were comparatively lethargic, as was industrial performance. In 1951, for example, manufacturing exports as a percentage of total production was just 6 percent. Over 1949–56 Irish national income grew just 8 percent compared to 21 percent in Britain and 40 percent in continental Europe. In these stagnant and stifling environs young men and women chose "exit" over struggling to remain and change the system.[63] "Emigration on the scale which obtained in Ireland creates a political vacuum in which all parties escape with cursory, superficial examination," Crotty sums up. "There are no angry young men in Ireland."[64]

People and capital fled – about 50,000 Irish citizens and £12 million in 1955 alone. That year Sean Lemass publicly proposed a plan to liquidate external Irish assets in order to fund creation of 20,000 jobs per year over five years, a proposal quickly quashed in the cabinet, however.[65] More characteristic of Fianna Fail attitudes and expressive of key interests in the party was Sean MacEntee's decree that it was only natural that a pool of unemployed people serve the whims of the marketplace, and that the state need only ensure "the operation of the free play of forces" in the market.[66]

A 1956–58 balance-of-payments crisis was exacerbated by fiscal orthodoxy. Deflationary responses impeded the growth of demand and productive capacity. Several commentators argue that, given signs of an export upturn, an expansionary policy instead would

---

[63] Albert Hirschman, *Exit, Voice and Loyalty* (Cambridge: Harvard University Press, 1970).

[64] Crotty, *Irish Agricultural Production*, p. 219. Population fell from 2,818,000 in 1951 to 2,599,000 in 1961. In a symptomatic folly the IRA revived ancient enmities in the 1956–62 "border war."

[65] See Bew and Patterson, *Sean Lemass*, chapter 4; Farrell, *Sean Lemass*, pp. 91–96; and George Gilmore, "The Failure of Republicanism," in *The Ripening of Time* 5, 1 (November 1976).

[66] Fianna Fail Minister of Finance, quoted in Rumpf and Hepburn, *Nationalism and Socialism*, p. 189.

have fostered a dynamic export drive off a protectionist base.[67] But by 1958, with the European Community forming, dollars converting, and transnational corporations roaming, Irish policy-makers abandoned the last shreds of autarkic ambitions for industrialization by invitation. As the legitimacy of economic nationalism bled arterially away in emigrants and capital, state managers were prodded by (and pounced upon) the crisis and the new pattern of global economic forces to subdue any resistance by a weak bourgeoisie – though sugaring the pill with reequipment subsidies and a formal discouragement of internal sales by grant-aided foreign firms. Nearly half the manufacturing assets in the Republic were British-controlled anyway.[68] Agricultural exporters were eager for access to EEC markets and prices. Since the anemic "propensity to defer" by a subordinate strata was expressed literally by resort to "exit," the "voice" in the policy switch was virtually monopolized by a highly lauded pragmatic state elite in this oft-labelled "Whitaker–Lemass revolution."

But "pragmatic" policy activity takes place within parameters imposed by both circumstance and the strategies and political influence of societal interests and external agents. In the mid-1950s Lemass had failed to stir support among manufacturers or within his party for launching a state-driven efficiency campaign designed to upgrade domestic industry, spur competitiveness, shift to exports, and generate full employment. "It is the height of nonsense," Lemass, forced onto the defensive even at this dire time, complained, "to say that the country is living beyond its means."[69] State activism – other than in the service of private property – was anathema. Only a few years earlier the Catholic Church, which dominated education and ran many hospitals and charity services, successfully aligned its organizational and ideological muscle with Irish physicians to oppose an expansion of the health system on the grounds that the state thereby infringed on the individual's right to fend for themselves or go untreated.[70] The next step, these opponents

---

[67] Kieran Kennedy and Brendan Dowling, *The Irish Economy Since 1947* (Dublin: Gill and Macmillan, 1975), p. 219, and Anthony Coughlin, "The Economics of Independence," *The Ripening of Time* 5, 1 (November 1976), pp. 41–45.

[68] See John Sweeney's estimate and method in his "Foreign Companies in Ireland," *Studies* 247, 62 (Autumn/Winter 1973).

[69] Bew and Patterson, *Sean Lemass*, p. 121.

[70] On the "mother and child" scheme, see Browne, *Against The Tide* and John H. Whyte, *Church and State in Modern Ireland* (Dublin: Gill and Macmillan, 1971).

implied, was Stalinist gulags. Within this very narrowly circumscribed political climate the only option available – other than
sitting tight – was to open the economy to ECLA-style development
schemes, which carried the blessings of the United States.

BREAKING WITH AUTARKY

The despair pervading the 1950s can hardly be exaggerated. T. K.
Whitaker, then newly appointed secretary in Finance, testifies with
perhaps a touch of color that he had been jarred by a *Dublin Opinion*
magazine cartoon captioned, "Has Ireland A Future?" which motivated him to initiate a comprehensive review of economic policy
that would become the basis for the first program for economic
expansion.[71] A Capital Investment Advisory Committee, established in 1956 and peopled with Keynesian-leaning economists,
submitted reports critical of indiscriminate tariffs, exposing shortcomings and gross inequities in the education system, exhorted the
state to undertake "productive" investment, and urged the courting
of foreign investment. Still in search of the elusive self-sustaining
industrial dynamic, the committee proposed:

A broad programme of economic development should be prepared,
designed to discover and implement productive investments and provision
should be made for its continuous and systematic review in the light of
changing circumstances. The essentials of this programme should be made
widely known: so far as is consistent with effective action, industrial,
farming, and trade union bodies should be kept fully informed about its
progress.[72]

Whitaker then composed *Economic Development*, published by the
government in November 1958 and at first ignored by the general
public. In it Whitaker scribbled an obituary for Sinn Fein reveries of
the past:

After 35 years of native government people are asking whether we can
achieve an acceptable degree of economic progress. The common talk
amongst parents in the towns, as in rural Ireland, is of their children having
to emigrate as soon as their education is completed in order to be sure of a
reasonable livelihood ... All this seems to be setting up a vicious cycle – of
increasing emigration, resulting in a smaller domestic market depleted of

---

[71] Interview with T. K. Whitaker.
[72] Third report of the Capital Investment Advisory Committee, reprinted in Chubb and
Lynch, *Economic Planning and Development*, pp. 77–99.

initiative and skill, and a reduced incentive, whether for Irishmen or foreigners, to undertake and organize the productive enterprises which alone can provide increased employment opportunities and higher living standards.[73]

Although studies tend to appraise the ideological shift of Fianna Fail (governing party from 1957 to 1973) as both dramatic and relatively smoothly conducted, the expressed objective all along had been the creation of an internationally competitive and productive economy. So it required very few rhetorical contortions within the party to justify a move to the next "stage" of industrial development.[74] The opposition parties taunted Fianna Fail for falling from autarkic grace and in the same breath approved of it.[75] The strong links between the largest "Irish" enterprises and Britain account, in part, for their acquiescence to the dismantling of tariff walls while small firms faced no immediate blast of trade competition and, as in the French case, were neither well organized nor well represented in the major employer associations, the Federated Union of Employers and the Confederation of Irish Industry. The break with autarky did not require any obvious enhancement of state power beyond the creation of an Economic Development unit within Finance. The "pragmatic elite" prudently and also predictably took the path of least resistance out of a crisis more of stagnation than of any serious social threat.[76]

But there were distinct variations possible within this single general policy direction. Bew and Patterson distinguish between the "Whitaker line," expressing the cautious anti-expansionist preference primarily of bankers, and the "Lemass line," encouraging progressive neo-corporatist experiments fueled with increased state interventionism and expenditure.[77] Over the next decades Irish governments would see-saw between these policy "lines" until the Whitaker variant achieved ascendence in the early 1980s.

CONCLUSION

The quasi-autarkic policies of 1932–58 ultimately proved incongruent with international market trends and so were insupportable

---

[73] *Economic Development*, pr. 4803 (Dublin: Central Statistics Office, 1958), p. 5.
[74] Mair, *The Changing Irish Party System*, pp. 140–80.
[75] Interview with Patrick Lynch.   [76] Academics played an important role.
[77] Bew and Patterson, *Sean Lemass*, pp. 164–68.

politically in terms of providing the "material bases of consent."[78] State managers – both party ministers and senior civil servants – were forced to break with autarky and to resort to fresh responses to the long-exhausted, "easy" phase of import-substitution. As Kuhn notes regarding scientific revolutions, the collapse of a paradigm (or, in this application, policy orthodoxy) only occurs when a full-fledged and *approved* successor appears.[79] In the absence of popular mobilization behind labor-oriented alternatives, the policy shift occurred in accordance with a wave of modern capitalist precepts regarding indicative planning, macroeconomic policy tools, and open trade. A weak labor movement espied the potential for both prosperity and augmented influence, and eagerly embraced the "Lemass line." After all, even socialists argued that there was hardly any point espousing the seizure of the means of production when there were barely any means of production to seize: let foreign industry in.[80]

State authorities backing the policy shift saw themselves in the role of aiders and abettors of private capital accumulation, whose mission was to enlighten and subsidize myopic entrepreneurs in the pursuit of their own – and presumably the nation's – best interests. Fianna Fail legitimately and legitimizingly portrayed the turn to industrialization-by-invitation as merely the next normal phase in the economic nationalist effort to create a competitive domestic industrialized economy promising jobs and higher living standards. Indeed, export-oriented industrialization soon generated a self-justifying stream of benefits. Overall the Irish policy shift and its social consequences accord with the verdict that "while the apparent determinants of state action may involve the political defeat of the bourgeoisie," the effect is "to reproduce and to reinforce that class."[81]

There was an alternative course to the "Whitaker–Lemass initiative," but only in the outermost reaches of counter-factual speculation. Emigration, which in the 1950s subtracted one-seventh of the

---

[78] See Adam Przeworski, *Capitalism and Social Democracy* (Cambridge: Cambridge University Press, 1985).
[79] Thomas Kuhn, *The Structure of Scientific Revolutions* (Chicago: University of Chicago Press, 1962).
[80] Interview with Donal Nevin.
[81] Gosta Esping-Anderson, Roger Friedland, and Erik Olin Wright, "Modes of Class Struggle and The Capitalist State," *Kapitalistate* (Summer 1973), p. 183.

population, was both signaler and dampener of crisis. No substantial support could be drawn from any quarter for more dramatic state activity, expansion of public commercial bodies, and more imperative measures to upgrade native firms so as to mount a home-market based export drive. Fianna Fail dared not indulge in directive development which might conflict with either local industrial interests or with – it is fair to say – a paranoiacally anti-statist climate reflecting the widely publicized concerns of the *petit bourgeoisie*, rural interests, and the Catholic Church. (One must add, however, that the patent success of statist "intrusions" in Britain *and in Northern Ireland* played a part in weakening such resistance.)[82] There was no choice politically but to turn to foreign enterprise.

[82] Interview with Noel Browne.

CHAPTER 4

The rising tide

It is a cliché to suggest that there has been a shortage of ideas rather than capital in Ireland. The situation might be better explained by saying that those with capital had no ideas and those with ideas had no capital.

Labour Party Outline Policy: Industrial Development, 1969

In 1962 Premier Georges Pompidou confided in the National Assembly that planning was "a little like the Kantian ethic: a text without obligation or penalty."[1] The role of the state was not to bully but to coax, guide, and enlighten investors and producer groups. French-style planning was manned by a congenial commissariat, not stern commissars. So in the 1960s Irish administrators squeamishly made way – minimal way – for a planning system designed to operate "only to the degree that it is compatible with the market."[2]

The French were exemplars but British behavior again dominated Irish actions.[3] British entry to the European Economic Community seemed imminent, and the Republic could not afford to exist outside a common external tariff. "We are too small to influence others," Lemass said, regarding EEC entry, "our link with England is first [priority]."[4] This threat of market loss furnished the government with a decisive degree of leverage over the protected private industries.

Like Chile and Uruguay in the 1960s the Irish aimed to improve a small-scale industrial base, expand and diversify exports, and thereby diffuse dependence.[5] Foreign firms were envisaged as

[1] Quoted in Lorraine Donaldson, *Development Planning in Ireland* (New York: Praeger, 1966), p. 34.
[2] *Ibid.*   [3] Chubb and Lynch, *Economic Development and Planning*, pp. 3–6.
[4] *Hibernia*, 15 January 1964, p. 5.
[5] See the contributions by Robert R. Kaufman, Albert Hirschman, and Guillermo O'Donnell in Collier, ed., *The New Authoritarianism in Latin America*.

"pump-primers" for an *Irish* dynamism. Some efforts were made to encourage primary export-substitution (exporting goods that previously had been substituted), but these shrank to a defensive posture against strong competitors swarming across lowering tariff walls. But the response of indigenous firms to free trade was sluggish, almost resistant. Because free trade was inevitable, Irish industry had to "mature" hastily. Sean Lemass, Premier from 1959 to 1966, had hoped for gradual immersion rather than a sudden plunge into the icy waters of international institutional calculations.[6] Lemass continued to insist that Irish-owned firms could and should become the center of dynamism in a fully modernized and competitive economy.

The Irish state commenced inducing local industry to modernize, attract foreign capital, set up quasi-corporatist institutions, and issued coordinated economic targets which timidly but accurately were euphemized as "programmes." In the late 1950s a politician hardly could breathe the word "planning," even at Labour Party gatherings, for fear of being drenched with holy water.[7] In that light the publication of *Economic Development* and the *First Programme for Economic Expansion* – methodical expeditions into wishful thinking – was "by the standards of the time, daring."[8]

The new approach arose with the succession to power of a post-revolutionary political elite which was concerned with "sound economic policy for steady economic growth."[9] The "boys of the old brigade" stepped rancorously aside as the "men in the mohair suits" whiz-kidded into ministerial posts.

The civil service, though, was rooted in "pre-revolutionary" values, structures, procedures, and codes, and the Department of Finance was a Gladstonian museum. Whitaker – who was appointed over many senior figures – was audacious by that Department's standards.[10] Civil servants, as Lemass bewailed, "did not move easily into the camp of change."[11] Likewise, the transfiguration of

---

6 Bew and Patterson, *Sean Lemass*, p. 91. Also see Susan Baker, "Nationalist Ideology and the Industrial Policy of Fianna Fail: The Evidence of the Irish Press," *Irish Political Studies* 1, 1 (1986).
7 A remark attributed to Jack McQuillan, a maverick left-wing politician.
8 Garret Fitzgerald, *Planning in Ireland* (Dublin: Institute of Public Administration, 1968), p. 39.
9 Al Cohan, *The Irish Political Elite* (Dublin: Gill and Macmillan, 1973), p. 73.
10 Interviews with T. K. Whitaker, Patrick Lynch, and Garret Fitzgerald.
11 Chubb and Lynch, *Economic Development and Planning*, p. 90.

interest groups into corporatist-style "social partners" would be a formidable task. Just prior to reunifying in 1959, the Irish Trade Unions Congress comprised sixty-four unions, while the Congress of Irish Unions had twenty-one unions.[12] In 1967, the proportion of unionized labor in the Republic was 56 percent (48 percent in Northern Ireland, 43 percent in the Netherlands, 34 percent in Japan, 32 percent in West Germany, 25 percent in the United States, and a matching 56 percent in Sweden). The Federated Union of Employers (FUE) reflected the obstinate individualism and authoritarian managerial style of small firms chiefly comprising the membership: "Only 31 establishments, or 1% of the total, engaged over 500 persons," according to a 1961 survey.

On the other hand, this 1 per cent of the establishments accounted for 27.7% of the total net output and for 20.9% of the total persons engaged. By contrast, the establishments employing on average less than 15 persons (which, as has been said, were just over 50% of the total number of establishments surveyed) accounted for 5.9% of total net output and for 7.6 per cent of the total employment.[13]

In the mid-1960s the FUE had 1,600 establishments (of some 5,000 manufacturing, building, and service industries), but could field only a dozen executive and research personnel. The Irish Congress of Trade Unions procured half as many.[14] The small industrial scale affected working-class organization and ideology adversely. Lee writes: "There were none of the great mining areas, of the great iron and steel centres which helped to tightly knit working-class communities together and to foster the vibrant working class cultures in some other countries." Moreover, not unlike the FUE, there is

a practice of preserving the autonomy and identity of individual unions whenever they band together for common purposes ... While recognized by Government as the national spokesman on all matters relating to Labour's interests, the ICTU is not itself a trade union, may not independently engage in collective bargaining, has no authority over the internal affairs of affiliated unions, and may not bind its affiliates in decisions or commitments without their concurrence.[15]

---

[12] Lyons, *Ireland Since The Famine*, p. 680.
[13] J. J. Lee, "Worker and Society Since 1945," in Donal Nevin, ed., *Trade Unions and Change in Irish Society* (Cork: Mercier Press, 1980), p. 16.
[14] Interviews with FUE and ICTU personnel.
[15] Chubb, *The Government and Politics in Ireland*, p. 109.

The National Farmers Association represented 60 percent of farmers (122,000 members) but the smaller organizations, the Irish Creamery Milk Suppliers Association (44,000) and the Sugar Beet Growers Association (25,000) were contentious rivals. So intense was conflict with and among farming associations that Fianna Fail omitted agriculture from the roster of "players" appointed to the new National Industrial Economic Council, the key advisory quasi-corporatist institution of the planning era.

Although Ireland was ideologically inclined toward at least a Papal brand of corporatism (*Quadragesimo Anno*), the nation was developmentally ill-suited.[16] The new Prime Minister, Lemass, who redefined self-reliance to mean "an economy sufficiently viable to enable all Irish to live in their own country," launched the society upon an export-led industrialization path along which the three programs for economic expansion become trail markers and revealing indicators of underlying economic trends, political conflict, and administrative turf wars.[17] The Irish state certainly held the initiative – with ministers, civil servants, and consulting academics propagating the gospel of "modern capitalism" and proposing a host of administrative reforms. But the Irish state relied largely on the protectionist era coalition and so, rather than confront even a divided group of industrialists, preferred to sidestep (and make side payments to) domestic capital. On the other side of industrial relations, organized labor was enticed into corporatist experiments that Lemass intended to flourish as the organizational basis for a dynamic economy, and to form a coalitional base for revitalized Fianna Fail hegemony.[18] If economic planning and neo-corporatist interest intermediation proved ineffective, the Irish merely were repeating British experience.[19]

The next section provides political anatomies of the three Irish program activities, and attends to international, administrative, and ideological constraints. As for the lattermost, Przeworski and Wallerstein note that it was not only the triumph of technical

---

[16] See John H. Whyte, *Church and State in Modern Ireland* (2nd ed., Dublin: Gill and Macmillan, 1982).

[17] Lee, *Ireland: Politics and Society*, p. 398.

[18] On this point see Mair, *The Changing Irish Party System*; Bew and Patterson, *Sean Lemass*; and Dick Walsh, *The Party: Inside Fianna Fail* (Dublin: Gill and Macmillan, 1986), pp. 66–76.

[19] On similarities see Michael Shanks, *Planning and Politics: The British Experience 1960–76* (London: Allen and Unwin, 1977).

economic theory that Keynesianism heralded but also a "frame-work" that installs consumption as "the motor force for production, and suddenly workers and the poor turn out to be representatives of the universal interest."[20] The politics of economic policy in the Republic are essentially struggles among social forces promoting or rejecting this crucial proposition, the basis of the "Lemass line."

The first program for economic expansion emphasized – like the first Free State government – agricultural exports. The second program focused on industrial upgrading. The third program acknowledged a key role for foreign investors. No fourth program materialized. These exercises ended with EEC entry and with the Industrial Development Authority (IDA) assuming the role of coordinator of industrial planning.[21]

THE "FIRST PROGRAMME 1958–63"

Pompidou had exaggerated the innocuousness of planning. By the 1960s French planning was "less than imperative, more than indicative."[22] The Irish fortified their own planning with an array of tax exemptions, grants, and subsidies (rather than cheap discretionary credit, which was little availed of by small industries). Nonetheless, the "First Programme" was a bundle of "vague, exhortatory statistics" and succeeded through little fault of its own.[23] As Whitaker explained in *Economic Development*, the program harbored no great ambitions, posed no threat to the bourgeoisie: "While I deprecate planning in any rigid sense, I am convinced of the psychological value of setting up targets of national endeavour, provided they are reasonable and mutually consistent," Whitaker wrote. "There is nothing to be gained by setting up fanciful targets. Failure to reach such targets would quickly produce disillusionment and renew the feeling of national despondency."[24]

The "First Programme" prepared by Whitaker was adopted without submission to parliamentary debate. Dail Deputies are acutely responsive to local demands within their bailiwick, but typically play a minimal role in reviewing policies and legislation.

---

[20] Adam Przeworski and Michael Wallerstein, "Democratic Capitalism at The Crossroads," *Democracy* 2, 3 (July 1982), p. 37.
[21] See chapter 5.   [22] Shonfield, *Modern Capitalism*, p. 148.
[23] Cullen, *An Economic History of Ireland*, p. 184; Fitzgerald, *Planning in Ireland*, p. 51.
[24] *Economic Development* (Dublin: Stationery Office, 1958), pr. 4803, appendix, p. 4.

Senior civil servants exerted power over cabinet members if only through selectively "weighting" alternatives presented to harried ministers.[25]

The "First Programme" emphasized agricultural output via: improving grasslands; eradicating bovine tuberculosis; financing research; improving access to export markets; and providing easier credit terms to farmers. In the industrial realm the program endorsed the attraction of foreign capital, upgrading local enterprise; tariff cuts; export tax relief; research subsidies; tourism encouragement; marketing aid; and vigorous government projects in vital areas where "it is considered unlikely that they will be initiated by private interest."[26] The program foreswore interfering in the private sector other than by the stimulus of public capital spending, directed especially into "productive" projects, productive "in the sense of yielding an adequate return to the community in competitive goods and services."[27] Building and construction fell from one-fifth of gross domestic capital formation over the period 1953–56 to one-eighth over the program period, the difference channelled more "productively." But Whitaker rather prematurely wrote of the "virtual satisfaction of needs" in social areas, and shortly after a severe housing shortage arose in Dublin.[28] Frugal standards evidently lived on in the civil service. Secondly:

in Ireland, projects which are primarily of a "productive" character have a relatively high import content (think of machinery and equipment), while the import requirements for redistributive investment (think of subsidised housing and public works) tend to be low. Hence the income multipliers attached to the latter exceed those applying on the former type of investment.[29]

"Productive" investment, by definition, is needed for long-term growth; "redistributive" spending is vital to maintain aggregate demand as well as to improve infrastructure. Apart from being a dubious distinction, one can note that the wrong "productive" investments can generate counter-productive effects. In 1961 Louden Ryan, an economist in the thick of everything, quibbled with the export-led productive strategy. Ryan stressed that

---

[25] Interviews with various personnel.
[26] *Programme for Economic Expansion* (Dublin: Stationery Office, 1958), pr. 4796, p. 34.
[27] *Ibid.*, p. 3.   [28] Fitzgerald, *Planning in Ireland*, p. 23.
[29] Desmond Norton, "Fiscal Policy – The Long View," *Administration* 2, 33 (Summer 1975), p. 197.

increased exports were likelier to result from successful development than cause it. He foresaw danger in

"export-import" enclaves – that is, industries which import the bulk of their materials and export almost all their output. Such industries might have no direct impact on existing activities – these latter would only benefit indirectly through the expenditure of the new incomes of the workers in the new industries. The new export industries might not be meshed into the existing industries structure – there might be no "backward linkages," and there might, therefore, be no strong pressures, emanating from the new activities, on existing industries to improve their methods and techniques. . . . Where this happens there may be less chance of a dynamic of economic development being released by them.[30]

But over 1959–63 the program coincided with a boom in trade and with internationalization of capital investment as the pattern shifted from portfolio to direct investment, from less developed to developed countries, and from raw materials to manufacturing. US investment alone expanded at an annual rate of 10 percent in the 1950s and 1960s. The upsurge of demand elsewhere boosted annual GNP growth to 4 percent in the Republic, which doubled the modes program target. Suddenly, an obscure government document became an object of celebration.

Fianna Fail had lost eight seats in the 1961 election yet clung to office due to independent support and the Labour Party's anti-coalition stance. Fianna Fail needed a savior, and the program served the purpose admirably. A second – and more ambitious and sophisticated – program was in preparation at the Economic Development Branch (established in 1959) of the Department of Finance. No serious commentator since can claim that the program itself was responsible for the recovery, but as Garret Fitzgerald suggested, it just may have maintained the momentum.[31]

The "leap forward" was driven primarily by 7 percent annual industrial growth, and largely by foreign enterprises lured to Ireland by incentives which the Industrial Development Authority and the Grants Board dispensed. (An External Investment Act in 1958 heralded the eventual total repeal of the Control of Manufactures Acts.) Of all firm start-ups, 70 percent were foreign; and 133 foreign firms accounted for 85 percent of new investment and

---

[30] Louden Ryan, "Investment Criteria in Ireland," *Journal of The Statistical and Social Inquiry Society of Ireland* (1961–62), p. 64.
[31] Fitzgerald, *Planning in Ireland*, p. 11.

77 percent of new employment.[32] To appease local industry, grant-aided firms were discouraged from competing in the domestic market; nearly all production was exported. The foreign industrial performance provoked a wide range of reactions in the Irish parliament, including a few apprehensive, if ugly, rural sneers. Quoth one discussant:

> The cry that industry is "away" and all because a few Japs, a few Jews, or a few Negroes come in here for the taxpayers to build factories for them, contribute to the cost of the machinery, give them slave labour – if it can be got – protect them on every side so that they can export their goods into other countries under the label "Irish." I warn the minister that they will pack their bags tomorrow or the day after and clear off, and they can tell this government, or any other government, where they get off. They can snap their fingers at any government because they care damn all except for what they can get as soft as they can get it from the people of our country. That is the kind of increase there is in industry.[33]

But Labour Party leader, William Norton, was more reflective of opinion among the Deputies and the populace in general in his chiding remark:

> There was a time when it was very unpopular to invite foreign manufacturers to come here and manufacture goods which we could not produce ourselves. Very many more than one member of the Fianna Fail Party nearly had apoplexy when they heard the idea. Now all these loves and hates are over ...[34]

Meanwhile, native industry underwent intense scrutiny (thirty investigations in all) conducted by the Committee on Industrial Organization (CIO), created in the summer of 1961 largely as a means of feeding subsidies and placating native industrialists. the CIO included representatives from the Federation of Irish Industries, the Federated Union of Employers, the Irish Congress of Trade Unions (though not at first), the Department of Finance, the Department of Industry and Commerce, the Grants Board, and the Industrial Development Authority (IDA). The CIO reports assembled a daunting list of industrial shortcomings; small scale, high import-content, low proportion of exports, meager marketing skills and contacts, low specialization and, put kindly, an anachronistic

---

[32] Donaldson, *Development Planning in Ireland*, pp. 18, 44.
[33] (Michael Donnellan), *Parliamentary Debates, Dail Eireann*, 15 Mar. 1961, col. 660.
[34] *Ibid.*, col. 650–51.

approach to management.[35] As a remedial measure, the CIO prescribed Adaptation Councils (which ideally would interact con-
structively with Trade Unions Advisory Bodies), a measure inspired
by the underdeveloped character of most existing industrial associations.[36] Because of the disinterest and distrust endemic among Irish
enterprise, the Adaptation Councils failed to make much impact.
However, the CIO did stimulate legislation for 25 percent adaptation and re-equipment grants, a redundancy payments scheme,
and was a sparring ground and prelude for later concertations. The
CIO reports also lifted the composers of the second program out of
the "stubby pencil and eraser" guesswork stage. A Federation of
Irish Industries report cited the inadequate preparations:

> Unfortunately, it is becoming clear that so far in this adaptation pro-
> gramme, the need for fundamental changes in product and marketing
> policy has not been given the prominence it deserved ... Effective adapt-
> ation must involve a great deal more than simply brightening up the
> industrial structure developed under protection.[37]

The Grants Board–IDA plausibly argued that the difference in
grant allocations which apparently favored foreign firms "was
simply the outcome of relative availabilities of concrete investment
opportunities."[38] It is a fair estimate that – with 20 to 25 percent of
the state funds – local industry matched foreign projects in overall
grant receipts.[39] The native bourgeoisie therefore appears to have
waged a fight against international interlopers by tapping state
financial resources. However, half the "home industrialists" were
themselves foreign (mostly British) firms that by 1973 had extracted
more "from the IDA through the aids offered to so-called 'home
industry' than through the aids offered to new investors."[40] So the
bulk of industrial aid flowed into non-Irish enterprises.

The inflow of foreign capital rose from under 1 million pounds in
1960 to 22 million in 1963, and higher still the next year as British
capital sought refuge from the electoral triumph of the Labour

---

[35] Fitzgerald, *Planning in Ireland*, p. 60.   [36] *Ibid.*, p. 61.

[37] *Challenge – Irish Industry and Free Trade*, a business study by the Federation of Irish Industry,
Dublin (1968), p. 41.

[38] F. Flynn, "The Development of Home Industry," *Administration* (Special IDA issue) 20, 3
(Summer 1972), p. 59.

[39] John Sweeney, "Foreign Companies in Ireland," *Studies* 247/248, 62 (Autumn/Winter
1973).

[40] *Ibid.*

Party. A survey of new businesses (36 percent UK, 27 percent German, 24 percent US, and 4 percent Dutch in investment) testified to the attractiveness of export tax relief, and variety of government subsidies.[41] Most foreign enterprises (71 percent) claimed they would remain after incentives expired, as long as twenty-five years away for firms locating at the Shannon Development Zone.

The program may have consisted of arithmetical incantations, but the psychological impact was indisputably exhilarating and influential. The program – allegedly "above politics" – was a powerful ideological potion reinforcing the Irish state's structural "predisposition" toward promoting private enterprise. Fianna Fail basked in the glory of progress to the extent that an opposition Deputy complained:

> In the years that have elapsed since the appearance of the grey book Economic Development signed by Mr. Whitaker, the two so called Programmes for Economic Expansion, which were very largely attributed to Mr. Whitaker, every folly that the government has perpetrated has been perpetrated under the alibi that it is in pursuit of the objectives of the programme, first and second for economic expansion, which was after all the handiwork of the detached and omniscient Mr. Whitaker.[42]

Political decisions glistened with a technocratic coating. Sean Lemass prodded bureaucrats and ministerial departments and civil service to shed their drab ways to become glittery "development corporations" – though to little effect.[43] Inside the civil service, and the nation as a whole, the ideological spectrum ranged roughly from St. Vincent de Paul to the mellower side of Lord Keynes. Pro-planning economists customarily sprinkled their conference papers with talismanic references to favorably disposed bishops. Fears of state tyranny had some slight grounding, at least in the economic sphere. At the start of the first program, the state directly allocated half of the industrial investment which, combined with private investment influenced by subsidies, amounted to three-quarters of total industrial investment in Ireland.[44]

Public enterprises were hamstrung by directives to supplement, not surpass, the private sector, by marketing deficiencies, and by

---

[41] Donaldson, *Development Planning in Ireland*, p. 54.
[42] *Parliamentary Debates, Dail Eireann*, 12 December 1963, col. 247.
[43] See Sean Lemass, "The Organization Behind The Economic Programme", in Chubb and Lynch, *Economic Development and Planning*.
[44] Donaldson, *Development Planning*, pp. 76–77.

their disjointed interactions. "There is no virtue in setting up state-sponsored agencies to meet particular needs as they arise," an economist reproached, "without according these organizations a prescribed place in a general economic plan."[45] An Irish counterpart of the Italian Instituto per la Ricostruzione Industriale (IRI) or the Swedish state holding company Statsforetag was never entertained by the Fianna Fail administration. A latent function of leaving the public sector uncoordinated may have been to deflect criticism from the conspicuous shortcomings of the private sector.

In this heyday programming and foreign investment were compatible inasmuch as mere forecasting creates no conflict. No single authority coordinated implementation of the program. The internal consistency and interrelation of targets were not examined. There was no genuine review of projections versus performance. Throughout the life of the program, short-term fiscal policy was not coordinated with long-term objectives, nor was this even contemplated. Uncomfortable discriminatory investment decisions were delegated to "neutral" state agencies, like the IDA. It was indeed "planning without tears."

THE NATIONAL INDUSTRIAL ECONOMIC COUNCIL AND THE ERA OF THE "SECOND PROGRAMME FOR ECONOMIC EXPANSION, 1964–69"

The "Second Programme" featured input–output tables, an iterative methodology, and a "First Programme" afterglow which was a force in itself. Minus parliamentary input, the encore effort (August 1963) covered seven years in which GNP was projected to rise at a 4.4 percent annual rate. (Auguries would soon turn to agonies.) The basis of programming was reiterated:

> Objectives and priorities are outlined but the programme does not in every instance specify how they are to be attained. Rather it is educative and indicative, combining help and guidance from the state for private enterprise with direct state action where this is needed to insure full productivity.[46]

Like the concurrent Fourth Plan in France, no provisions were made or margins allowed for balance-of-payments difficulties or

---

[45] Patrick K. Lynch, "The Economics of Independence: Some Unsettled Questions of Irish Economics," *Administration* 7, 2 (1959), p. 166.

[46] *Second Programme for Economic Expansion* (Dublin: Stationery Office, 1964) Pr. 7239, Para 4.

international market disorders, and it was based explicitly on the assumption of EEC entry by 1970.[47] After De Gaulle's veto, Lemass enacted unilateral tariff cuts in 1964 and 1965, and negotiated the 1965 Anglo-Irish Trade Agreement which swapped duty-free access of Irish manufactures to Britain for progressive annual 10 percent reductions in Irish tariffs. The agreement affirmed the pro-EEC orientation, intensified pressures on "home industry" to adapt and modernize, and enhanced Ireland's appeal to foreign investors. (The second program acknowledged the substantial – if not premier – contribution by foreign industries to export-led development.)

The responsibility for composing the program again centred in the Economic Development Division of the Department of Finance. Aside from the CIO, no official consultative network provided the planning staff with – cybernetic jargon was infectious – input and feedback. On Fianna Fail's initiative, the National Industrial Economic Council (NIEC) was not just another instance of institutional mimicry but a response to internal difficulties. Though welcoming the NIEC as a "bold and imaginative approach," the ICTU withdrew from the bi-partite National Employer–Labour Conference in 1963 in reaction to a White Paper urging wage restraint – minus a *quid pro quo* – to boost productivity.[48] (A wage agreement, however, was reached the following year, inaugurating a series of annual or biannual employer–labor negotiating rounds.) Lemass wooed trade unions by inviting participation in planning via the NIEC. The underlying purpose was to secure a stable incomes policy, and eventually the NIEC would dissolve over this recurring issue. Lemass declared that the Council would prepare:

reports from time to time on the principles which should be applied for the development of the national economy, and for the realization and mainte- nance of full employment at adequate wages, with reasonable price stabi- lity, and reasonable long-term equilibrium in the balance of external payments. In these reports the Council will have regard to the level and trend of incomes, from whatever source. The Council will not deal with agricultural matters ... [because] agricultural policy is determined to a

[47] *Ibid.*
[48] *Closing The Gap* (Dublin: Stationery Office, 1963) and see the account in Charles McCar- thy, *The Decade of Upheaval: Irish Trade Unions in the 1960s* (Dublin: Institute of Public Administration, 1973), pp. 50–75.

large extent by external conditions, which we cannot hope to alter by decisions taken here.[49]

The NIEC was geared to create consensus, not new policies. The terms of policy debate were defined such that the stakes were no more than a matter of "nibbling at the extra 2 per cent or 3 per cent growth in the economy."[50] A participant characterized the NIEC as a sounding board for Lemass' initiatives:[51] "Here it is," Lemass, in effect, would say. "Show me why I can't do it!" And the Council issued more than two dozen well-researched, occasionally pungent replies. Like the British NEDC, the Council was an "outsider" with respect to the normal channels of policy-making. The Council was inserted into the administrative environment by the chair, T. K. Whitaker, who retained his post as Secretary of the Department of Finance, which was "not well-disposed toward trespassers."[52] According to interviewees, interdepartmental feuding was rife in the government and in the civil service. After Lemass stepped down from the premiership in 1966 and Whitaker departed for the Central Bank there would be left behind "a vacuum of leadership and skill."[53]

Unlike the NEDC, Irish trade union leaders and the state planners attest to the growth of a mutual respect and rapport which exceeded the lifetime of the council. But no *economie concertée* emerged. Instead, the Trade Unions took an active hand in promoting and criticizing socio-economic policy initiatives while the employers associations pressed primarily for an incomes policy. Like the ICTU, employers associations were not equipped to make very informed or truly binding agreements. Their vistas were limited by the short-term and cramped perspective of the small firms.[54]

To surmise that trade unions *dominated* the Council would be unwarranted inasmuch as the NIEC itself dominated nothing, and influenced little. Employers and the civil servants merely conceded the concertative "sound and fury" to the ICTU representatives.

---

[49] Quoted in Meenan, *The Irish Economy Since 1922*, p. 157.
[50] Interview with Louden Ryan.
[51] Interview with Charles McCarthy.
[52] See Ronan Fanning, *The Irish Department of Finance 1922–58* and Lee, *Ireland: Politics and Society*. Also Jack Hayward's comments on ill-disposed attitudes regarding planning as expressed within the British Treasury and the French Ministry of Finance in "The Politics of Planning in France and Britain," *Comparative Politics* 7, 2 (January 1975), pp. 285–98.
[53] Interview with Garret Fitzgerald.
[54] NIEC, *Report on Economic Planning*, no. 8 (1965), p. 19.

Ironically, one tangible achievement for the trade unions was the creation of a route of ministerial access – the Department of Labour. Fitzgerald found in the 1960s that Irish industry always had "the last word" in "genuine consultations" with the Department of Finance planning staff.[55] The role of Finance increased due to the lack of resources among the employer associations. There was, instructively, no direct link between the NIEC and the Adaptation Councils.[56]

The 1965 NIEC's *Report on Economic Planning* does disclose strong traces of trade union apprehensions about the venture:

economic planning must be *active* as well as *being* indicative ... If the targets are to be accepted as a guide to action, those who make the attempts to achieve them must be involved in fixing the targets and in indicating the assistance they will require from policy in solving the problems and overcoming the obstacles they see in the way of reaching them. If the plan is to maintain a continuing influence on action, managements and workers must be involved in the periodic reviews of performance and in the modification of targets to take account of unforeseeable events ...

The danger in purely *indicative* planning ... is that the industrial targets will be neither accepted nor understood, that their relevance to decisions by individual industries or firms will not be appreciated and that the decisions required at all levels to ensure that the targets are achieved will not in fact be made.

The admonitions were for naught. The British balance-of-payments crisis in the mid-1960s capsized the Irish as well as the British National Plan. Deflation, and a sterling devaluation adversely affected demand for Irish products and so slackened growth in the Republic. By 1967 the original program targets were deemed unreachable. The second program suffered the predicted problems of adherence, not to mention *coherence*. The public service was not compelled to comply with the program's objectives, let alone take initiatives to fulfill them. The ICTU could not cope with rising strike activity over wage disputes, status claims, and less economistic sources of dissension in critical services. The private sector extracted what suited its short-term purposes from the modernization effort or else, astonishingly, ignored advantages it might reap. By 1968, a Labour Deputy beheld the industrial adaptation efforts:

[55] Fitzgerald, *Planning in Ireland*, p. 128.   [56] *Report on Economic Planning*, p. 31.

I notice in all such undertakings that it is those who need the exercise the least who partake in them the most. Those who need the exercise do not avail themselves of it. Some more compelling method should be used to induce these firms who go their own way and take little notice of efforts such as this to participate. In the long run, it is the employees of those industries who will suffer. Some firms I know are very slow to shake themselves down ... they are afraid of change and new ideas. When the crunch comes, they will just go into liquidation and the workers will be thrown on the scrapheap.[57]

In 1967 the second program was abandoned quietly, partly because Whitaker acknowledged the inevitable, and partly because Fianna Fail couldn't live electorally with it.[58] In the 1965 election, the Labour Party matched its historical high of twenty-two seats, struck a socialist stance, and was poised – so its members believed – to overtake Fine Gael as second largest party.[59] Meanwhile, Declan Costello's social democratic wing in Fine Gael hoisted its "Just Society" program onto the 1965 party platform. The prospects for a new Fine Gael–Labour coalition were enhanced enormously. Internally, Fianna Fail underwent a leadership struggle from which compromise candidate Jack Lynch eventually emerged as Prime Minister in 1966. Labour's "go it alone" strategy precluded any threat of coalition, but Fianna Fail declined to donate electoral ammunition to its opponents. Rather than revise the sinking second program, a third program was conjured.

As planning euphoria waned along with the prospect of admission to the Common Market, the effective instruments of modernization in the late 1960s dwindled down to two essential elements. In 1969 industrial policy became concentrated in the reorganized and expanded Industrial Development Authority. In an appraisal of the second program, Crotty casts the second element into macabre relief:

when they were setting targets of a 43 per cent increase of cattle and a 17 per cent decrease of people in the countryside; the truly awesome thought does not appear to have occurred to the economic planners of the Republic that in only one previous recorded decade did changes of this order and

---

[57] *Parliamentary Debates, Dail Eireann*, 6 March 1968, para. 203 (Seamus Patterson).
[58] Interview with T. K. Whitaker.
[59] The Labour Party crept upward electorally from 9 percent of the 1957 vote to 17 percent by 1965, and believed it was poised to overtake a sluggish and outworn Fine Gael as second largest party.

nature take place in the cattle and human population of Ireland. The decade was 1841–1851.[60]

The development strategy can fairly be depicted as "paying and praying." That is, *paying* foreign firms to locate in the Republic while subsidizing improvement of local firms, and *praying* for EEC admission which would boost agricultural fortunes. The upshot is that the Irish Republic increased its dependence on external forces through planning processes which, paradoxically, were premised on substantial but shrinking internal autonomy.

According to a 1967 survey of "Grant-Aided Industry" (80 percent foreign-owned), these firms were responsible for 11 percent of industrial output, 9 percent of employment, and 42 percent of industrial exports.[61] Between 1960 and 1966 they contributed 90 percent of increased exports and 70 percent of new employment in the Republic. Another investigator credits foreign direct investment with 80 percent of private manufacturing investment and 90 percent of new manufacturing jobs between 1954 and 1971.[62] The pre-1970 wave of foreign investors were, relatively speaking, "smalltimers." Between 18 and 30 percent of firms belonged to parent corporations which owned six or more subsidiaries.[63] But most newcomer firms were taking their first toddling steps into the international marketplace. Nonetheless, foreign investment became the primary driving force of modernization in Ireland – North and South.[64]

Despite glittering GNP growth (4.2 percent per year from 1960 to 1970) and industrial export sales (17 percent per year from 1964 to 1974), the most troubling aspect of the growth strategy shows up in the employment statistics. Over the period 1958–74, the rural drain alone exceeded jobs created in industry and services, 154,000 to 132,000. Total employment in the Republic eked upward at a 0.2 percent annual pace from 1961 to 1968, and then dropped at a 0.4 percent rate from 1968 through 1972.[65] At half the 1950s level emigration was certainly diminished but hardly staunched.

---

[60] Crotty, *Irish Agricultural Production*, p. 204.
[61] *Survey of Grant-Aided Industry* (Dublin: Stationery Office, 1967).
[62] John Teeling, "The Evolution of Offshore Investment in Ireland" (Ph.D. diss., Harvard Business School, 1975), p. 9.
[63] *Ibid.*, p. 84.
[64] On Northern Irish economic strategy see, for example, Richard Ned Lebow, "Ireland", in Gregory Henderson, Richard Ned Lebow and John Stoessinger, eds., *Divided Nations in A Divided World* (New York: David McKay, 1974).
[65] Kennedy and Dowling, *The Irish Economy Since 1947*, p. 257.

Among the many benefits multinational firms were enlisted to bring, jobs were the key political criterion and the crucial legitimizing element of economic policy. "There can be no doubt that the policy of attracting firms from abroad must be maintained in the years ahead," the NIEC concluded in 1967.[66] The NIEC calculated that the industrial sector must generate 70 percent of new jobs within a projected 5.5 percent annual GNP growth in order to attain by 1980 full employment – which was then defined as 2 percent unemployment. The council reckoned with the realities of international capitalism:

For example, the rate of return that would call forth the amount of new investment needed in the private sector to realize full employment may not be the same as the rate that would establish a universally acceptable relation between changes in profits and in other incomes such as wages and salaries. Since much of the finance and enterprise that will be needed must be attracted from abroad, there can be little control over the minimum rate of return which must be available, for externals with money to invest or technical know-how that can be put to use in new industries are under no obligation to use them in Ireland.

To *maintain* competitiveness, the relationship between increases in total money incomes and increases in national production must be the same here as in the countries with which Ireland trades. To improve competitiveness, the rate of increase of money incomes relative to productivity must be somewhat slower here than in neighbouring countries.[67]

Hence Irish workers were advised to accept the peculiar proposition that in order to "catch up" with wages of affluent continental labor, they must remain steadfastly behind Dutch, Danish, or German workers as to the rate of wage increases won. The formula promised a long hard haul particularly for less skilled workers in the absence of any guarantee by industrialists to reinvest the extra profits in domestic production rather than in foreign securities and ventures, real estate, speculation, or Veblenesque conspicuous consumption. Although several trade unions and the Labour Party asked for stronger measures, the report did not demand that the state sector, which accounted for a third of manufacturing output and employment, diversify and expand commercial activities. This omission may reflect a more moderate stance taken by ICTU leaders at

[66] NIEC, *Report on Full Employment*, no.18 (Dublin: Central Stationery Office, 1967), p. 64.
[67] *Ibid.*, pp. 57, 64.

Table 8. *Living standards, productivity, GNP growth, and unemployment rates in the EEC, various years*

	1973 GDP per capita (living standards)	1973 GDP per person employed (productivity)	1961–71 Avg. annual GNP growth (constant pr.)	1970–72 % of unemployment
Belgium	219	191	4.9	2.1
Denmark	260	187	4.6	0.9
France	229	192	5.8	1.4
Germany	266	213	4.6	0.7
IRELAND	100	100	4.0	6.1
Italy	120	116	4.9	3.4
Luxembourg	247	204	3.1	0.0
Netherlands	212	210	5.4	1.7
UK	147	114	2.7	2.8

Source: **Kennedy and Bruton,** *The Irish Economy,* p. 9; J. W. O'Hagen, ed., *The Economy of Ireland: Policy and Performance* (Dublin: Irish Management Institute, 1975), p.125; Gibson and Spencer, *Economic Activity in Ireland,* p. 93.

Table 9. *Indicators of prosperity in the British Isles*

	Republic of Ireland	Northern Ireland	Scotland	Wales	England
GDP at factor cost, 1967 per capita	304	419	564	532	653
as % of England	46.6	64.3	86.5	81.6	100
Percentage unemployed avg. for 1966–71 incl.	7.4	7.2	4.1	4.0	2.3
Net emigration: annual rate per thousand, 1966–71	5.0	5.0	6.3	3.4	0.003
Percentage of labour in agriculture, 1966	30.8	9.9	5.2	5.3	2.8

Source: David Law, "Ireland, Scotland, and Wales," in *Economic Sovereignty and Regional Policy: A Symposium,* ed. John Vaizey (Dublin: Gill and Macmillan, 1975), p. 236.

Table 10. *Average wage rates in selected countries for all workers in manufacturing (cents per hour)*[a]

	Ireland	Puerto Rico	Taiwan	Singapore	Hong Kong
1963	58	112	15	33	21
1964	64	118	15	33	21
1965	68	123	16	33	23
1966	76	129	17	34	24
1967[b]	80	139	18	35	25
1968	75	155	21	35	25
1969	85	165	22	33	26
1970	100	176	23	32	28
1971	115	187	25	33	32
1972	131	200	27	35	38

[a] Data was not available to accurately estimate total hourly labor costs. Fragmentary evidence suggests that fringe benefits in Taiwan and Singapore are higher than the 22 percent Irish rate but the difference will not change the relative rankings.
[b] Exchange rates: £1 Irish = $2.78 until 1967; thereafter $2.35
$1 Singapore = 35¢
$1 Hong Kong = 17.5¢
$1 Taiwan = 2.5¢

Sources: International Labor Office *Annual Yearbook*, 1971 and 1972. Geneva; *Annual Report of the Central Bank of Ireland*, Summer 1974; Various issues of the *Oriental Economist*, January–June 1974.

council meetings than many rank-and-file members would have liked. An International Labour Organization report perceptively noted at the time that Irish trade union leaders "were afraid of being branded as 'arms of the government'."[68] But not *that* afraid.

On the whole, however, the ICTU leadership probably was very much in tune with majority opinion. The "working-class Tory" phenomenon in Britain had a somewhat muted counterpart in Ireland where some workers were more devoted to rosary beads than to little red books, to republican symbols instead of the crown. Irish socialists generally endorsed the sober appraisal that the country had yet to complete its capitalist stage of development.[69] Therefore, foreign firms, and the developmental strategy inviting

[68] *The Restructuring of Irish Trade Unions* (International Labour Organization, 1974), p. 11.
[69] Interviews with members of the Labour Party, the Socialist Labour Party (1977–82), The Workers Party and The Communist Party of Ireland. There were plenty of exceptions within and outside these organizations.

Table 11. *Export oriented foreign direct investors established in Ireland 1954–1971*

Year	No. of industries	No. of projects	Fixed investment (£000s)	Gross output (£000s)	Numbers employed
1954	2	2	164	580	81
1955	1	1	250	450	150
1956	–	–	–	–	–
1957	2	2	1,805	4,000	870
1958	5	5	794	2,269	971
1959	10	10	2,448	13,731	2,782
1960	6	11	5,680	12,009	3,407
1961	12	18	3,090	4,847	1,753
1962	10	14	2,745	6,991	1,858
1963	14	16	4,883	16,306	4,161
1964	8	14	2,102	8,879	888
1965	10	24	5,201	13,961	1,957
1966	12	25	6,459	20,421	4,061
1967	14	43	4,885	11,077	2,575
1968	17	46	11,642	27,058	3,948
1969	21	68	41,671	59,907	6,038
1970	20	59	27,051	121,368	8,069
1971	10	15	42,438	35,744	4,222
Total		372	163,308	361,598	47,791

Source: IDA files.

Table 12. *Number of projects by nationality 1954–1971*

Country	In operation	Starting up	Failures[a]
United Kingdom	119	7	19
United States	100	19	8
Germany	80	10	20
Holland	14	1	0
South Africa	15	0	1
Sweden	6	1	3
France	9	0	2
Other countries	29	6	1
Total	372	44	54

[a] The nature of IDA grants means that they become repayable if a plant closes within ten years of start up. This provides a powerful incentive to companies to sell their business rather than to close it. An active IDA Rescue Division assists in this work. Therefore some "failures" have in fact been taken over by new owners.
Source: Teeling, "The Evolution of Offshore Investment."

them, were welcomed by leftists in labor. In any case, Irish laborers had scant reason to feel deep loyalty to native industry, as the testimony below hints:

I started my apprenticeship in 1960, the beginning of the boom period, but I was always being told about the hard times of the previous decade. With the shortage of work in contracting employers could pick whom they wanted and treat them as they wanted. The boat to England was the only alternative. There were stories of people being paid less than the union rate, of non-labour unions being used, of men having to queue up to apply for a vacancy. As the boom continued, the attitude of many of the lads was to screw the employers for as much as they could, as after the boom they would start screwing the workers again.[70]

This "legacy" of antagonism played a role in soaring strike levels in the mid-1960s although the NIEC reported that "the immediate causes of 40% of industrial disputes were disagreements about wages and hours of work, and over 30% were the result of disputes about the engagement or dismissal of workers."[71] Within a weak and fragmented working class, the predictable tendency was for skilled workers to prefer to concentrate on maximizing their gains in the labor market rather than to commit themselves to political bargaining with employers and the government. This narrow view stirred an ICTU general secretary in 1968 to complain:

If we are not moved by the belief that in the mass organization of the trade union movement we have an instrument in the hands of the workers which they can use to revolutionize the society in which they live; if we are content to let society evolve in another direction, and compete with each another for the choicer crumbs on the master's table, then possibly small sectional trade unions or sections which demand recognition by unions of their selfish acts, are the kind of union which is most suited to our purpose.[72]

Meanwhile, the Labour Party – once mocked by Lemass as a "nice, respectable, docile, harmless body of men" – had undergone revitalization and devised a critique and programmatic alternative to the development orthodoxy.[73] Their plan for full employment, ironically, shared many features with the stillborn initiatives of Lemass.

---

[70] Quoted in McCarthy, *Decade of Upheaval*, p. 104.   [71] *Report on Full Employment*, p. 104.
[72] Quoted in *Restructuring of Irish Trade Unions*, p. 18.
[73] Michael Gallagher, *The Irish Labour Party in Transition, 1957–82* (Manchester: Manchester University Press, 1982), p. 70.

The 1969 party policy document drew a bead on the basic presuppositions of state policy:

planning has been confined to the "indicative" or so-called programming approach. The public controls have been the normal orthodox measures that would have been applied anyway in the absence of a programme. The major criterion has not been an increase in the numbers at work but rather stability in the balance of payments and growth in our external reserves. The interests of the monied class have been put at a premium.[74]

The party customarily cited the danger of British neo-colonialism but "equally important," it found that Irish capital consistently had flowed away and out of reach. "The capital inflow produced by foreign investors over a period of eight years," the party noted, "is less than the increase of our external reserves in the one year of 1967."[75] Capital controls were absolutely essential as were, on the carrot side, incentives to retain savings for local use.

On the directive side the Labour Party intended to equip the state with a "super-ministry" of economic development to devise a national plan and preside over sub-agencies (a National Planning Authority, a State Development Corporation) charged with implementing "detailed action programmes." Labour proposed that regional development authorities and an industrial manpower authority be established. "In general," the document stated, "the strategy will be to create complexes of large scale advanced technology projects based on the exploitation of native resources."[76] Here was a formulation – thin on detail – of a counter-hegemonic development scheme, a scheme at odds with the new "pragmatic" state managers, the major parties, the financial sector, the urban and rural bourgeoisies and, off in the distance, the EEC. After a disappointing 1969 electoral result, Labour, which had gained votes yet lost several seats, treated the documents as the wish lists their opponents said they were.

"THE THIRD PROGRAMME, 1969–1973"

Viewing target shortfalls Finance judged that the second program had been "overly concerned with detail." The next exercise must be more selective and far more modest about goals: a 3.8 percent

---

[74] *The Labour Party Outline Policy: Industrial Development*, Labour Party Annual Conference, January 1969, p. 140.
[75] *Ibid.*, p. 137.   [76] *Ibid.*, p. 139.

growth rate, 4,000 new jobs per year, and a decline of emigration
from 18,000 to 12,000. A social program was included. Whitaker's
stress on "productive" over "redistributive" expenditure never
really had taken hold in practice, and public expenditure had
expanded through the 1960s. The program aimed to facilitate
investment by centralizing industrial policy in a reorganized Development Authority. Thus, a "secondary" feature of the first program
grew to dominance by the advent of the third, whose authors
cautioned that "since most economic decisions are taken outside the
government's immediate sphere of influence, there is no guarantee
that the aims set in this programme can be reached, or that its
policies and purposes will not be frustrated by private decisions or
indifference."[77]

The NIEC bit the consultative dust in 1970. The immediate cause
was the aggravating unlikelihood of ever devising a satisfactory
incomes policy. An important underlying reason was a bureaucratic
territorial feud: the Department of Finance "did not suffer rivals
gladly."[78] As in France and Britain the institutional resistance to the
anticipated ascent of a comprehensive planning agency was fierce.[79]

The NIEC was from the beginning emasculated as a political
force. As a Fine Gael observer observed, the NIEC was caught in an
exquisite Catch-22 plight *vis-à-vis* the government. Garret Fitzgerald ruefully relates that when the NIEC was faced with the government's decision to abandon the second program in 1967, "the
Council could not find it easy to take any effective action, as any
such action could have been construed as political in character, and
*the effectiveness of the Council depends largely on its being, and being seen to
be, apolitical.*"[80] (my emphasis)

Insofar as corporatism refers not only to functional representation
in policy-making but also to "the state's *reciprocal* influence on
interest groups, and their consequent employment as agencies of
mobilization and social control for the state *vis-à-vis* their members,"
the NIEC, after a long and vigorous audition, has to be judged a
disappointment.[81] Neither the state nor employers extracted the

[77] *Third Programme For Economic Expansion* (Dublin: Stationery Office, 1969), Ch. 1.
[78] Interview with Louden Ryan.
[79] Hayward, "The Politics of Planning," p. 54.
[80] Fitzgerald, *Planning in Ireland*, p. 189.
[81] Leo Panitch, "The Development of Corporatism in Liberal Democracies," *Comparative
    Political Studies* 10, 1 (April 1977), pp. 65–66; and see Niamh Hardiman and Stephen Lalor,
    "Corporatism in Ireland: an Exchange of Views," *Administration* 32 (1984).

incomes policy they wanted from labor, and labor failed to acquire any substantial influence over policy implementation. Nonetheless, the NIEC did function successfully as a forum for, and consecrator of, what I termed in chapter 2 a "consensual satisfice." The dissolution of the NIEC in no way jeopardized the legitimacy of the development policy.

The third program lingered – escaping abortion but not oblivion – until 1972. A fourth program never appeared. Preoccupied in 1969 with the Ulster crisis Fianna Fail was rocked internally by the removal or resignation of ministers whose republican sympathies allegedly extended to arms smuggling. The programs literally got lost in the subsequent cabinet shuffle, and the approach of the EEC by 1972 focused administrative attention elsewhere. The Employer-Labour Conference from 1970 onward assumed the function of providing a semblance of wage policy. In retrospect, economic programming had been a *conservative* exercise, endorsing the terms set by the socio-economic order, concerned with "equitable distribution of *increasing* wealth," a reformist rather than a transformational force which sought to harmonize the state sector with private requirements. (By 1970, public enterprises accounted for 8 percent of GNP, 6 percent of total employment, 37 percent of public sector employment, 15 percent of total gross investment, and 46 percent of public gross investment.)[82] "Manufacturing exports of any sort arguably require policies which threaten a variety of domestic populist interests," Kaufman observes, "devaluation and subsidy burdens on urban consumers; requirements of low labor costs and union discipline; liberalization of import policies; and stable expectations about price and exchange level – in short, many of the requisites of predictability and stability that O'Donnell suggested were necessary for deepening."[83]

In the 1970s the next step in programming would have been insertion of "teeth" into tripartism – that is, to experiment with directive forms of planning. Since the trade unions balked at an incomes policy – which would have restrained wages more vigor-

---

[82] John A. Bristow, "Public Finance and Fiscal Policy," in Norman Gibson and John Spencer, eds., *Economic Activity in Ireland: A Study of Two Open Economies* (Dublin: Gill and Macmillan, 1977), p. 194.

[83] Robert R. Kaufman, "Industrial Change and Authoritarian Rule In Latin America: A Concrete View of Bureaucratic-Authoritarian Model," in Collier, *The New Authoritarianism*.

ously than capital income – the Irish state was unwilling to cede authority to the NIEC. (In fact, it appears that no such *quid pro quo* ever was proposed.)

Neither "imperative" forms of planning nor coordinated network of public enterprises were congruent with the most dynamic element of the programming era: foreign investment. The argument that state-aided industries provided the otherwise unemployed with the privilege of paying taxes seemed pragmatically sound, if not strikingly equitable. But this tactic was not supposed to become a substitute for the vaunted upsurge of private initiative that the policy was intended to trigger. So the Industrial Developmental Authority (IDA) ingested funds and issued "job projections" which, while credible, conferred political kudos on incumbent governments. Studiously ignored was the public sector's role in supporting demand, exploiting local resources, improving infrastructure and "socializing" private sector risks, so that the highly ideological and economically illiterate cry that "four private jobs support each public job" would be quite resonant, and one potential alternative thus effectively derided and dismissed.[84]

If, as Watson writes, economic planners accommodated the prerogatives of oligopolistic interests (thereby driving out smaller ones), this process occurred in Ireland with foreign firms taking the prerogatives and small firms taking the leftovers or else their leave of the industrial world.[85] Although few foreign firms were in the mammoth multinational category, IBM, Ford, General Electric, Texaco, Philips, Mitsui, and Tate & Lyle located there while only two Irish companies ranked in Europe's top 500. The disgruntled would argue that those were two too many Irish firms inasmuch they began to invest abroad too.

CONCLUSION

Given the logic of export-led industrialization (combined with a "catalytic" or "enabling" state), the fact that programming ushered in a dominant foreign sector should have surprised no one. Indeed, warnings were issued all along the political trail toward the policy of

[84] A remark made by 1973–77 Finance Minister Richie Ryan.
[85] Michael Watson, "A Comparative Evaluation of Planning Practices in Liberal Democratic States," in Hayward and Watson, *Planning, Politics and Public Policy*, p. 474. Also see Hall, *Governing The Economy*, chapter 1.

economic openness. "Sinn fein" economic sentiments were now a quaint and curious fragment of forgotten lore. In May 1972 the Irish Republic lunged into the promised land of plenty in the Common Market with an 83 percent majority vote. In a subtle yet vital sense the surge in state activity had been a prologue for the consummation of EEC membership on 1 January 1973. The Labour Party cobbled together a counter-hegemonic economic strategy but, in the "rising tide" of prosperity, was resoundingly ignored.

The Fianna Fail-led state plausibly portrayed export-led industrialization as a practical matter of promoting economic nationalism "by other means." The state gained the capacity and the legitimacy to deploy its administrative and financial resources – though not just as it pleased.

The Fianna Fail government revived a mouldering capitalist structure and benefited from the creation of a hegemonic ideology that depicted global economic shifts as irresistible forces requiring a single best response from the blameless private sector and reluctant *dirigiste* state. This characterization of circumstances, while credible, sustained a high degree of deference, of a high propensity by non-elites to defer to policy prescriptions.

CHAPTER 5

Pushbuttons and pragmatists

> The truth that nobody would admit is that we are not indepen-
> dent, that except for that enormous river, called the Irish Sea,
> that runs between the two countries, we are effectively,
> economically an integral part of Great Britain.
> Dr. Noel Browne, *Parliamentary Debates, Dail Eireann* (1970)

The Common Market vote in 1972 expressed a resounding recognition of circumstances perceived by the electorate to be beyond
national control.[1] Few Irish believed that their island could thrive
outside the Treaty of Rome. An official mission to Brussels became
the economic equivalent of a pilgrimage to Lourdes. Thereafter an
infirm economy should revive, shriveled regions flourish, and benign
investors spread capital abundantly in the fair hills of Eire. So said
the major parties and virtually all the media.

This chapter delves into the motives and interests underlying the
enormous pro-EEC vote, which reaffirmed the legitimacy of the
export-led industrialization strategy; then we examine the political
and ideological role of the Industrial Development Authority, the *de
facto* central planner. The chapter concludes by treating issues of the
late 1970s: the disposition of new-found mineral resources, and the
revealing furor stirred by the closure of the largest foreign manufacturing employer in the Irish Republic. By the end of the decade the
consensus favoring the development scheme began to crack – but
not crumble – and neo-corporatist experimentation flickered out.
The Right seized the political initiative, successfully imposing
within both major parties a policy diagnosis prescribing deflationary
discipline.

---

[1] No one propagandized so tirelessly on behalf of EEC entry as Garret Fitzgerald. See his
Toward A New Ireland (Dublin: Torc Books, 1973).

SELLING THE COMMON MARKET

The EEC, a necessity, was transformed into a virtue. The government, public agencies, and the media trumpeted the good news that the Common Market had something for everyone. Farmers anticipated increases in beef and dairy output at guaranteed high prices. Economists expected export growth and diversification and the diffusing of Irish dependence among many EEC members. Politicians expected manna to flow from the EEC regional fund to the distressed Western counties in particular and the country as a whole (which was defined as an "underdeveloped region" *in toto*). Remarkably, Irish industrialists displayed few misgivings over their ability to meet the challenge of European competition. Competing manufactured imports already stood at 23.6 percent in 1973, up from 13.4 percent at the launch of the first program. Not a heartening trend. But Irish industries certainly teemed with defects, which the Labour Party emphasized in its futile anti-EEC campaign. Hence, the accurate refrain by a Labour Deputy that:

Every Minister for Industry and Commerce, and the present minister is no exception, in his estimate speech has admitted that certain firms have not adapted as rapidly as desired. The present minister has admitted that certain sectors of industry do not seem to be concerned that the outcome of our entry to the EEC may be to diminish the number of jobs and close many firms.[2]

The Deputy delivered the Labour Party's verdict on the Common Market courtship.

It is true that any enlarged market area will give us further export opportunities but what has influenced the party's attitude to the possibilities of free trade and what has made us oppose the measures suggested so far has been our realization that we have a low level of development. We are not in the same category as our future partners. We require a different relationship with any free trade area than those countries would.[3]

Although EEC entry was a foregone conclusion the Labour Party waged a spirited fight, arguing that few industries would withstand the sudden stern competitive conditions. While foreign firms should

---

[2] (Michael O'Leary) *Parliamentary Debates, Dail Eireann*, 9 June 1970, col. 669–671.
[3] *Ibid.* In an earlier debate a Fine Gael Deputy answered "We either export profits or we export people" – a political refrain. (Mark Clinton) *Parliamentary Debates*, 4 December 1969, 243, col. 2249.

wax as native industry waned, Labour judged that new employment was unlikely to offset combined redundancies and an increased rural outflow due to EEC farm modernization policy.[4] Emigration would shift to the continent (the pro-Marketeers giddily forecast the creation of 50,000 net new jobs within five years by sheer virtue of membership).[5] Instead of revitalizing agriculture, the Common Agricultural Policy would plump up a small fraction of the farmers and only until urbanized EEC members found it expedient to enact a modern "repeal of the Corn Laws." (In 1971 only Italy's agricultural sector population at 19.5 percent was near Ireland's 26.5 percent; France had 13.5 percent and other EEC members came in at 10 percent and the UK at 2.7 percent.) Anti-Marketeers claimed that the EEC levy could be leaped easily by Irish cattle and that favorable trade agreements were negotiable for other exports.[6] Community Regional Policy was dismissed as a cosmetic device. In effect, the anti-Marketeers argued for a revitalized Sinn Fein policy wherein the Irish state would promote *native* industrial exports, liberalize trade at a more accommodating speed, and retain control over policy instruments in order to deal with specific economic weaknesses.[7] In an alternative scheme state-sponsored bodies would expand their commercial role in coordinated conjunction with actively "guided" private firms. The anti-Marketeers aimed to maximize policy discretion, puncture cornucopic illusions and dispel the pervasive attitude that there was "no alternative." But, outside the trade unions, their argument won few adherents.

The pro-Market campaign by Fianna Fail and Fine Gael was endorsed by "a well-organized agricultural lobby, the bulk of industrial interests, and nearly all professional economists."[8] The Labour Party appeared as a quixotic force against the unstemmable tide of progress. Several state bodies – notably the Industrial Development Authority – unabashedly promoted the pro-EEC case too. The idea of "going into Europe" was graced by an air of high purpose, as if

---

[4] *Economic Freedom* (Irish Congress of Trade Unions, April 1972), p. 1.
[5] A White Paper, "The Accession of Ireland To The European Community," predicted that Irish industry would easily "hold its own." See Alan Matthews, "The Economic Consequences of EC Membership for Ireland," in David Coombes, ed., *Ireland and The European Community: Ten Years of Membership* (Dublin: Gill and Macmillan, 1983), p.114.
[6] *Economic Freedom*, p. 2.
[7] Anthony Coughlin, *The Common Market: Why Ireland Should Not Join* (Dublin: Common Market Study Group, 1970).
[8] Patrick Keatinge, *A Place Among The Nations* (Dublin: Gill and Macmillan, 1977), p. 142.

the Irish were voting to promenade into continental cathedrals, not a marketplace where the going could get quite rough. But the pro-Market case appealed to voters to whom the pseudo-autarkic policies of the past were synonymous with a stagnant economy and a suffocating culture.[9]

The EEC vote too reflected diffuse socially progressive yearnings, the specific material interests of aforementioned groups, and political party loyalties which the referendum result mirrored exactly. (Fine Gael and Fianna Fail's 83 percent versus Labour's 17 percent.) Still, the most potent argument for entry replicated earlier arguments favoring an "open door", i.e., that Ireland was simply impotent in the international economic arena. A Fianna Fail Minister curtly replied to Labour pleas for self-reliant policies:

> I do not think we have a chance. This is an academic question. We have to go ahead to industrialize as fast as we can ... The aspect of access to markets is the vital one. We could be strained if we were to provide all the capital ourselves, but I believe it could be done. The technical know-how is more difficult; in some areas you can buy it; in others you cannot, but you cannot buy access to markets and this is the big fallacy in the argument that we should rely solely on our own resources, be they private enterprise or state enterprise.[10]

As for entry terms, Irish negotiators extracted a five-year phase-out of tariffs, a delay on opening Irish fishing zones, and permission to retain export tax reliefs and incentives – plus guarantees that any revised incentive scheme required by EEC codes would be equally effective. Irish negotiators were amazingly confident that the Republic was immune to short-term losses: "In this respect, Ireland's position was exactly opposite that of the United Kingdom, whose fully predictable and concrete short-term economic losses had to be weighed against speculative 'dynamic' long-term economic gains."[11] Allegedly, there was nothing to fear but the panic-mongering of the Labour Party. As pro-Marketeers asserted, Ireland would escape its primordial dependence on British markets, enjoy the novelty of a voice in marketing arrangements and exchange a tenuous sovereignty for assured prosperity.

---

[9] For a vivid portrait of the toll taken, see Terence Brown, *Ireland: A Social and Cultural History* (London: Fontana, 1985).

[10] (George Colley) *Parliamentary Debates, Dail Eireann*, 4 December 1968, 243, col. 580.

[11] Dermot McAleese, "Ireland in The Common Market," in John Vaizey, ed., *Economic Sovereignty and Regional Policy* (Dublin: Gill and Macmillan, 1978), p. 135.

N.B.

Several years after entry an Irish economist could concede that: "In or out of the EEC, Ireland would still have enjoyed free access to the European market" via European Free Trade Area (EFTA) agreements; that agricultural gains, while substantial, had been overestimated (the beef crisis of 1974 injured the small farmers particularly); that change in net manufacturing exports was negligible because the lifting of the Common External Tariff was offset by the loss of preferential position in British markets; and that "it must be admitted that a substantial part of Ireland's older established industrial sector – for example, the footwear, shirt-making, woolen and worsted, and toy industries – may prove highly vulnerable against low-cost competition from LDCs" (not to mention capital-intensive continental firms).[12] The Common Agricultural Policy price system drenched large farmers in filthy lucre. But all farmers paid higher prices for inputs, especially foodstuffs. Inexorably, these were transmitted into food prices which, as in Britain, fueled increased wage demands and, in turn, affected industrial competitiveness.[13]

Price rises were felt quite acutely in the lowest wage member of the EEC. In 1973, for example: "Irish households on average spent thirty-two percent of household expenditures on food, compared to about twenty-two per cent in West Germany" but two-thirds of Irish households actually spent more than 40 percent on food.[14] "Catching up" quickly to European prices, Irish performance was less fleet in the realms of productivity and wages. In retrospect, the trade unions were justifiably suspicious, and the Labour Party along with official Sinn Fein and other EEC opponents had performed the role of Cassandra consummately.[15]

Quite pertinent here is the weight imputed to foreign firms in tilting the decision to join the EEC. If Ireland should enjoy access to the Market anyway, the question nags whether "the anxiety

---

[12] *Ibid.*, pp. 143, 157.

[13] Desmond O'Rourke, "An Unofficial Appraisal of The Irish Economy," *Studies* 267, 2 (Autumn 1978), p. 175.

[14] *Ibid.*, p. 174.

[15] *Ibid.*, p. 175. O'Rourke points out that this CAP "bonanza" is "financed by the diversion to Brussels of national import levies on imports of agricultural products from third countries. The import levies surrendered by the Irish government must be offset against any savings in direct expenditure on agriculture. Further, to the extent that domestic food prices of Irish agricultural products are held by CAP at levels higher than the Irish exchequer would have been willing to support, the added cost is a hidden tax on Irish consumers."

expressed by bodies such as the Industrial Development Authority about the necessity of EEC entry for the continued expansion of foreign industrial investment was misplaced?" One possibly vindicating reply is:

> On balance, we think not, *for the simple reason that foreign investors would not regard the two situations as equivalent.* Membership of the Community carries with it a security of access which no trade agreement can quite replicate. The gradual harmonization of economic and social policies to which the EEC aspires, with the ensuing removal of many non-tariff barriers to trade must also appeal to the foreign investor. As has been often stressed before, uncertainty and incomplete information constitute no less serious an obstacle to international exchange than tariffs and quotas.[16]

Since 1958 the Irish state had "artificially created a low-risk environment for offshore investors" in what became by default more than design the core of the Irish developmental strategy. Would foreign investors snub an island unchristened by the EEC? Would the capital "sunk" in the economy surface and drift away sooner than the fifteen-year export tax holiday allowed? Noting the capital outflow after passage of the 1964 capital gains tax in Britain, Irish leaders were acutely aware of how mobile funds can be.[17] The Republic was so responsive to the foreign investors that the latter could be "conspicuously absent from the normal channels of interest expression" yet exercise influence on public policy.[18] In this anticipatory sense, foreign capital "ruled but did not govern" economic policy. In the 1970s the Irish all but abandoned any pretense to "self-sustained, indigenous development" in favor of repeated

---

[16] McAleese, "Ireland In The Common Market," p. 158.

[17] On the plight of the 1964–70 Labour government, Coates writes: "Because the Labour Government depended on . . . foreign loans to maintain the flow of essential imports, it had to fit its domestic policy to the terms on which the loans were granted. . . . The law of anticipated reaction is everywhere visible in Government policy in this period. And because so many of those foreign and domestic holders of sterling were big multi-national corporations, the Labour Government found both that it was necessary repeatedly to raise domestic rates of interest to attract in their cash flows, and also vital that Government policy on prices and incomes, on industrial relations and on the free movement of trade and money was congruent with the requirement of the multi-nationals themselves." David Coates, *The Labour Party and The Struggle For Socialism* (Cambridge: Cambridge University Press, 1975), p. 107. Krieger adds: "The decision to retract minimalist social democratic programs in a highly visible campaign to win IMF approval . . . destroyed the tenuous basis for cohesion within the Party and signified the end of Keynesian society in Britain." *Reagan, Thatcher and The Politics of Decline*, p. 58. Also Kathleen Burk and Alec Cairncross, *Goodbye Great Britain: The 1976 IMF Crisis* (New Haven: Yale University Press 1992).

[18] Philippe C. Schmitter, *Interest Conflict and Political Change in Brazil* (Stanford: Stanford University Press, 1971), p. 371.

injections of foreign capital, which provided tangible political and economic dividends. But, far from lessening dependency, EEC entry intensified the "conditioning situation" in terms of which Ireland industrialized. Dependent industrialization enabled "the features of the political structures essential to their insulating function to be largely preserved and, hence, to prevent shifts to alternative development strategies."[19]

Contrary to stereotyped *dependista* formulations, the international market and foreign firms dictated nothing; rather it was indigenous interests, converting "market signals" into persuasive programmatic messages, that determined the precise form policy took. The state direction urged in Labour's program was shunned. Hence, this analysis is consistent with the "recurring dependency syndrome" which is an inverse relation between growth and state entrepreneurial activity, that the demand for a more directive form of state intervention falls as prosperity rises (and likewise the "capacity" of private capital to resist or buffer adverse state policy).[20] I argue that this syndrome is best explained as the result of outcomes of a broader (and continuing) social struggle to gain the power to define the developmental project. Given the adopted policy imperatives of export-led development and EEC entry, policy entrepreneurs exploited the limited scope available for adjusting the structure and organization of the state and economy to the new circumstances.

The anti-EEC forces waged a vigorous but unconvincing campaign. If EEC entry would be a "disaster," it looked to be a handsomely mitigated one. Over 1973–79 farm output, starting from a low base, led the EEC with a 5 percent growth rate, though output per labor unit, acre, or cow remained well below Community standards.[21] Seventy percent of farm profits were reaped by 30 percent of Irish farm operators. Nonetheless, an English critic of the EEC observed that "by maintaining support prices at a level which enables the least efficient producers to survive, the Common Agricultural Policy has certainly given monopoly rents to the large farmers in agribusiness, but has also frustrated that centralisation which otherwise would have occurred through the working of the

---

[19] Andrew Martin, "Political Constraints on Economic Strategies in Advanced Industrial Societies," *Comparative Political Studies* 7, 4 (October 1977), p. 350.
[20] Duvall and Freeman, "The Technobureaucratic Elite," p. 333.
[21] Interview with Seamus Sheahy.

market."[22] While 60 percent of land holdings were beneath the viable 50 acre mark, economists foresaw a 21 percent drop in farm employment between 1976 and 1985.[23] (Farm employment fell 32 percent during the 1960s.) The rural drain was to enhance the productivity and profitability of remaining units. Because farm profits were virtually tax-free into the mid-1970s (and in 1980 only 15 percent of farmers paid tax), the ranchers' wealth intensified friction between themselves and small farmers and also stoked a conflict between "country" and "town" over the issue of the tax burden.[24]

Equity aside, agricultural prosperity certainly contributed to aggregate demand which "appears to have been essential for the growth of the output of older industries" which lagged behind in the export-led modernization race.[25] The fabled rising tide failed to lift all boats. Many small business dinghies in the home market harbor stayed afloat although this was often a reprieve, not a pardon, for industries "largely confined to sectors such as those using simple or standardised mature technology, and having characteristics such as labour-intensity, local craft-intensity, low value-added to local primary resources, a low value/bulk ratio (giving natural protection due to transport costs), and clear advantages arising from regular contact with the local market."[26]

THE INDUSTRIAL DEVELOPMENT AUTHORITY

An assessment of Irish industry, foreign enterprises or of any aspect of Irish industrialization requires scrutiny of the role of the Industrial

---

[22] Holland, *Uncommon Market*, p. 108.

[23] Robert O'Connor and Philip Kelly, "Agriculture: Medium-Term Review and Outlook," in Brendan R. Dowling and Joe Durkan, eds., *Irish Economic Policy: A Review of The Issues* (Dublin: Economic and Social Research Institute, 1978), p. 78.

[24] *Trade Union Information*, nos. 237–241 (Winter 1978), p. 23. In a study of the social consequences of industrial activity in the West of Ireland, Lorelei Harris noted that the PAYE tax protests of 1979–80 "highlighted a division of loyalties based on a conflict of class interest. Thus, on the day of the second PAYE demonstrations, when 7000 workers took to the streets of Ballina and closed the town's businesses for the afternoon, many of the female participants attempted to disguise their identities with sunglasses, hats and scarves in order to avoid recognition and the possibilities of their photographs appearing in the local papers,' "Class, Community and Sexual Divisions in North Mayo," in Chris Curtin, Mary Kelly, and Liam O'Dowd, eds., *Culture & Ideology in Ireland* (Galway: Galway University Press, 1984), pp. 157–58.

[25] NESC Report no. 56, *Industrial Policy and Development: A Survey of the Literature from the Early 1960s* (Dublin: Stationery Office, December 1980), prepared by Eoin O'Malley, p. 26.

[26] *Ibid.*, pp. 58–59.

Development Authority, which became after 1969 the key coordina-tor of industrial policy and the most significant planning agency in the Irish Republic. Ideally, the IDA aimed to generate full employ-ment (or a pacifying proportion of jobs) by inducing foreign and local investment, encouraging joint ventures, nurturing small business (94 percent Irish), funding research and development, aiding promising entrepreneurs and products, and performing a host of other functions. The IDA is the institutional crucible in which the terms of dependent industrialization were worked out, and the centripetal center of political tugs-of-war over policy.

A 1967 survey of grant-aided industries spotlighted a trend afflicting not only "less developed countries" but all industrial societies:

the rapid technical advances in production equipment and the continuing trend toward capital-intensiveness rather than labour-intensiveness is perhaps the greatest challenge to any industrial promotion campaign having for its primary aim the provision of additional job opportunities. It seems that as time goes on a progressively greater volume of new industrial activity will be needed to provide a given number of jobs . . .[27]

Asked how he foresaw Ireland – given this trend – in the year 2000, an IDA representative replied that because the Republic was so compact and boasted so educated a population, it was possible to insert every able-bodied Irish man and woman into employment pushing buttons on new technologies.[28] Hence there was nothing to fear from automation. Nor was he disturbed by the fact that – if trends of the mid-1970s continued – most capital-intensive gadgetry would be of foreign ownership. Foreign enterprises would hold fast because of Irish financial advantages, the affable culture, and other charms. If there is a touch of eschatology in the IDA's mission, this push button vision expressed it.

Similar optimism informed the "new strategy" of the People's Nationalist Party and Fomento in Puerto Rico, which hoped to lure a critical mass of high-tech firms so as to emerge as the "technologi-cal axis" of the Caribbean.[29] South Korea and Taiwan undertook "statist" direction of their economies concentrating on production

---

[27] *Survey of Grant-Aided Industry* (Dublin: Stationery Office, 1967), p. 33.   [28] Interview.
[29] See Raymond Carr, *Puerto Rico: A Colonial Experiment* (New York: Vintage, 1984), p. 227, and Jose J. Vilamil, "Puerto Rico 1948–1976: The Limits of Dependent Growth," in Vilamil, ed., *Transnational Capitalism and National Development* (Atlantic Highlands, NJ: Humanities Press, 1978).

of high-tech equipment, and other Third World states followed despite this route being "just about the most difficult and least effective way of entering industrial production."[30] The dice are loaded against the newcomer that has a small home market, is short of capital and skilled manpower, and is rich in unskilled labor. Even the experience of relatively privileged Scotland, an early "peripheral postindustrial" path taker, duplicated, in often a more aggravated way, Irish adversities.[31]

The Industrial Development Authority was established in 1949 as a promotional body. Two decades later it absorbed the funding function of the Grants Board and was reorganized as an autonomous state-sponsored organization. That foreign investors prefer to haggle with quasi-autonomous agencies was by then well appreciated.[32] The "civil service climate" was swept away and the new managing director populated the IDA with new talent on contractual terms akin to "venture management" – they were public servants with flair.[33] The IDA was to fill an "increasing need to evolve a viable and properly integrated industrial structure based on a major input of foreign capital, technology and entrepreneurship to supplement [not supplant] native resources." To that end, the IDA engaged in

(1) The preparation and implementation of Regional Industrial Plans which accord with national, social, and economic goals as laid down in various Government policy statements.

(2) Making grants to manufacturing industry towards the cost of fixed assets, re-equipment, manpower training, research and development of new products and processes, reduction of loan interest and factory rental.

(3) Guaranteeing loans and where appropriate taking equity participation in industrial enterprises.

(4) The encouragement of diversification through associations, licensing agreements, and joint ventures.

---

[30] Clark and Cable, *I.D.S. Bulletin*, p. 29.

[31] For overviews see Tony Dickson, ed., *Scottish Capitalism* (London: Lawrence and Wishart, 1980), Norman Hood and Stephen Young, *Multinationals in Retreat: The Scottish Experience* (Edinburgh: Edinburgh University Press, 1982) and Philip McDermott, "Multinational Manufacturing and Regional Development: External Control in The Scottish Electronics Sector," *Scottish Journal of Political Economy* 26, 2 (1979).

[32] Interviews with IDA personnel.

[33] Only 21 of the original 131 staff members transferred out, but the IDA doubled its staff by December 1970 according to *Industrial Development Authority Review 1952–70 and Annual Report for 1969–1970* (Dublin: IDA publication, 1970).

(5) The carrying out of promotion and publicity campaigns at home and abroad.

(6) Securing the provision of physical infrastructure for industrial development, i.e., land, services, factories, and housing.

Related operational programs were:

(1) To assist the development of new large and medium sized industry by both home and foreign based enterprise.

(2) To modernize, strengthen, and expand existing industry.

(3) To develop existing and new small industries (i.e., with up to fifty employees and 100,000 in fixed assets in designated areas and up to thirty employees and 60,000 in non-designated areas).

(4) To provide industrial estates, advance factories and housing for key industrial workers.[34]

What the IDA did not do is hardly worth mentioning. (The Shannon Free Airport Development Company continued to operate independently, as did Gaelterra Eireann which oversaw development in Gaelic-speaking regions.) The IDA enjoyed a great deal of autonomy in order to perform its formidable assignments; but paradoxically it also is the most monitored organization on the island. Over the 1970s job creation figures were a highly dramatic device in any Irish government's arsenal, so the IDA's performance was subjected to intense scrutiny by politicians worried that their constituency would be slighted in factory location, and by interest groups.[35]

The managing director established a remarkable degree of freedom for his organization.[36] This freedom of maneuver is partly attributable to the traumatic cabinet shuffle during the 1970 "Arms crisis" which ushered in an inexperienced Minister of Industry and Commerce; partly institutional design; and partly because of any prudent minister's desire not to tamper with a good thing. The first minister testifies that the new IDA ran itself remarkably well.[37] The managing director describes the succeeding 1973–77 coalition minister – who evoked as much love among Irish industrialists as Tony Benn among the British – as cooperative, "an asset" to the

---

[34] P. S. McMenamin, "The Industrial Development Process in The Republic of Ireland, 1953–72," in John Vaizey, *Economic Sovereignty and Regional Policy* (Dublin: Gill and Macmillan, 1976), p. 182.

[35] Interviews with IDA personnel and numerous politicians.

[36] N. S. Carey, ed., *Politics, Public Enterprise, and The Industrial Development Agency: Industrialization Policies and Practices* (London: Croom Helm, 1974), p. 43. A pair of reports by A. D. Little Consultants Agency prodded the IDA reorganization.

[37] Interview with Patrick J. Lalor.

industrial promotion campaign.[38] In effect, the success (of however limited scope) of the IDA at generating jobs lulled ministers and led to benign abdication of responsibility for policy initiatives. However, the IDA, as any investigator becomes aware, protrudes ultra-sensitive "antennae" into the political environment – the personnel pore over every critique – which in turn stimulates internal initiatives.[39]

The tone and content, if not always the style, of IDA activity adheres to dauntingly econometric criteria and technocratic values, i.e., that one is solving an utterly technical problem through the best means at hand. Studies weighing the impact of industrialization in Irish society in forms other than statistical tables are rare – as are questions about the long-term consequences of the development path.[40] Left unquestioned, as Dr. Noel Browne pointed out sharply, the alleged "idiocy of rural life" might be succeeded by a more fairly appraised "idiocy of urban industrial development."[41]

The ideology of modernization "reflex modernization") pervaded this public administrative structure. The IDA is the institutional spearhead for the political elite of pragmatists who embraced the myth along with the myth of developmentalism in the sixties and seventies. "The myth of modernization," according to a critic of French planning,

is a complex collection of motivating images which insists upon the importance of increasing national production, modernizing production processes, industrial structure and product lines, and upon the responsibility of ranking civil servants to guide and insure such developments.[42]

The IDA drew fire away from incumbent governments while shielding itself with a persuasive image of technical neutrality and very real expertise. Nonetheless, in politicized realms the degree to which technical advice is accepted and *which* form of technical diagnosis is favored "depends less on its validity and the competence of the expert, than on the extent to which it reinforces existing positions, and the power of those holding them."[43]

---

38 Interview with Michael J. Killeen.
39 Personal observations in the IDA offices and library.
40 This is no longer true. Critical studies have been appearing since the mid-1980s with increasing frequency.
41 Interview with Dr. Noel Browne. 42 Cohen, *Modern Capitalist Planning*, p.135.
43 Dorothy Nelkin, quoted in Alvin W. Gouldner, *The Dialectic of Ideology and Technology* (New York: Seabury Books, 1976), p. 256.

In view of dependency propositions that foreign investment (1) bestows too few benefits to the host country; (2) distorts the local economy (by, for example, "crowding out" local industry); and (3) interferes with the political processes in the host country, the performance of the IDA is assessed and developmental problems examined.

THE PRICE OF IRISH PROSPERITY

The dependence of Irish industrialization on foreign firms is highlighted by comparing data from the 1967 and 1977 surveys of grant-aided industry.[44] In 1966, grant-aided industry (of which foreign firms comprised three-quarters) accounted for 9 percent of total manufacturing employment, 42½ percent of manufactured exports, and 11 percent of gross output. By 1973, the figures bulged to 29 percent of total manufacturing employment (compared to 10.3 percent in the UK, 22.4 percent in Germany, and a whopping 52.4 percent in Canada), 62 percent of manufactured exports (compared to 24 percent in the UK and 30 percent in Belgium), and 30 percent of gross output (versus 63 percent of GNP in that branch-plant paradise, Canada).[45] The dominance of British capital was surpassed in the 1970s by American investment. Though British firms outnumber US firms over the 1960–75 period, American investment exceeded the British and the Germans (in third place) in capital and in jobs. The trend continued into the early 1980s. In 1976 US firms generated 68 percent of foreign sector job "approvals" in the Republic. In 1979, the figure passes the 70 percent mark while the US provided 80 percent of all new foreign fixed asset investment as well.[46]

As the 1967 survey foretold, the cost per job created through IDA auspices simply soared – rising 32.6 percent in 1977 alone over the prior year (by which time grants per job doubled the 1960–73 average).[47] Even the "lag" period between announced projections and jobs provided as industries come "onstream" nullifies employment potential through intervening technical advances. In 1966, job

[44] *Survey of Grant-Aided Industry* and Dermot McAleese, *Profile of Grant-Aided Industry in Ireland* (Dublin: IDA, 1978).
[45] McAleese, *Grant-Aided Industry*, p. 26.
[46] *Industrial Development Authority Annual Report 1979* (Dublin: IDA, 1980), p. 17.
[47] *Irish Times*, 25, 26, 27 December 1977, p. 12.

projections were fulfilled at a rate of 80 percent; ten years later that critical figure declined dismayingly to 59 percent.

The Institute of Industrial Research and Standards reported that throughout the late 1970s recession employers were more interested in improving production processes (which shed labor) than in developing new products – which augured poorly for the "push-button for every fingertip" utopia. The corrosive character of automation – which cut jobs in the short run, and perhaps in the long term too – hampered the Irish strategy for creating employment and prosperity. Over the 1966–74 period, new grant-aided industries (foreign and native) "accounted for 59–68% of the increase in gross output and 24–33% of the increase in exports, all of which was *achieved with a lower labour force than in 1966.*"[48]

Capital-intensive technology is not necessarily villainous since the capital surplus which it generates ought to be made available for other social purposes. In practice, however, the surplus is controlled by private elites whose interests do not coincide with those of subordinate groups, or even with one another. Where reinvestment occurs, international competition dictates that firms invest in labor-shedding processes and equipment. Noting this tendency of investors to aim at cost-reduction measures instead of capacity expansion, Durkan observes:

A feature of the Irish economy in the period 1960–73 was the very high level of investment averaging 19½ per cent of GNP over the period and the poor performance on total employment which rose from 1,052 thousand in April 1960 to 1,066 thousand in April 1974 (non-agricultural employment rose from 783 to 712 thousand over the same period). In the more recent period, 1974 to 1977, investment has averaged almost 25 per cent of GNP.[49]

In that "more recent" period total employment sank to the lowest level in the history of the Irish state. What went wrong? The IDA was running too many races: races against demography (boasting "the youngest and fastest growing population in the EEC"), job loss from import competition, rising expenses of capital intensive technologies, and rivals for footloose capital.

Regarding concerns over a final-assembly bias and the abysmally

[48] McAleese, *Profile*, p. 25.
[49] Joe Durkan, "The Irish Economy: The Recent Experience and Prospective Future Performance," in Durkan and Dowling, eds., *Irish Economic Policy*, p. 47.

low local linkages by foreign firms, the IDA responded in the mid-1970s by targeting foreign high-tech electronics firms for siting in Ireland to create a secure web of industry that might transform the Emerald Isle into a silicon Isle. However, obscured by energy crises and global recession, the benign consensus-generating basis of the "peripheral postindustrial" project was eroding as a result of systematic technology gaps – systematic in terms both of internal socio-economic organization and of international exchange relations. The sources and effects are identified briefly:

(1) *Foreign control over the terms of technology transfer* is the most familiar problem. Duty-free import of technologies gives rise to balance-of-payments strain. Imported with the technologies is their "interest-composition," i.e., their design embodies the criteria of potent social interests elsewhere. Among potentially inappropriate criteria are:

(2) *Capital-intensity bias and "segmentation."* Though never attaining full employment in its history, the Irish state is not situated so badly relative to labor-suplus Third World economies. Trends toward industrial and service automation are not necessarily disadvantageous in a relatively developed society that produces a surplus of science and engineering graduates in addition to a skilled labor force. Nonetheless they have taken a toll. Segmentation is the allocation by parent firms of partial, specialized production processes among a variety of sites. If "final assembly," they are low-skilled, as early critiques had noted. Segmentation retards host state capacity to make Vernon's "obsolescing bargain" obsolesce, and also militates against linkage. A related concern is:

(3 *The "volatility" of new technologies* also hampers any turn of bargaining advantage to the host. That parent firms of foreign affiliates retain control over R & D for rapidly changing sophisticated products is too well documented to dwell on here. If local firms and the state are unable or unwilling to match (presumably in product lines of specific competitive advantage) these R & D outlays and organization, product cycle virtuosity suffers. If so, reliance on high-tech foreign affiliates will only exacerbate these effects. Finally:

(4) *(1), (2), and (3) are interrelated*, and their negative impact is intensified by global economic downturns *and* by global competition, especially so when the state is restricted to a catalytic

role and the local bourgeoisie lacks what Evans nicely terms a "vocation for hegemony." In downturns R & D is devoted to tasks of rationalization (producing a similar level of output with less labor) rather than product innovation which provides a basis for capacity-extension (and more jobs). But in the latest upturn, high tech firms are more likely to locate affiliates in Asian or even East European low-wage areas. The competition for the quantities of mobile capital to fund the "peripheral post-industrial" path is keener than ever. The greater the competition for these firms, the more remote the possibility that this strategy can succeed.

The impact of automation was highly evident in Ireland long before the oil embargoes and price rises. As the McAleese survey noted, new exporting firms achieved increases of 60 percent or more in output and of 24 percent or more in export growth over 1966–74 with an accompanying reduction in the work force. Over 1973–79 manufacturing output went up 5.1 percent while jobs edged up 0.7 percent.[50] Over 1979–84 output grew on average 4.3 percent as jobs fell by more than 3 percent (and in 1984 alone a 13 percent export increase was associated with a drop-off in job creation).

Despite a rise of investment to 30 percent of GNP (compared with 14 percent in the United States, 17 percent in the United Kingdom, and 31 percent in Japan) in the 1970s, employment fell to the lowest level in the history of the Irish state. Even in the 1960s–73 heyday of the "economic miracle," unemployment averaged 6.5 percent – a figure which at the time was still deemed unacceptable in both UK and USA contexts. High unemployment meant more taxation for relief schemes. State spending increased from 36 percent of GNP in 1962 to 53 percent by 1974 through regressive taxation that triggered massive demonstrations in 1979 (and afterward). Capital taxes were less than 1 percent of tax revenue while the share contributed by Pay-As-You-Earn (PAYE, instituted in 1963) workers ascended aggravatingly from 62 percent in 1970 to nearly 90 percent in 1980.[51] In the mid-1970s the ICTU affirmed support for "state action to expand employment," and explicitly rued an "over-reliance on multi-national companies for job creations."[52]

[50] Kieran Kennedy and Tom Healy, *Small Scale Manufacturing in Ireland* (Dublin: Economic and Social Research Institute, November 1985), paper no. 125, p. 158.
[51] *Irish Times*, December 1980, p. 1.
[52] *ICTU Annual Report 1975* (Dublin: ICTU, 1976), pp. 72, 171.

In Ireland the "easy" export-led industrialization phase was rapidly coming to a close. The consensus-generating aspects of the development strategy were eroding. A fiscal crisis was looming (Ireland moved into debtor status in 1972–73). A coalition of foreign investors, local exporters (and their suppliers), parts of the state bureaucracy, the main political parties, and skilled elements in trade unions was in the process of consolidating just before the onset of sustained adversities in the 1980s. And the IDA would retain much of its strength as implementer and propagator of the policy orthodoxy.

THE BALANCE SHEET IN THE 1970S

The IDA encouraged attraction of science-intensive industries such as pharmaceuticals, chemicals, electrical and general engineering, and synthetic fibers. "Labor-intensive" industries were synonymous in the IDA view with sweatshops.[53] Subsidies favored capital over labor inputs but the IDA was "prepared to pay higher than normal grants for industry with high skill content" and which met "basic criteria of commercial viability," reasoning that capital-intensive "growth industries" will provide fewer but durable jobs.[54] Nonetheless, the IDA rejected very few "realistic" projects. The DeLorean plant was one illustrious exception.

The IDA bore the brunt of the outcry for jobs. Over 1971–74, 58,500 jobs were created in IDA sponsored industries, but 53,000 jobs were lost in the old manufacturing sector – a quarter of all manufacturing jobs.[55] Competing manufactured imports rose from 19 percent in 1965 to 31 percent by 1973 because of tariff reductions with Britain *alone*. The McAleese Survey found "the average import-content of overseas firms' purchases in industries other than food (58 percent in 1974) exceeds that of Irish firms" (48 percent) that were never themselves parsimonious importers.[56] Exports increased from 29 percent of GNP in 1958 to 35 percent in 1969; imports rose even faster from 39 percent of GNP in 1958 to 54 percent. In the 1970s economists noted that because 56 percent of imports were materials for production and a further 16 percent were

---

[53] Interviews with IDA personnel.
[54] John McKeon, "Economic Appraisal of Industrial Projects in Ireland" (mimeo, IDA 1980), p. 12.
[55] *Ibid.*   [56] McAleese, *Profile*, p. 46.

producer capital goods imports, the structure of this economy made it difficult for the government to deflate without harming output.[57] The vertical integration of foreign firms militated against linkages and multiplier effects. A Science Policy survey concluded that grant-aided industries had *"not* generated much secondary employment, with the exception of the effects which direct income generation (in the form of wages and salaries) may have had on raising consumer demand in Ireland."[58] While this helps home industries, balance-of-payments pressure increases because import consumption is high. This food-producing country imports about 60 percent of supermarket-shelved food.[59] Export-led development was reliant on import-gorging manufactures that exert steady and sometimes severe pressure on the balance-of-payments. In deflationary episodes the victims are not only workers but small firms having neither the resources of foreign firms nor recourse to the Eurodollar market. Deflation may relieve the profit squeeze on "home industries" but simultaneously reduce the local demand which they require. The contradiction is exquisitely painful. The support for deflationary policies by business associations (of which foreign firms are members) probably indicates the ascendance of new exporting industries over the old home market firms.[60]

The wage-earning population is urged to exercise restraint so that capital can "renew, remunerate, and expand" though no demonstrable relationship between profit levels and job-creating investment exists which would make sense of the exhortations. The top 5 percent of the population of "poor auld Ireland" own 63 percent of the wealth; the top 10 percent 74 percent.[61] (In Northern Ireland, the top 5 percent account for 47.5 percent of wealth; in Britain 52 percent.) Few among these 5 or 10 percent are wage and salary earners on the Pay-As-You-Earn tax system who in 1977 contributed 87.5 percent of income tax – up from 62 percent in 1970 while

---

[57] Kennedy and Dowling, *The Irish Economy Since 1947*, p. 127.

[58] OECD, *Review of Science Policy: Ireland* (Paris: OECD, 1971), p. 25.

[59] *Irish Times*, 1 April 1977, Supp., p. ii.

[60] See Derek Chambers' contribution on behalf of the Confederation of Irish Industry to The "Symposium on Increasing Employment," in *Journal of The Statistical and Social Inquiry Society of Ireland* 23, 2 (1975), pp. 69–74.

[61] P. M. Lyons, "The Size of Personal Wealth in The Republic of Ireland," *Review of Income and Policy*, ser. 20, no. 2, 1977. Also see P. T. Geary, "Wages, Prices, Incomes and Wealth," in Gibson and Spencer, *Economic Activity in Ireland*, and Breen, Hannan, Rottman, and Whelan, "The State and the Distribution and Redistribution of Income," in *Understanding Contemporary Ireland*.

manufacturers, large farmers, and non-PAYE professionals chipped in an incredibly shrinking share. This issue would explode into political view with the huge demonstrations in 1979.

The integrated sourcing and marketing of international firms exacerbates growth of a "dual economy." That is, of two sectors having "unequal access to resources."[62] There was evidence of the foreign sector "bidding away" capital and skilled labor. In 1972 two-thirds of capital was raised for foreign firms from domestic sources. A 1975 US Chamber of Commerce survey of American firms in Ireland disclosed that they paid an average weekly wage of £58 Irish compared to a local average of £42.8.[63] A sample of sixty-two US firms revealed that 32 percent of output on average was sold locally. Irish manfacturers also grumbled that the subsidies conferred on foreign firms allowed them to engage in a form of "internal dumping." Although there was little data on takeovers, investigators infer it was a fairly brisk activity.[64] The neat notion that native firms should benefit eventually from the "rollover" of products of foreign firms, i.e., that the latter surrender products, processes, and leadership due to the product-cycle was disconfirmed. As Cooper points out, there often was a "critical minimum level" in R & D activity below which commercially usable results do not appear.[65]

R & D and "control" functions stayed centered in parent companies while Irish (and a few small foreign) firms tended to rely on the Institute for Industrial Standards and Research whose director in the 1970s followed the rule: "Let others do basic research, while we concentrate on adapting it and making it widely available to industry."[66] In 1975 the IDA "advertised" a 60 percent surplus of science and engineering graduates as one of the boons for foreign employers contemplating Ireland. After small net inflows early in the decade there was a new upturn of emigrating by 1977.

New industries generate demand for technical expertise, but an OECD team warned that the degree to which skill formation takes

---

[62] NESC Report *Industrial Policy and Development*, pp. 65–68.

[63] US Chamber of Commerce (Ireland) *Annual Report*, 1976, p. 10. This may be a classic example of the inability of multinationals to please their hosts no matter what they do. High pay is not normally regarded as a defect.

[64] See OECD, *Review of Science Policy* (Paris: OECD, 1980).

[65] Charles Cooper, "Science, Technology and Development," *Economic and Social Review*, 2, 2 (January 1971), pp. 184–85.

[66] Quoted in *Irish Times*, 22 June 1978, "Special Report on R & D," p. 17.

place "depends to a large extent on the stage of production at which manufacturing plants are set up. Final stage and (to a greater extent still) assembly production, have fewer beneficial effects of this nature."[67] There was evidence of a world-wide trend of "rationalization of work processes" which in conjunction with increasing capital-intensity diminish the quality of work (and labor's power in the workplace) as well as the quantity.[68]

The IDA strived to "marry" foreign firms with local suppliers; shift out of simple assembly operations; and hike job projections. But the international competition of Development Agencies for footloose capital induced the IDA to race at an Alice-in-Wonderland pace in the fine art of plant location. Closures did not pose an alarming problem, but the fact that only 20 to 25 percent of grant-aided industries expanded their facilities forced the state to resort to "repeated injections of new overseas firms."[69]

Tax on *all* manufacturing was cut from a nominal 45 percent rate to 10 percent as of January 1, 1981, thus mollifying local business. While the IDA assured the population that foreign firms will remain fastened to Irish soil after the tax holiday expires, no risks were to be taken. In Belgium eighty-one foreign companies closed down because of rises in the cost-of-living over 1970 to 1975.[70] In Puerto Rico 20 percent of foreign companies quit once incentives expired. These aren't all flimsy "fly-by-nighters." Illustrious names like Siemens, General Electric, and British Petroleum left Italy.

Social spending rose at a 12.9 percent rate between 1958 and 1972, exceeding the budget rate, which was 9.8 percent.[71] The rural outflow increased demand for urban services. "Agricultural employment [since 1946] has declined by 300,000; while only 60,000 new jobs in manufacturing have been added [up to 1974], an average of 2,200 jobs a year" for a nation that needs ten times as many.[72] The

[67] OECD, *Review of Science Policy*, p. 25.
[68] There is a vast and still growing literature here. See J. K. Jacobsen, "Microchips and Public Policy: The Political Economy of High Technology," *British Journal of Political Science*, 22, 4 (October 1992).
[69] See McAleese, "Capital Inflow"; Teeling, *The Evolution of Offshore Investment*, and *Industrial Policy and Development*.
[70] Turner, *Multinationals and The Third World*, p. 120.
[71] P. R. Kaim-Caudle, *Social Policy in The Irish Republic* (London: Weidenfeld and Nicolson, 1967).
[72] Anthony Coughlin argued that the Irish industrialization strategy has, among other defects, distorted the product mix in local output. See his "In Perspective," in *The Irish Economy: What Is To Be Done?* (Dublin: ASTS Publication, 1976), pp. 3–12.

industrialization strategy exacerbated the very problems that proponents hoped it would solve.

The Irish state created demand with expenditures which rose
from 36 percent of GNP in 1962 to 53 percent by 1974, mostly debt
creation, of which the foreign component rocketed in the recession-
ridden 1970s. Only the UK among OECD countries incurred higher
debt over 1969–74 (60.5 percent of GNP versus Irish 58.2 percent).[73] Foreign borrowing was relatively cheap, but there were
abundant signs that the state was on collision course with borrowing
limits.[74] Foreign lenders got a negative real interest rate on Irish
borrowings. But, as of 1977, Ireland paid "410 million pounds in
servicing its debt – and that equalled 130 pounds from each man,
woman and child and absorbed 28 percent of tax revenue."[75]

Moreover, borrowing (92.8 percent of GNP in 1978) was criticized for being applied to prodigal current spending rather than to
"productive" outlays. However, state spending probably prevented
a sharper decline in investment by foreign and especially local
sources. Still, long-term current deficits can discourage private
investment or lead to capital flight. The efforts of Irish governments
to juggle the dual imperatives of preserving the conditions for
accumulation ("remunerating, renewing, and expanding") and of
legitimating the socio-economic system are examined in chapter 6,
as are shifts in IDA performance and industrial policy.

The IDA's role as the premier policy instrument of the state is
reflected in a recitation of achievements in a nineteenth anniversary
report:

The Authority employs nearly 700 persons.

Planned investment in IDA grant-aided industries was £2,677 million in
the 1970s compared with £130 million in the 1960s; grants totalling
£831 million were committed to these industries.

Job approvals associated with this investment amounted to 192,380 [net of
known cancellations] compared with 45,000 in the 1960s, 99,000 or 51
per cent of these were in domestic firms [including the expansion of
existing overseas companies].

Average grant cost per job approved declined by 17 per cent in real terms
from 7,592 in 1970 to 6,279 in 1978 (1979 prices).

Job approvals in small firms increased from 1,190 or 9 per cent of total

[73] Jeff Frieden, "The Indebted Emerald Isle" (mimeo, 1984).
[74] *Irish Times*, 6 September 1978, p. 2.
[75] *Irish Independent*, 8 June 1978, p. 12.

approvals in 1970/71 to 8,244 or nearly 25 per cent of total in 1979 and are planned to rise to nearly 10,000 or 30 per cent in 1980.

Investment commitments by Irish firms to re-equip and modernise their plants under the IDA's Re-Equipment and Modernisation Programme totalled 450 million.

IDA backed research and development programmes totalled 21.4 million for the decade; assistance under the scheme grew steadily from 0.1 million in 1970/71 to 3.1 million in 1979.[76]

The celebratory list cites a "Service Industries Programme," regional planning, linkage-producing activities, and other endeavors. The IDA claimed that each new manufacturing job it midwives produces 1.3 jobs elsewhere, that the "shake-out" of industries was nearly completed, and that the basis of a strong diversified economy was laid.[77] On the other hand, industrial job losses rose from 15,000 in 1979 to 25,000 in 1980, 40 percent of "jobs projected" were phantoms, the interaffiliate trading of foreign firms (68 percent of exports and 55 percent of imports) militates against linkage, and the official failure rate increased from 10 percent of grant-aided projects in the 1952–60 period to 16 percent over the 1960–73 period.[78] The grant cost per job for *foreign* firms increased substantially in real terms. While the lower cost per job reflected a trend toward small business, nearly two-thirds of "jobs projected" in 1979 were new foreign projects or the expansion of existing subsidiaries.[79] Nonetheless, the pressures of intensifying competition for footloose capital, closure rates, rising costs per foreign sector job, and political lobbying by Irish business were nudging the state and the IDA toward a more indigenized development track.[80]

At the outset of the 1980s the economy was more vulnerable than ever to international maladies while trade dependence upon Britain remained substantial. (Britain still accounted for half of exports and two-thirds of all trade.) One minor but telling expression of dependency was a decision in 1981 by the state-owned television station to drop a current events program syndicated overseas because it projected a "negative image" of Irish people who had the temerity to

---

[76] IDA, *Annual Report 1979*, p. 3.

[77] Padraigh White, "Industry in Ireland Today," in *Ireland in The Year 2000* (Dublin: An Foras Forbatha, 1980), p. 37. White succeeded Michael Killeen as IDA managing director.

[78] McAleese, *Profile*, p. 78. The export tax relief, it was argued, inhibited linkage. Yet the state first had to attract "linkable" firms through that lure. Within the logic of the strategy there was no recourse.

[79] IDA, *Annual Report 1979*, pp. 5–9.   [80] *Industrial Policy and Development*, pp. 84–85.

engage in industrial disputes as well as in hurling matches and more picture postcardable pastimes.[81] The state had industrialized the economy but the links of dependency had been redefined, not altered.

The notion that Ireland is a floating grassland devoid of mineral wealth was dashed in the 1960s by a plethora of discoveries:

In 1974 the minerals industry accounted for 7 per cent of gross output, 12 per cent of the net output (value added), 10 per cent of the total payroll of industry and 11 per cent of our exports. When the Navan mines come onstream, Ireland will be the third largest exporter of metals and *will probably replace Australia as the third largest exporter of metals in the world* ... Silvermines is the biggest zinc-lead ore producer in Europe. Northgate is one of Europe's largest silver producers and in Magcobar we have one of the world's largest producers of high quality barytes. The Navan deposits will constitute one of the ten largest mines in the world in proven reserves and potential extraction rates.[82]

This geological wealth could provide the basis for heavy industrialization by generating downstream industries in die-casting, galvanizing, and so on. Because of the vertical integration of multinational mining companies in conjunction with the generous terms of Irish authorities, nothing of the kind occurred. The Resource Protection Study Group of Ireland estimated that 97.5 percent of the wealth-generating potential of minerals was realized outside the country. Inasmuch as the multinational companies enjoyed a twenty-year tax holiday on mines with "extraction lives" less than that, the Irish state subsidized its own plundering.[83] Besides ore deposits, a natural gas strike off the southern coast was tapped while offshore oil had been located – though not, at this writing, in commercial quantities.

Amid accusations by Fianna Fail shadow ministers that "the end of private property" was nigh the Labour Minister for Industry and Commerce in the coalition government announced in 1973 that the

---

[81] *Sunday Tribune*, 27 December 1981, p. 2.

[82] Martin Cranley, "The Natural Resources of Ireland," *Administration* 8, 1 (1976).

[83] Several interviewees hinted at dark goings-on with regard to the conduct of negotiations with multi-nationals, but no evidence of illegal suasion surfaced.

mining tax holiday was to be repealed.[84] Mineral development is an area in which host countries most successfully have honed their negotiating skills and increased bargaining power over time.[85] Coalition ministers discovered to their relief that mining companies did not resist rises in taxation and royalty rates to what were, after all, international levels.[86] A year after the repeal the Minister for Finance rejoiced that "not one whisper of complaint from investors" had been heard.[87] The Minister's hearing aid may have malfunctioned, but the point here is the immense caution with which Fianna Fail behaved toward investors. A good deal of maneuver for tougher bargaining went untested and was unexploited. The repeal had no adverse impact at all on the IDA's industrial programs.[88] Manufacturing investors were reassured profusely that their own holiday was not endangered. But, looking back, a coalition minister did feel that they "could not get away with it again."[89]

The repeal actually meant very little because the state retained no control over processes, extraction rates, or destinations of the minerals. There was no viable state mining company and no smelter for domestic value-adding. (The Irish politely declined a Soviet offer in the late 1970s to build a smelter in exchange for a percentage of the output.) Defending his controversial deal over disposition of an ore discovery in Navan, Minister of Industry and Commerce Keating explained: "There is not the mass of public support in Ireland to have the state run the mines ... I wanted an indigenous mining group as a countervailing force to the multinationals ... there was tremendous thrust to deliver the Navan ore body to private multinationals. I opposed it."[90]

A private "Irish" consortium would not necessarily operate differently than foreign companies. Many finds will likely be near exhaustion before the appearance of a smelter or downstream industries. As of 1989 the Bula mines were in receivership. The Navan mines were bought in 1985 by a state-owned Finnish company.[91]

---

[84] (Charles J. Haughey, the Fianna Fail minister who introduced the mining tax holiday in the mid-1960s), Parliamentary Debates, Dail Eireann, 5 April 1974, 271, col. 1788.

[85] But see Jenkins, "Reexamining The 'Obsolescing Bargain'."

[86] Interview with Garret Fitzgerald.

[87] (Richie Ryan) *Parliamentary Debates, Dail Eireann*, 11 February 1975, 278, col. 420.

[88] Interview with Michael Killeen.

[89] Interview with Garret Fitzgerald.   [90] *Irish Independent*, 15 January 1978, p. 6.

[91] Tim Pat Coogan, *Disillusioned Decades: Ireland 1966–87* (Dublin: Gill and Macmillan, 1987), p. 138.

FERENKA: INTIMATIONS OF INDUSTRIAL MORTALITY

"IT ALL STARTED WITH ROW OVER CLEANING TOILET," a headline declared in the wake of an announcement in November 1977 by the Dutch parent that it would shut down its Irish subsidiary (Ferenka), the largest manufacturing employer in Ireland.[92] In one stroke 1,400 jobs vanished in Limerick (population 63,000). The nation shivered in the shock waves. The Dutch company departed in the midst of an inter-union dispute, and a duel erupted between those blaiming the "bloody-mindedness" of trade unions and those pointing to an ultimate clash of national goals with the strategies of large multinationals.

This steel-cord manufacturing plant had received £8.3 million (of 12 million promised) since 1969. Dutch parent ENKA was part of the larger multinational corporation AKZO headquartered in Arnhem from where it conducted operations in forty-five countries.

AKZO is the 37th largest company in Europe and it produces a wide range of products. In terms of turnover, it is third largest in the European paper and paper products industry, it is fifth largest in food manufacturing industry, tenth in engineering and electrical goods and eleventh in chemicals and plastics ... Before the depression in 1974 its total assets stood at almost 2000 [million pounds] and equity capital totalled 700 [million pounds].

However, even in its last good year, which was 1974, AKZO group was performing poorly. The profit earned ... represented only 3% of sales and 3.1% of net assets ... By October 1975 a major rationalization was being implemented throughout the group ... the company planned to reduce its European workforce from 43,000 to 37,000 by the end of 1977. In the company as a whole, employment fell from 103,000 in 1974 to 87,000 in [1977].[93]

Although the Irish plant was troubled by labor discontent the foregoing facts must be weighed when assessing the company's spokesman's complaint that: "We have had an ongoing struggle with personnel over five years. It has cost the company a lot of money. In my opinion no guarantees were offered by the Irish government or the unions that there would be a period of peace."[94]

[92] *Irish Independent*, 30 November 1977, p. 1.
[93] Vincent Browne, John Feeney and John Howard, "Don't Cry Just Yet For Ferenka," *Magill* 6, 1 (December 1977), p. 18.
[94] *Irish Times*, 2 December 1977, p. 1.

In fact, AKZO had been channelling investment into workers' paradises in Czechoslovakia, Bulgaria, and Brazil ever since an attempt to dismiss 5,000 workers in Holland, Belgium, and West Germany in 1972 had been thwarted by trade union resistance.[95] In Ireland Ferenka had incurred a loss of £15 million, a 25 percent labor turnover rate, and 26 unofficial disputes. But even the worst year in terms of lost man-hours only amounted to 2 percent of the total and was marginal relative to overall losses stemming from the international recession. By 1977 the market for steel cord for radial tyres was buoyant but AKZO's loss-cutting strategy went ahead.

Ferenka's work regime was notoriously authoritarian. The four-cycle shift imposed enormous strain. Many commentators who ascribed industrial conflict to the "cultural unpreparedness" of a rural work force did not pause to reflect on the kind of education system required to persuade workers to adjust themselves placidly to conditions inflicted on migrant labor on the continent.[96] Dissatisfied with the ITGWU's apparent passivity, two-thirds of Ferenka's workers opted for the Marine, Port and General Workers Union (MPGWU), whereupon the ITGWU threatened a strike if the company recognized the "interloper."[97] According to a Limerick correspondent:

The relationship between the workers and the Irish Transport and General Workers Union (which had been given the right of sole representation for production and general workers) began to deteriorate about 1974. A link which had been created between top officials and the man on the floor through a part-time official disappeared. Communication seemed to have broken down and union decisions were not always passed on to the men. For that reason there was a loss of confidence in the ITGWU and this provided a perfect pitch for the dissidents who succeeded in swinging the workers away.[98]

A new militant shop steward was elected; the result being that all but four of the sixteen shop stewards were opposed to the ITGWU and the workers' committee wanted the Marine Port and General Workers Union. Yet this inter-union rivalry did not alone precipitate the final fatal strike.

---

[95] Brian Trench and Niall Kiely, "Why Azko Axed Ferenka," *Hibernia*, 2 December 1977, p. 3. On the 1972 incidents see the *Irish Press*, 22 September 1972.

[96] Browne, Feeny and Howard, "Don't Cry Just Yet," pp. 20–21, for description of working conditions. The workers tell their side in *The Bottom Dog* 95, 5 (11 November 1977).

[97] *Irish Times*, 29 November 1977, p. 14.   [98] *Ibid.*

In September 1974 a production worker who refused to clean a toilet was suspended. An unofficial picket ensued. The worker was reinstated but seven shop stewards who led the picket were suspended. When one steward was fired the strike began. The strike was compounded by the inter-union dispute, but a settlement was reached *before* the announcement that AKZO was shutting Ferenka.

Neither a pleading Minister of Industry and Commerce nor a beseeching Bishop of Limerick could win a reprieve – which reportedly would have cost the IDA half again as much as the original grant. Ferenka workers occupied the factory for several days. Remarkably, new Fine Gael leader Garrett Fitzgerald called for the establishment of a "workers' cooperative" on the premises – a dizzying rhetorical departure from the party's traditional views. But even socialists acknowledged that any such venture would be thwarted by the marketing "lock" which private companies held. In any case, Fianna Fail Minister of Industry and Commerce O'Malley ruled out public ownership. The IDA was assigned the task of searching out another industry for the Limerick site.

The Republic erupted into debate over the premises guiding industrialization policy. On one hand, the trade unions were excoriated and likened to the "Bourbon dynasty which learnt nothing and forgot nothing."[99] On the other hand, the alternatives of public ownership and a small-scale approach entered the public discussion. The ideology of "reflex modernization" was for the first time widely questioned. The Ferenka crisis exposed how precarious was the basis of Ireland's industrialization. Perhaps the depths of insecurity were best illustrated by the hysterical anti-trade union tracts in "Letter To The Editor" columns. One exemplary contribution argued that:

If the disaster of Ferenka's closure would shock the Government into introducing legislation to make unofficial strikes illegal and shock the unions into supporting this legislation, some good might come out of this business. *Whatever the real reason,* the Dutch parent company puts down the 15 unofficial strikes since the factory opened as a major cause for its closure.[100] (Emphasis mine)

The presupposition inside this text is that when dealing with multi-national firms, only unconditional surrender will do. The bargaining power of the state is nil; so the power of Irish unions in turn *must*

[99] *Irish Times*, 8 December 1977, p. 13, Letters Column.
[100] *Irish Times*, 5 December 1977, p. 14 Letters Column.

be made nil. The producer is always right because business can be taken elsewhere to a more subservient welcome.

The peripheral nature of Irish industrialization could not have been cast into sharper relief. A gossamer of grants and relatively cheap labor – wages 40 percent below West German counterparts – "anchored" Ferenka, not raw materials or any other natural advantages. Still, Ferenka was somewhat exceptional among foreign firms in blending a shallow base with an atrocious industrial relations record. Upon Ferenka's departure, the Minister of Labour pointed to the overall record:

Of the externally-owned manufacturing firms operating in Ireland the great majority – more than 80% – had no strike problems at all in the period 1972–1976. In that period of five years only 13 firms out of a total of over 500 could be said to have had significant labour problems ... The strike experience of British firms operating in Ireland could be said to be markedly better than in Britain. As regards US firms ... the situation is significantly better than in the US – an annual average of 500 man-days lost per 1000 workers against an average of 804 days ... in the US.[101]

But the Republic was vulnerable to the opprobrium which the Ferenka management (AKZO) might conjure. *Kiplinger European Newsletter* discouraged investors from dallying in Ireland due to what was an exaggerated strike rate. The strain of maintaining an "attractive business climate" was indeed beginning to show. In an image-making age public relations mattered more than the actual state of industrial relations. The Irish state was confined by reliance upon the good graces of foreign enterprises. But the Ferenka affair certainly had exposed a distressing faultline economic policy.

There were few, if any, cries of "multinationals *delenda est!*" With 30,000 jobs a year as the objective, foreign investment remained a vital contributor but was adjudged as one which "should be used so as to complement not substitute for native technology."[102] The tricky part is going about doing, or making noises about doing, just that.

Reviewing progress at the end of the 1960s, an Irish economist sagely cautioned that one "cannot set a distorted economy right in just a decade."[103] Two decades clearly had sufficed to distort the

---

[101] *Irish Times*, 10 December 1977, p. 1.
[102] Charles Cooper and Noel Whelan, *Science, Technology and Industry in Ireland* (Dublin: National Science Council, 1973), p. 40.
[103] This was Patrick Lynch.

Irish economy *differently*. Multinational firms preempted development of an indigenous economic base in the dynamic sectors even
though the Irish economy undeniably made industrial strides. As
Mandel argues, a crisis in contemporary capitalist societies stems
from

the shortening of turnover-time of fixed capital, the acceleration of technological innovation, and the enormous increase in the cost of major projects
of capital accumulation due to the third technological revolution, with its
corresponding increase in the risks of any delay or failure of the valor-
ization of the enormous volumes of capital needed for them. The result of
these pressures is a tendency in late capitalism towards an increase not only
in State economic planning but also in State Socialization of costs (risks)
and losses.[104]

Yet these activities do pose risks for the beneficiaries, which are cited
concisely by a French observor:

The Irish bourgeoisie embraces only one project [which is the promotion of
optimum economic growth through private enterprise and the profit
motive] but it involves the defence of very different interests. The carrying
out of its project demands very delicate choices among interests: whether to
align itself with international capitalism and risk being swallowed up by it
or whether to depend upon an ever increasing State intervention and risk
engendering a State capitalism which would subordinate it to its
interests.[105]

Foreign firms control 60 percent of Irish manufacturing, propel the
economy briskly along the runway (at a high price in fuel) but offer
no prospect of a "take-off." A 1984 report by independent consultants indicated that of 96,026 jobs approved and funded between
1970 and 1978, only 28,937 materialized by 1981.[106] The state
ritually responds to sluggish industrial job creation by encouraging
wage restraint. "The actual outcome of 11 years wage restraint is
there for anyone to see," writes Derwin, "under central bargaining
agreements from 1970 to 1981 the basic wage rises for a worker on
£20 (in Dec. '70) amounted to 298.8 per cent (before tax, etc.). The
Consumer Price Index rose by 327.8 per cent between November
1970 and August 1981."[107] Tax inequities are a potentially

104 Ernest Mandel, *Late Capitalism* (London: New Left Books, 1975), p. 484.
105 Michel Peillon, *Contemporary Irish Society: An Introduction* (Dublin: Gill and Macmillan,
    1982), pp. 147–48.
106 NESC, *Survey of Industrial Policy* (Telesis Report), p. 29.
107 Des Derwin, "Talk Bread, and The Bakery," *Left Perspectives* 2, 2 (Summer 1982), p. 25.

Table 13. *Trends in government borrowing and spending, 1972–1978*
(Irish Republic)

	1972/3	1974	1975	1976	1977	1978
% rise in current spending	16.3	17.6	42.9	23.8	17.1	20.9
% rise in current revenue	15.7	7.2	28.4	36.6	19.5	11.7
Current deficit	5.5	94.9	258.8	201.4	102.0	405.0
Deficit as % of GNP	0.3	3.2	7.0	4.5	3.7	6.4
% of borrowing financed						
abroad	17.0	44.6	27.2	64.0	15.8	–
Total Gov't debt	1421	1957	2743	3612	4210	–
Overseas as % of						
Government debt	8.9	15.9	17.2	28.8	24.9	–

Source: OECD, *Economic Survey of Ireland* (Paris: OECD Publication, May, 1978), p. 20.

Table 14. *Adjusted earnings rate on return (%) on US manufacturing*
investment in 1975 and 1976

	1975	1976	Average 1975–76
IRELAND	29.9	29.2	29.5
Germany	15.5	27.7	21.6
Denmark	11.4	29.8	20.6
Belgium & Luxembourg	9.8	12.6	11.2
Netherlands	9.5	12.5	11.0
Italy	7.1	12.4	9.7
France	12.0	7.3	9.6
UK	5.4	5.5	5.5
World	11.2	12.3	11.7

Source: Irish Times, 18 October 1977, p. 21.

explosive issue. If accumulation is a self-legitimating activity raising living standards and creating jobs, the Irish economic strategy is corrosive. The success of grant-aided industries might be weighed against the fact that "the number of employees under State control, 265,800 in 1976, was 30% greater than the official figure for total employment in manufacturing for that year."[108] Public sector

---

[108] Ross, "Regional Policy," in Dowling and Durkan, *Irish Economic Policy*, p. 314.

employment increased from 18 percent of the total in 1965 to
27 percent in 1979.

Irish elites kept public enterprise firmly in a very subordinate
place. The power of market ideology is revealed in the back-handed
tribute paid in an NESC report recommending expansion of public
sector activities:

A great deal of public money is now being put into private sector enterprises and this has not given rise to any call for state control over their
activities. It can be argued, therefore, that if a state enterprise is receiving
no more assistance than that which would be given to a private sector
enterprise, it should not be impeded by unnecessary supervision.

The point is that alternative economic arrangements are possible, if
not politically feasible. The "bottom-line" argument advanced by
opposition groups was not that foreign investment be shunned but
that unless the state readjusts policies the industrialization strategy
must suffer diminishing returns.[109]

As noted in chapter 2 the Irish Republic presented in the mid-
1970s a case of a state whose "potential sectoral power" increased
while it languished in the weakest realm of the four-cell bargaining
chart. National savings (variable I) rose from 7 percent in 1960 to
over 24 percent by 1975 – an ample amount by contemporary
standards. Arguably, technological capacity (variable II) improved
as state enterprise entrepreneurs (in, for example, the Sugar
Company, Bord Na Mona (Peat), and the Electricity Supply Board)
acquired the expertise to generate technologies suited to the local
milieu. The Irish situation certainly improved in regard to valuable
resources (variable v). The Republic remained handicapped as to
domestic market size (variable IV) and persistently weak in marketing capacity (variable III).

These cumulative improvements enabled the Irish state to edge
toward "imposing greater controls or exacting greater rents" as
indeed occurred in the case of the repeal of the mining tax holiday,
and to move toward the status of controlling foreign capital in
sectors "at some economic and political cost." But this form of action
presupposed political shifts within the Republic in addition to new
elite and public perceptions that the costs of foreign capital in a

---

[109] James Wickham, "The Politics of Dependent Capitalism: International Capital and The
Nation State," in Austen Morgan and Bob Purdie, *Ireland, Divided Nation, Divided Class*
(Dublin: Ink Links, 1980).

sector out-weighs its value. Otherwise, there is nothing to motivate the state to apply improvements in its "potential sectoral power" to the task of developing an autonomous policy for directing the economy, to act even slightly at odds with private economic agents. There is no alternative.

Irish industrialists hardly appeared to be a robust bourgeoisie. Certainly, the prerequisites for "lessening dependency" improved – in part thanks to foreign firms. The mineral discoveries (and potential downstream industries), underutilized land (and food processing prospects), fishing grounds of which the Irish fleet nets just 15 percent, and local entrepreneurs might combine with more adventurous public enterprises to create a sturdy economic base. State industrial expansion would be justifiable as part of a pragmatic tradition of tapping unutilized resources.[110] However, a "re-mix" of these elements of economic strategy can occur only in a political climate where explicit conflict over allocative and redistributive issues was intensifying.

CONCLUSION

The Irish, so said the Fianna Fail party, swapped one economic nationalist strategy – autarky – for another version, export-led foreign investment-fed development. The widespread welcome for the stream of benefits generated by the "new" strategy indicates that economic nationalism was not just a flexible concept but a means to other ends (jobs, higher living standards, etc.), and could rely on a large fund of public support (a "consensual satisfice"). Even the tiny opposition made few complaints about foreign industry or the export emphasis *per se*, and objected only to the *role* of multinational firms – fearing that economic dynamism might shrink to these enterprises alone unless the state orchestrated development.[111] No alternative scheme could make political headway in this climate.[112]

The state effectively ceded its "strength" to the Industrial

---

[110] For an overview of SSBs, see John Bristow, "State Sponsored Bodies," in Frank Litton, ed., *Unequal Achievement: The Irish Experience 1957–1982* (Dublin: Institute of Public Administration, 1982), pp. 165–82.

[111] Interviews with Eamonn Smullen and Cathal Goulding.

[112] See the industrial blueprint published by Sinn Fein – The Workers Party (later, The Workers Party) in 1977, which relies heavily on public sector commercial expansion and which denounces "a Trotskyite paranoia about state bureaucracy." *The Irish Industrial Revolution* (Dublin: Repsol, 1977), p. 140.

Development Authority, an organization which successfully depoliticized debate over development in the 1970s. The IDA was virtually autonomous with respect (and within limits determined by "job-creation" performance) to state officials. As for the anticipated "take-off," analysts found that "the preferred path for profitable Irish firms is not to invest in export-oriented industries at home but to buy into similarly domestic-oriented industries in other countries."[113] Neither the IDA nor the state were equipped or willing to interfere with market choices. The public good was insistently identified with private profit, regardless of owners or their locale. But this highly ideological notion would show signs of strain by the decade's end.

State policy-makers did not innovate so much as they responded incrementally to the unfolding logic of economic openness. The "choice" of openness arguably was thrust upon them, inasmuch as places as diverse as South Korea, Mexico, Taiwan, Puerto Rico, and the Philippines took the same path with the same timing but differing degrees of state direction. The state elite, and the new cadre of economic consultants, *transmitted* economic ideas (EOI, indicative planning, Keynesian notions) which actually emanated from powerful exogenous actors. Nor was much inventiveness displayed in adapting these models to Irish conditions so as to maximize local benefits and to consider carefully the long term. Through the 1970s – with few exceptions – the new economic elite in and outside government embraced a unanimous right-of-center set of diagnoses and prescriptions. "It is certainly true," an historian archly noted, "that Irish economists have devoted little time to pondering their own assumptions."[114] The 1972 Common Market vote signified public ratification of the new elite orthodoxy. So there was no pressure to scrutinize the assumptions informing the economic strategy.

The state pursued what was domestically a deceptively costless course. State capacity certainly grew but the whole point of taking the EOI path was to accommodate, not challenge or change, the policy preferences of private capital. The Ferenka case and the mining negotiations exemplify how potently that premise operated. They also signal the beginning of public misgivings over the content and implementation of development policy. Chapter 6 examines the political implications.

---

[113] Alan Matthews, "The Economic Consequences," p. 126.
[114] Lee, *Ireland: Politics and Society*, p. 582.

CHAPTER 6

Governability and corporatist compromise

> There was a time in official economic circles when planning was fashionable. We had some good shots at it. Then we had some that came unstuck and we abandoned it altogether. We had serious thoughts about full employment at a period which now seems not just a few years ago but an infinity away. Nobody talks about it anymore. Is it a dirty word?
>
> Justin Keating, *Parliamentary Debates, Dail Eireann* (1972)

In the context of a neo-colonial dependency this chapter examines governmental "bargaining" with producer groups and "bidding" for consumer group support at the polls from 1969 through 1984. We concentrate on the period from 1978, when industrial policy hit its highwater mark, to 1984 when the Telesis Report signaled the end of the strategy. Samuel Beer argues – or says he is tempted to argue – that just "as great retailing organizations manipulate the opinion of their markets, creating the demand of which in economic theory they are supposed to be the servants, so also the massive party organizations of Collectivist politics create the opinion which in democratic theory they are supposed merely to reflect."[1] Parties shape and condition the voters' sense of possibilities and alternatives. Anderson describes "paradigms of public choice" which specify the grounds appropriate for making claims within a given political order, defining the boundaries of admissible argument, and which are themselves at stake in political struggle.[2] In Ireland these ideological boundaries provided a cramped space for dissidents to operate within or against. Irish parties do not match their American or British counterparts in organization or media manipulation, but

---

[1] Beer, *British Politics in The Collectivist Age*, p. 331.
[2] Charles Anderson, "Public Policy and The Complex Organization: The Problem of Governance And The Further Evolution of Advanced Industrial Society," in Leon Lindberg, *Politics and The Future of Industrial Society* (New York: David McKay, 1976), pp. 192.

the Irish electoral pattern has been steadfastly one of a Tory party –
in Fianna Fail's post-populist era – and another Tory-led coalition
alternately governing and reinforcing a deep cultural conservatism
while dissenters and "surplus" citizens kept going up gangplanks. As
a socialist recalls:

The fact that there was a continual drain from Ireland of the potential
dissident meant that you had a marvellously complacent society. Beauti-
fully coordinated. Three or four pounds got you a ticket to Liverpool and a
job. You had to be a really determined revolutionary to stay here and go
hungry on the dole as it was. So the result was that you had a fair amount of
contentment all the way down the line. Like my mother they put it all
down to the will of God and his Holy Mother and accepted their cross.
That was where the Church came in. Then up the line they had a
wonderful life, a sort of eighteenth-century squirearchy. Ireland is a marvellous place to be if you have money. Nowhere like it.[3]

Emigration is the traditional means for allaying and postponing
problems of economic organization with which an Irish state otherwise would be compelled to grapple. Given strong demographic
pressure even the "right" economic decision – as ordained by
conventional market criteria – can turn out to be the wrong political
decision and therefore the wrong economic decision.

The Irish growth strategy crested in 1978. Until then the "open
door" policy toward investors appeared to be paying off, and at least
was satisfying key groups. Since 1960 annual growth averaged
4 percent and Ireland even led the EEC in 1978 with a 6 percent
performance. Manufacturing output rose 10 percent and manufactured exports rose 11 percent (though the latter had dipped from a
17 percent increase over 1964–74). The Irish Republic was cited by
the US Department of Commerce as a most profitable location for
American industry with a 25 percent rate of return (versus a 14.3
percent average in the EEC). The book value of American investment soared 186 percent between 1973 and 1977 while world-wide
book value rose 47.7 percent. About three-quarters of US profits
were reinvested in Ireland although not necessarily in productive
facilities.[4] Both UK and US capital were dissuaded by their
domestic tax laws from *immediate* repatriation of profits.

"Grant-aided industries" generated virtually all growth in industrial output and employment over 1973–76 when the cost of living

---

[3] Interview with Dr. Noel Browne.   [4] *Irish Times*, 12 October 1978, p. 6.

was doubling and the unemployment rate – averaging 6.5 percent over 1960–72 – followed suit. By then Ireland had industrialized significantly through an influx of more than 600 foreign firms over 1960–75 and even approached the 50 percent mark in service employment, which is sometimes cited as a threshold figure for a society entering the "post-industrial" phase.

Farm income increased 20 percent in 1978 although one-third of farmers accrue 70 percent of agricultural profits. That year the IDA announced further fruits of the nation's pragmatic path in the form of 27,000 jobs "projected" in grant-aided industries – which was in line with the job creation deemed necessary by the National Economic and Social Council for attaining full employment.[5] (Ireland possessed the fastest growing population in the EEC together with the youngest age structure and highest dependency ratio.)[6] Even tourism receipts jumped 20 percent in real terms in 1978.[7] Inflation and unemployment both dipped under double figures in a polity consenting to a "jobs at any cost" imperative. Possibilities for a shift in the "paradigm of public choice" were minimal, if not entirely nil. Measuring "overall Life Satisfaction" and "Happiness," a European Community survey in the midst of the recession (May 1975) testified to the durability of this "marvellously complacent society." The Irish Republic ranked second in "Life Satisfaction" (defined as "a rational evaluation of one's situation, weighed against reasonable expectations") while limping in at eighth place in "Happiness" (implying "an absolute state of being, something more emotional and less cognitive").[8] (Northern Ireland ranked *second* in "Life Satisfaction" and *sixth* in "Happiness" – which perhaps reflected its link to the more generous British welfare system.) Nonetheless by 1979 the investment paradise so painstakingly fashioned by government policy was teetering.

In the largest demonstrations in the history of the Republic, on 20 March 1979, 150,000 citizens marched through the streets of Dublin (and 40,000 more marched in Cork) to demand that the government

[5] NESC Report *Population and Employment Projections 1986: A Reassessment*, no. 35 (Dublin: CSO, 1977), p. 11.
[6] The IDA in the 1980s made the youthful profile a selling point in advertisements in business periodicals.
[7] The Irish too were traveling abroad and spending more in some years than they received in tourism.
[8] Ronald Inglehart, *The Silent Revolution* (Princeton: Princeton University Press, 1977), p. 165.

reform the tax structure to "ease the intolerable burden on the working class" so that "all would pay their fair share."[9] On May Day 50,000 Irish workers subject to the PAYE system – income tax "checked off" from pay packets – again demonstrated in Dublin. Three weeks later the Irish Congress of Trade Unions rejected – temporarily – the National Wage Agreement proposed by the government, by 318 votes to 119. Under severe rank-and-file pressure the ICTU withdrew from negotiations until tax reform was assigned to a bargaining agenda which had never before ranged outside the provinces of wages.[10]

The PAYE contribution to total income tax had risen from 61.8 percent in 1969–70 to nearly 90 percent. The street protest was ignited by capitulation by the government to the refusal by the rancher-dominated farmers' organizations to pay a 2 percent levy. The Fianna Fail administration had displayed scant regard for urban working-class interests after replacing a Fine Gael–Labour coalition in 1977. The government and mass media framed the tax dispute exclusively in the urban–rural terms, though the issue potentially was a more incendiary and class-oriented one. In the EEC Ireland sported the lowest income, lowest level of social services, highest debt, lowest wages, longest working-hours, and – though one would never guess from government and business admonishments – the lowest rise in unit wage costs. The Irish cost of living in 1978 was 12 percent higher than Britain and 5 percent higher than Northern Ireland, though wages were 12 percent *lower* than the UK (and 139 percent below the EEC leader, Netherlands). Given governments bent solely upon wage restraint to augment "competitiveness," the stage was set for new outbreaks of industrial conflict.[11]

Appalled at a 65 percent unofficial strike rate Prime Minister Jack Lynch in June 1978 scolded the work force for their wicked, wicked ways: "It is particularly unacceptable if those with secure jobs use their position in such a way as to destroy the job prospects of others worse off than they are," he said. "An accentuation of this trend

[9] *Hibernia*, 23 March 1979, p. 7.
[10] Interview with Manus O'Riordan, ICTU research officer.
[11] The ICTU in 1975 "affirmed its support for a co-ordinated policy for planned economic expansion and social development including a policy for the planned development of incomes. Such a policy would exclude any arbitrary controls or limitations on wages and salaries ..." *ICTU Annual Report 1975*, p. 181.

would call for the most fundamental reappraisal."[12] Indeed strikes hit the water supply, building materials, bus transport, electricity, air travel, garbage collection, and most spectacularly in 1979 the postal services, which rendered the Republic incommunicado for four months. The motivation, however, was far less a matter of greed than sheer neediness. "How could any family man, be he postman, busman, binman, or whatever," an Irish editor rhetorically asked, "exist with dignity on £60 per week at today's prices?"[13] As in Britain public workers grew militant because their wages were more easily "contained" than those in private industry. To compound the government's difficulties, the electorate indulged in environmental issues – pollution control, a nuclear power debate, preservation of historic landmarks – with an energy unbecoming for a developing nation.[14]

THE NATIONAL COALITION, 1973–1977

In 1969 the Irish Labour Party proclaimed with rare confidence and the widest inaccuracy that "the Seventies Will be Socialist." Infused in the mid-1960s with fractious luminaries like Justin Keating, Noel Browne, David Thornley, and Conor Cruise O'Brien, the party ventured into the political landscape wielding for the first time in thirty years an explicitly socialist program.[15] But new-found enthusiasm fizzled in a disappointing 1969 electoral performance – picking up votes but losing four seats – and after the anti-EEC campaign fiasco in 1972. As giddy visions for a solely Labour government receded party leaders shed their "no coalition" pledge in 1973 to aid Fine Gael (which harbored a social democratic wing) in displacing Fianna Fail after sixteen consecutive years in office. Just in time for the recession.

The coalition government was forced to jettison its policy designs – and good intentions – which included an embryonic fourth economic program. In the 1975 Budget speech Minister of Finance Richie Ryan would deride economic planning: "Of all the tasks

---

[12] *Irish Times*, 29 June 1978, p. 11.   [13] *Hibernia*, 9 March 1979, p. 3.
[14] See chapter 7.
[15] In 1936 the Labour Party fleetingly featured a program calling for public ownership of basic industries, state control of banking, the five year plans. Giving in to clerical outrage, the party dropped its slogan in favor of a "workers' republic." See Maurice Manning, *Irish Political Parties: An Introduction* (Dublin: Gill and Macmillan, 1972), p. 73.

which could engage my attention, the least realistic would be the
publication of a medium or long-term economic plan based on
irrelevancies of the past, hunches as to the present and clairvoyance
as to the future."[16]

To maintain social services and stimulate the sagging economy
the coalition increased borrowing from £134 million in 1972/73 to
£500 million by 1976 (23.2 percent from foreign sources). The
Coalition intrepidly introduced a very modest wealth tax and a
capital gains tax with the consequence that a £141 million capital
inflow in 1974 swiftly shifted to a £68 million outflow in 1976.[17]

The mining tax holiday was repealed. Farmers were snared in the
tax net for the first time. Pension age was lowered and social welfare
expenditures increased. Value added tax was removed from food
and medicine and well-heeled tax evaders were sometimes hunted.
But Labour's idea for a national development corporation to coordinate the private and public sectors and expand state-owned
commercial operations was shelved along with all other potentially
radical policy proposals. Prime Minister Liam Cosgrave insisted
that although he had "no ideological prejudice one way or the
other" as to deployment of state bodies:

it is a different thing to use these bodies as a precedent for something
completely different. It is essential that any new agency should not actively
discourage or displace private initiative. *We cannot risk alienating the investment on which our future depends.*[18] (Emphasis mine)

In the coalition's 1976 Green Paper the Labour Party advocacy of a
national development corporation was impaled on the proviso that
it "not compete unfairly with the private sector." Rather "income
restraint ... must be a first priority."[19] The Labour Party's trade
union link was useful to achieving that delicate end. As a chronicler
observed of Fine Gael:

It is interesting to note that the main reason for the taxation advanced by
Richie Ryan was that it would encourage the more productive use of
wealth – people would invest money rather than let it accumulate and be
taxed. Rarely was the argument of the more equal distribution of wealth
put forward, which tended to confirm an Irish Times opinion that the
whole exercise was "headline socialism and small print capitalism."

---

[16] Quoted in *Economic and Social Planning* (ICTU Summer Course, Wexford, 18–22 July 1976),
    p. 53.
[17] *Irish Times*, 16 June 1978, p. 7.   [18] *Irish Times*, 2 May 1978, p. 15.
[19] *Economic and Social Development 1976–1980* (Dublin: CSO, 1976), p. 36.

However, two reasons for persisting with the proposals were at work behind the scenes: first Liam Cosgrave's commitment to honouring the deal with Labour to the letter. Second, wage-restraint could never be sold to the unions unless capital too was taxed.[20]

Labour's *quid pro quo* for minor reforms was Fine Gael's zealous security policy which alienated many citizens. The "Blueshirt" heritage was evoked at the 1977 Party Convention where Cosgrave thundered out threats against unspecified "blow-ins." The supreme testament to the fatally arrogant style of the coalition was the insouciant lack of preparation with which it approached the 1977 election. Inflation and unemployment still were paramount issues and the electorate would "not accept arguments about the overriding importance of the international economic situation."[21]

Armed with a forty-seven-page manifesto, Fianna Fail swept into office with an unprecedented 84 of the 148 parliamentary seats. Bearing the scars of the recession and bereft of a counter-manifesto the coalition collapsed as Fianna Fail reaped support across the occupational and class spectrum by making a host of offers the electorate couldn't refuse.

FIANNA FAIL RESURRECTED, 1977–1981

To "get the country moving again" Fianna Fail abolished property tax, road tax on small cars, the wealth tax, shifted capital gains to a sliding scale and sweetened their bid for the youth vote with £1,000 grants to first-time home purchasers. Fianna Fail also proposed to raise borrowing to 13 percent of GNP to trigger a Keynesian recovery. The manifesto centerpiece was a pledge to create 20,000 jobs in a year – and at least as many in each subsequent year. The party strategy was the soul of simplicity – forcefeed profits to private industries which in turn should gratefully create jobs through productive investment.

The spending spree accelerated.[22] Wages doubled the government guideline so that the purchasing power of the average married worker rose 7 percent in 1978. Consumer spending rose 9 percent

---

[20] Brian Harvey, *Cosgrave's Coalition: Irish Politics in The 1970s* (London: Selected Editions, 1980), p. 96.

[21] Richard Sinnott, "The Electorate," in Howard Penniman, ed., *Ireland at the Polls: The Dail Election of 1977* (Washington: American Enterprise Institute, 1978), p. 57.

[22] An interview in 1982 with Martin O'Donoghue yielded, of course, a very different opinion.

and the exposed economy was deluged by imports – a 30 percent hike in the trade deficit (August 1977 to August 1978).[23] By Autumn 1978 Fianna Fail began squeezing credit and resuming the campaign for wage restraint. Fianna Fail now intended to reduce borrowing (debt service absorbed 30 percent of tax receipts) and social spending. Except for trade union resistance the £8 million formerly gained in wealth tax would have been offset by a tax on Children's Allowances – a critical sum in a country where 14 percent of married women worked (versus 60 percent in France and 67 percent in Britain).[24] Property revenue would have been offset by removing the food subsidies originally introduced by the coalition in 1975 to induce wage agreements and to protect urban workers from price rises after EEC entry. Union leaders retorted to wage restraint pleas that if low wages mattered so much India would be a full employment paradise.[25]

A "work-sharing" scheme really amounted to a proposal for sharing among a work force living on overtime and debt. Minister for Finance George Colley wanted to create a new agency which would cast off the dole anyone who refused the first available form of employment. But this measure would have harmed marginal Irish employers who, in Speenhamland fashion, paid "supplemental" wages to temporary labor from the dole queues.[26] Fianna Fail trumped up a welfare fraud hysteria to pare dole payments even as a survey (April 1971 to December 1973) disclosed 332 instances of individual fraud versus 1,222 cases of employers who, failing to register employees, evaded social welfare contributions.[27] Children's Allowances were frozen despite an 80 percent rise in the cost of living since 1974. However, Minister for Health Charles Haughey – waging a battle to succeed Prime Minister Lynch – deviated from this Dickensian style by introducing a progressive hospitalization scheme in 1978. But ministers incessantly admonished unions to moderate demands since their wages – and their wages alone – squeezed the profit margins of Irish firms and motivated substitution of machinery for manpower.[28] The Minister for Finance derided the

---

[23] *Irish Times*, 19 December 1978, p. 11.   [24] *Irish Times*, 22 November 1978, p. 9.

[25] Interview with Matt Merrigan, General Secretary of the Amalgamated Transport and General Workers Union.

[26] Mairan De Burca, "Clamping Down on The Dole," *Hibernia*, 16 November 1978, p. 6.

[27] Rosheen Callender, "The Green Paper: No Women Need Apply," *Irish Times*, 21 July 1978, p. 10.

[28] For a rebuttal, see *Jobs and Wages: The True Story of Competitiveness* (Dublin: Socialist Economists, 1983).

idea of a National Development Corporation and any prospect of extending the commercial activities of state bodies.

An independent Department of Economic Planning and Development was set up under Martin O'Donoghue, composer of the manifesto. The Department was empowered to devise and appraise economic and social plans but – like the defunct British Department of Economic Affairs – lacked the "purse string" power to enforce implementation.[29]

At the end of 1978 Fianna Fail plaintively announced that while it supervised the creation of 30,000 jobs, redundancies sadly had nibbled the net total to 17,000 – a 3,000 job shortfall. Unemployment declined by 11,000 but emigration alone accounts for the difference. Emigration was 13,800 in 1977 after net inflows in the early seventies. The tally is an especially anemic one considering that the state created 10,000 jobs directly in the public sector. So despite the engineering of a consumer spending spree, private enterprise contributed only 7,000 jobs to the net total. Blaming wage hikes and strikes for target shortfalls, the government managed to maintain very civil tongues with regard to the poor performance of private firms. Prime Minister Lynch resorted to gentle reasoning with reluctant investors:

While he commented that the substantial increases in the profitability in private companies had not been reflected in increased employment, Mr. Lynch said he felt sure that "industry will themselves appreciate that it is to their own long-term interest that further expansion is reflected in significant job creation."[30]

"The correct approach," declared the undaunted Minister for Economic Planning and Development, "is to intensify our efforts and to press ahead with an even faster rate of job creation in 1979."[31] Yet Irish workers hardly could be blamed for detecting a Swiftian modest proposal beneath sweet reasoning tones. The job creation strategy was unraveled by the opening of the Irish market to the EEC and by the world-wide trend toward capital-deepening which is an earmark of "the third technological revolution."[32] The Industrial Development Authority doubled expenditures from £63.2 million in 1976 to £121 million in 1977 but "projected jobs" increased one-third, from 17,893 to 24,028. Over 1973–77 the IDA

---

[29] Interview with Martin O'Donoghue.
[30] *Irish Times*, 18 November 1978, p. 11.
[31] *Irish Times*, 11 October 1978, p. 1.
[32] See Mandel, *Late Capitalism*.

claimed the creation of 57,500 jobs, but vanishing local industries neutralized the gain with 55,600 redundancies. This net rise of 1900 jobs was a rather sickly silhouette against the backdrop of the original IDA target of 38,000 jobs.[33]

The wage restraint regime demanded by government and business was likely to come about only if the 1972 ICTU motion on Democratic Economic Planning was met:

The ICTU conference resolves that ... a movement towards meaningful industrial democracy at both national and company level must be a prerequisite for any form of prices and incomes policy which could be regarded as being truly democratic and comprehensive, embracing all forms of income without exception. Conference holds that all workers must be guaranteed that their wage restraint will lead to productive and beneficial investment and not toward even further increases in the personal incomes of the privileged sections of society, and that the only effective guarantee of this would be democratic control by workers over the utilization and allocation of such investment funds.[34]

Fianna Fail resolutely fended off schemes for industrial democracy. However, a distinctly "invest or else" tone insinuated into government comments about private enterprises. In 1978 the Minister for Finance implored

Our producers must grasp the opportunities which the government's strategy is throwing open to them. They must exploit the advantages flowing from the enhanced competitiveness which moderate income increases will yield.

They must plough rising profits back into their businesses and raise investment and output. And it is imperative that they develop also a keen sense of responsibility in relation to the overriding need to create more jobs and reduce unemployment ...

We have a mixed economy, and both the public and the private sectors have contributions to make to its development. We expect that the initiatives in the budget will receive a positive and energetic response from the private sector ... Our approach is a pragmatic one. It is not dictated by ideological dogma. *If there is an inadequate response from either sector, we shall take appropriate action in the interest of the whole community.*[35] (Emphasis mine)

33 *Irish Times*, 1 August 1978, p. 1.
34 Cited in Manus O'Riordan, *Economic and Social Planning* (Dublin: Irish Congress of Trade Unions 1976).
35 *Irish Times*, 2 February 1978, p. 7.

In turn business spokesmen complained "the private sector is very gradually being nudged into the dock" and said that it was unfairly "portrayed as a whipping boy, a position which is inappropriate to it."[36] The Fianna Fail "pump-priming" strategy had flopped resoundingly and expensively.

A European Monetary System was mooted whose most appealing feature was the rigid discipline Fianna Fail imagined it would instill on prodigal wage earnings. Scarcely a cross word was uttered in the media about the lamentable job performance of "state stimulated" private enterprise. The tempting option for a government burdened by precise election promises to keep was an EMS scheme which might enable it to elude confrontation – by diverting blame for austerity elsewhere – with trade unions. Even if adding to foreign debt by the inducement of "soft" loans – instead of a real transfer of resources – seemed a curious way of going about curbing inflation, the government was determined to join. Certainly, the wisdom of a link-up with currencies which historically have appreciated against sterling was not altogether compelling. Small Irish firms relying on the British market stood to suffer most if the punt rose against sterling, or from any deflationary measures to maintain the punt in the band of EMS currencies. But the Irish government went ahead.

The PAYE demonstrations in March 1979 and in February 1980 were a consequence of industrialization policies consensually pursued by parties in charge of the Irish state. The Minister for Finance indignantly stated that "no one is going to push the government around by threatening strikes," but the state acknowledged the need to appease what was after all the bulk of the electorate through some symbolic tinkering with tax reform. (PAYE contributions to total tax moved even upward anyway.)

In 1979 a National Understanding agreement swapped wage restraint for tax concessions, social welfare increases, new farm taxes and a state pledge to increase job creation – including an Employment Guarantee Fund partly financed by insurance surcharges on employers. But unemployment rose from 82,000 in October 1979 to 101,000 in July 1980. Premier Jack Lynch, the

---

[36] Eugene McCarthy of the Federated Union of Employers, quoted in *Irish Times*, 14 April 1978, p. 12.

opposition rejoiced in reminding, had declared during the 1977 electoral landslide that if unemployment surpassed 100,000 at the next election the government did not deserve to survive.[37]

In December 1979 Charles Haughey succeeded Lynch and commenced his administration by propagating the theme of fiscal rectitude because borrowing exceeded 13 percent of GNP and debt servicing absorbed 27 percent of all revenue. In July 1980 Haughey argued "we cannot any more provide employment just for the sake of providing employment, by government expenditure."[38] Nonetheless, industrial and internal party conflicts forced a "pragmatic" U-turn in government plans.

Approaching the 1981 elections Haughey doubled IDA funding, instituted employment subsidies for labor-intensive industries, subsidized farm income (which fell 40 percent over 1978–80), restored some food subsidies, imposed import curbs, and tried to invigorate an ineffectual "buy Irish" campaign. Haughey directed the chairmen of the semi-state bodies to provide blueprints for creating work and wealth in exchange for which he vowed to "free the commercial state bodies from the centralized control which has stifled initiative and prevented risk-taking in recent years."[39] The IDA was supposed to work with semi-state bodies to coordinate policies across the private–public divide.

These abortive escapades into "*ad hoc* radicalism" and "debt-driven" industrialization were responses to the cumulative adversities of industrialization. A 10 percent manufacturing tax in January 1981 ruled out that source of potential revenue. Farming incomes were in steep decline and so were untappable.[40] PAYE demonstrations deterred income tax increases. So the path of least resistance was borrowing – which by 1980 increased to 18 percent of GNP. Debt expansion and new industrial policy measures were a "pragmatic" response to short-term, and intensifying, problems deriving from the pattern of industrialization. Unemployment hit 12 percent in June 1981 when Fianna Fail was nudged out of office

---

[37] The misfired pledge hardly was the whole reason for stepping down. See, for example, the account in Bruce Arnold, *What Kind of Country? Modern Irish Politics 1968–1983* (London: Jonathan Cape, 1984).

[38] *Hibernia*, 24 July 1980, p. 3.   [39] *Irish Times*, 16 July 1980, p. 1.

[40] Robert O'Connor, "Agriculture and Other Natural Resources", in Kieran A. Kennedy, ed., *Ireland in Transition: Economic and Social Change Since 1960* (Cork and Dublin: Mercier Press, 1986).

by a Fine Gael–Labour coalition prepared to take the "rough, stony path" toward a balanced budget.[41]

PLANNING AND MANIFESTOES

Whether voters in 1977 displayed an admirable "issue orientation" or else merely "descended into the marketplace" as coalition members complained, a political party willing to risk crucifixion on a quantified plan – the 1977 manifesto was the strongest such excursion – obviously also might leap into power by that device. The lesson was clear. Garret Fitzgerald contended years before that the impact of planning exercises on policy-making could be more profound than was yet appreciated. As extant policies sputtered, alternatives were likely to be cast into sharper relief. Bell forecasts "post-industrial society will involve *more* politics than ever before, for the very reason that choice becomes conscious and the decision-making centers more visible."[42] That is, value commitments and interests formerly "hidden" within the market and embedded in institutional arrangements are flushed out onto the political stage by an attentive electorate demanding more responsive government. But this only comes to pass if parties with persuasive policies have the wits and the resources to overcome the dominant political coalition.

The plight of the Irish state is aptly captured in Lindberg's prediction about Western democracies that "policy makers will be caught between the need for international cooperation and coordination in more and more policy areas, and the mounting domestic demands for more centralized national planning and control, and for action to deal with resource scarcities and internal distributional issues."[43] If governments undergo increasing fragmentation of policy-making due to the specialization of roles and functions required by expanding intervention (which tends to insulate elites), demands for a "higher-order integration" of policy instruments and for a more participative process should increase.[44] But of course groups can also intensify their invocations of the "magic of the

---

[41] A Fine Gael deputy supplied the penitential image.
[42] Bell, *The Coming of Post-Industrial Society*, p. 286.
[43] Leon Lindberg, "Introduction," in *Politics and The Future of Industrial Society*, p. 272.
[44] Lindberg, "Energy Policy and The Politics of Economic Development," *Comparative Political Studies* 10, 3 (October 1977), p. 357.

market" as the ideal remedy. Diverting responsibility for local woes to external agents like Brussels, the UK, and international financial forces cannot be persuasive forever as the dole queues lengthen. One outcome of the foregoing factors would be a widening of the margins of what a government deems "permissible" in coping with severe economic squeeze, thereby reducing barriers to alternative designs for capital formation. Another likely outcome is ideological and fiscal retrenchment.

EEC membership undeniably exerts a progressive influence on Irish attitudes and values. (A partly frivolous argument can be made that BBC television reception accounts for attitude change more so than all EEC programs combined.) The secular power of the formidably conservative Catholic Church has waned, despite occasional waxings in the 1980s.[45] Socialism is not a dirty word when social democratic practices are deemed the norm. Still, a "dramatic and forceful" corporatist outcome should not be ruled out. As Schmitter writes:

> the decay of pluralism and its gradual replacement by societal corporatism can be treated primarily to the imperative necessity for a stable bourgeois dominant regime, due to processes of concentration of ownership, competition between national economies, expansion of the roles of public policy and rationalization of decision-making within the state to associate or incorporate subordinate classes and status groups more closely within the political process.[46]

The foreign industrial presence aggravates this tendency. Any "interference" with development draws heavy official fire. In 1978 a multinational chemicals firm took its business elsewhere when planning permission was delayed because residents sought pollution control assurances. "These people have a right under the law as it stands apparently to object," the Minister for Industry, Commerce and Energy grumbled, "but I feel their democratic right should not extend beyond a democratic right to object."[47] Dismissing the barbaric local dissenters as "unrepresentative," the IDA anyway threatened to drop the Co. Clare district as an industrial zone. Deference was declining.

[45] In the mid-1980s the Church lost a contraception vote but triumphantly opposed abortion and divorce.
[46] Philippe C. Schmitter, "Still The Century of Corporatism?" in Schmitter and Gerhard Lehmbruch, eds., *Trends Toward Corporatist Intermediation* (Beverly Hills: Sage Publications, 1979).
[47] *Irish Times*, 14 October 1978, p. 16 (Desmond O'Malley).

Societal corporatism was a fragile and intermittent trend trade unions tried to nurture. The "National Understanding" in 1979 held out promise that agreements might one day encompass investment policy. An ITGWU research officer anticipated:

If, of course, the trade union movement is to demand a decisive say in economic planning it will be faced with the challenge of specifying its priorities in far greater detail in the decade ahead with regard to the appropriate balance to be struck between increasing employment and improving living standards and the proper proportions of national output which must be allocated between consumption, investment, and public expenditure.[48]

The formulation and promotion of counter-plans – not "counter-manifestoes" – is an ideal way for a peak organization or political party to clarify, specify, and assess the support for its objectives. But organizations that are not as rich as Croesus can't afford to be as wise as Solomon – as informed and effective as would be desirable. Resource and organizational deficiencies hamper construction of a corporatist structure and impede any movement in an industrial democratic direction.

PAYE-ING THE PIPER?

The first PAYE demonstrations in March 1979 hardly were the equivalent of the "moment of madness" in France in May 1968.[49] No one – least of all trade union leaders – wanted a showdown, although the potential was apparant. A government impelled to expand interventionist activity to cope with rising unemployment and inflation would try to reach accommodation with unions because the wage bargaining process "cannot proceed on an autonomous basis without conflicting with the aims of the particular plan," or at least not very smoothly.[50]

However tempting a more "dramatic and forceful version" of corporatism may be, the uncertain capacity of the state to enforce such arrangements against the urban work force counsels a more moderate course to muster support not only in "getting the country

---

[48] Interview with Manus O'Riordan of the ICTU.
[49] Aristide Zolberg, "Moments of Madness," in Ira Zatznelson, David Gordon, Philip Brenner, eds., *The Politics and Society Reader* (New York: David McKay, 1976).
[50] Olympios Katsiaouni, "Administrative Arrangements For Planning: Some Aspects of The Irish Experience," *Administration* 26, 1 (Spring 1978), p. 64.

moving" again, but in getting the incumbents re-elected. For their part trade unions seek participation in formulating policies for which their members are asked to sacrifice living standards, in effect investing these foregone benefits in new development.[51] A struggle conducted exclusively on the wages front is patently counter-productive.

Can an open economy, which is, moreover, a member of a free trade area, be planned? There is latitude which the Irish have not tested regarding the balance-of-payments. Lively debates over the terms of EEC membership will recur as "community needs" are perceived to clash with national needs regarding financial controls, energy policy, fisheries, regional development, and a Common Agricultural Program that cannot prop up prices or store a massive amount of surplus produce forever.

"Rolling plans" often are advocated as supple devices suited to adjusting national goals to balance of payments constraints. More directive forms of planning which apply controls on capital flows, investment locations, and forge "planning agreements" between state and private industry must reckon not only with internal class opponents but with a European Community whose structure is inscribed with the "ideology of liberal capitalism, or the assumption that the self-interest of enterprise could be harnessed in the public interest through a liberalization of trade, capital, and labour movements."[52]

No Irish government can defy the EEC. Rather, a small nation might exploit scavenging advantages available in the interstices of the international economic order. A sudden *volte face* toward national capitalism simply isn't in the cards. Put another way, a socialist Irish Republic is unimaginable without the prerequisite of a socialist Britain or a European Community with "a socialised rather than a privatised market in which common objectives and the public welfare predominated over uncommon divisions and private interests."[53]

In the view of some analysts, progress toward democratic planning presupposes the centralization of trade unions to enhance their

---

[51] Peter Lange, "Unions, Workers, and Wage Regulation," in John Goldthorpe, ed., *Order and Conflict*, pp. 98–123. Also David R. Cameron, "Does Government Cause Inflation? Taxes, Spending and Deficits," in Leon Lindberg and Charles Maier, eds., *The Politics of Inflation and Economic Stagnation* (Washington: Brookings Institution, 1985), pp. 224–79.

[52] Holland, *Uncommon Market*, p. 4.   [53] *Ibid.*, p. 17.

power within corporatist arrangements so that pay restraint can be translated credibly into investment controls and policy influence.[54] But "just why the ruling class would concede to demands for the social control of investment when they won't allow wages and social services to rise," a shop steward pertinently objects, "is not explained." Still another analyst counters:

the workers' concept of relativities is too narrow. Their comparative criteria are not ambitious enough. Only when Irish workers lift their eyes from parochial preoccupation of petty relativities at home and in Britain and ask about wider relativities between Irish society as a whole and the other Western European societies, and of the role of the worker in them, will they finally wrench off the mental chains riveted on them by the dead hand of the stagnant generations.[55]

Relativities did not narrow over the two decades but an investigator finds that over 1971–77 the "real pre-tax earnings of the average male industrial worker would have remained stagnant unless special increases were secured" even as unemployment rose nearly 2 percent each year.[56] Invocations by employers of "inability to pay" clauses in pay agreements were much more frequent than publicized and pilloried unofficial strikes. In the absence of a link to a vibrant social democratic party unions will resort to the small but not insignificant advantages of "free-for-alls." Jessop observes:

Where unions are decentralized and shopfloor bargaining is widespread, it is hard to sustain a corporatist system without substantial material concession to organized labour to induce voluntary compliance or to compensate for statutory restraint. Alternatively, where no strong social democratic party exists, a dominant bourgeois party may prefer to ignore unions and consult only with business interests, continuing to pursue a welfare state programme and employing a mixture of *dirigiste* and *sozialmarktwirtschaftlich* policies in maintaining economic stability and securing industrial reorganization.[57]

The likeliest scenario was not one festooned with gaudy departures into economic planning but, in incremental fashion, one in which variations of retrenchment are practiced. Hence, native employers

---

[54] See fns. 46 and 51.   [55] Derwin, "Talk Bread and The Bakery," p. 24.

[56] Peter J. Mooney, "Incomes Policy," in Joe Dowling and John Durkan, *Irish Economic Policy* (Dublin: Economic and Social Research Institute, 1978), pp. 239, 243.

[57] Bob Jessop, "Corporatism, Parliamentarianism and Social Democracy," in Philippe Schmitter and Lehmbruch, eds., *Trends Toward Corporatist Intermediation* (New York: Sage, 1984), p. 208.

continued a publicity campaign attributing all industrial faults to wage-earner greed. Corporatist bargaining goes off the agenda entirely.[58] The foreign sector – which can afford a free-for-all – goes along. As IDA literature noted: "Irish wage costs remain significantly below those of virtually all other industrialised countries. Because of the lower base in Ireland, higher percentage increases do not necessarily yield higher absolute increases in pay in Ireland over other countries."[59]

The claim that foreign investment and economic planning in a dependent economy are conflicting and *politically* contradictory processes proved true in Ireland by the late 1970s. Foreign investment *coupled with adverse shifts in the international economy* rendered Irish "programming" superfluous and ruled out strong planning exercises for fear that they might ruin the ideal investment climate. The key determinants are political and so one cannot claim this proposition is proven *in principle*. Outward-oriented growth was generating unheeded popular pressures for more directive planning to meet productive and welfare needs. Thus, if the autonomy of the state is constricted by reliance on foreign investment, so too in a fragile industrializing economy is the power of the state (and the "pact of domination" comprising it) eroded by non-elite pressures upon the policy process. But these effects can be quashed by elites if adverse economic events are construed according to orthodox wisdoms. Struggles over adjustment policies are intrinsically and sometimes decisively *ideological* struggles over diagnosis and prescriptions. In the early 1980s the orthodox ideology of economic liberalism held up very well.

EXTERNAL DEPENDENCE, FISCAL CRISIS, AND CORPORATIST COMPROMISE

From June 1981 to November 1982 the Irish Republic underwent three elections – an overdose of electoral entertainment in which the major parties played on the theme of "stability" to shed the indepen-

---

[58] In the early 1980s Peter Murray and James Wickham noted that recently arrived foreign firms tended to oppose trade unionization, and especially so in the electronics sector on which the second stage of the development strategy was reliant. See their "Technocratic Ideology and The Reproduction of Inequality: The Case of the Electronics Industry in The Republic of Ireland," in G. Day et al., eds., *Diversity and Decomposition in The Labour Market* (Aldershot: Gower Press, 1982).

[59] *General Information IDA–Ireland* (Dublin: IDA, 1975), p. 8.

dent Deputies and fringe parties with which they allied after the June 1981 and February 1982 contests. Fine Gael and Fianna Fail competed for the right to impose the least agonizing cuts necessary to stave off the specter of IMF domination. The Labour Party, Sinn Fein – The Workers Party (later the Workers Party and independents were unable to slow down the momentum toward burdening the working class with the heaviest cost of adjustment. The niggardly terms in which the debate was set were illustrated by a blunt prophecy by the IDA chairman: "The standard of living will fall further, unemployment will rise, the tax burden will be increased. In short, things will be worse before they get better."[60] Yet, if economic progress is the "sole justification of profit, and the credibility of the Irish bourgeoisie as leader of the economy and promoter of progress resides entirely in its ability to develop the economy," as Peillon writes, then Marxists, in mechanistic glee, can expect a "legitimation crisis."[61]

Investment expenditure in 1981 was a robust 30 percent of GNP, and exceeded in democratic states only by Japan's 31 percent (compared to 14 percent in the USA and 17 percent in Britain) while manufacturing productivity rose 6.5 percent in contrast with 0.5 percent in the USA, 3.4 percent in Britain, and 1.0 percent in Western Europe as a whole.[62] Irish unemployment increased to 13 percent by 1982 with no sign of halt in a country with the lowest wages and highest percentage of households beneath the poverty line in the Common Market (excluding Greece). The PAYE protests produced no substantial change in the tax structure; a Fine Gael Minister ruled out redistributive reform because the Republic could not afford to frighten capital by "the kind of wealth tax we had before" – which was effective at a derisory 1.0 percent rate.[63] Capital taxes accounted for a grand total of 0.7 percent of total tax revenue as the PAYE share rose, indirect taxes increased, and cries for "belt-tightening" bombarded the union halls and dole queues.

The 1981–82 Fine Gael–Labour coalition introduced an upwardly redistributive budget and instigated its own electoral downfall when independent Deputies – appalled by a measure taxing childrens' apparel – withdrew support. "The whole thrust of the budget was to

---

[60] (Michael Killeen) *Irish Times*, 18 October 1982, p. 10.
[61] Peillon, *Contemporary Irish Society*, p. 53.
[62] *Irish Times*, 18 October 1982, p. 10.   [63] *Investors Chronicle*, 11 July 1981.

get the money needed from the workers," a Workers Party Deputy fumed, "through increased social welfare contributions, income taxes which automatically increase with inflation ... and indirect taxes."[64] The Economic and Social Research Institute estimated that the budget would add 6 percent to inflation because of the indirect taxes and the subsidy cuts which the ESRI predicted would provoke wage demands from trade unions. The General Secretary of the ITGWU angrily observed that "over the last 15 months ... the consumer price index went up 26% while wages and salaries went up only 13% to 14%."[65] The budget was an awesomely frank device for picking the pockets of the less nattily attired population. It included severe spending cuts, higher and more indirect taxes, increased VAT, abolition of food subsidies, curbs on public sector pay, taxing shorter-term social welfare benefits, and only a hint that the government would try to relieve the burdens described below by ESRI:

The net direct tax burden (income tax and PSRI contributions, less children's allowance) on the average industrial worker have increased 2.5% since June 1979. On the other hand, the net direct tax burden on the well-off taxpayer, earning four times industrial earnings (27,000 pounds per annum) has fallen by 4.6%.[66]

A youth employment program added a percentage point to tax. IDA funding increased 7 percent despite 23 percent inflation. As for corporatist dalliances the Fine Gael wing of the coalition had decided that "social partners have no right to decide economic and social policy."[67] The coalition lost the February 1982 election by a hair to Fianna Fail, which had attracted crucial support from an Independent and three Workers Party Deputies by promising a "more humane way" toward balancing the books.[68]

Haughey's government accepted the bottom line that the budget deficit be slashed to £715 million (half that of the previous year) but kept food subsidies and promised not to impose VAT on food and clothing or to tax welfare benefits. Fianna Fail imposed once-off taxes on banks and insurance companies, advanced the date of corporate tax payments, and devised an important deposit scheme

---

[64] (Paddy Gallagher) *Sunday Tribune,* 7 March 1982, p. 3.
[65] Interview with John Carroll. This quote cited in J. K. Jacobsen, "Chasing Progress: The Politics of Industrial Development in Ireland" (Ph.D. dissertation, University of Chicago 1982), p. 297.
[66] *Irish Times,* 9 June 1981.   [67] *Irish Times,* 3 February 1982, p. 1.   [68] *Ibid.*

to quicken collection of VAT. But Haughey reversed course and soon was imposing cuts in Health and Education as well as courting a civil service strike by imposing pay limits. A final straw for fringe party supporters was publication in the autumn of Fianna Fail's economic plan, "The Way Forward." Like the Fine Gael coalition budget it was based on the premise of the imperative of redirecting wealth upward. ESRI economists noted that, if successful, the Fianna Fail plan intended that by 1987 "the share of profits (and self-employed income) in Domestic Product will rise to 22% compared to 14% in 1982; over the same period the share of wages and salaries will fall from 75% to 68%."[69] The "key ingredient" of the plan was the ancient refrain – wage restraint. But the economists questioned:

the assumption (or vision) that increased competitiveness will lead to a higher output volume. On the basis of the plan's figures, wage rates would rise by 9% per annum in manufacturing industry while output prices would rise only 7½%. Thus employers are faced with wages rising relative to output prices. The plan assumed that they respond by expanding output, so driving up productivity and reducing unit wage cost growth.

But in the absence of strong external demand stimulus and with domestic markets contracting is it not more likely that employers will do as they have done since 1980 and reduce labour input as a way of maintaining competitiveness?[70]

The Workers Party published a counter-plan, bolted and brought down the government on 4 November 1982. Riven with internal struggles and by a spate of scandals the Haughey government registered an all-time high level of public dissatisfaction (67 percent) two months before the decisive no confidence motion. The fact that Fine Gael profited from the 24 November election – forming a government with Labour – might well be a tribute to the potency of free market ideology (not to mention Garret Fitzgerald's *personal* popularity). Alternatively, it was testimony to the Labour Party's lack of a distinctive and persuasive "project" of socio-economic development. "They are offering the same hair shirt," cried a Workers Party member with regard to the choice, "the only difference is the buttons."[71]

---

[69] Brendan Dowling and Brendan Walsh, "The Way Sideways," *Irish Times*, 10 November 1982, p. 2.
[70] *Ibid.* The Haughey government recorded an all-time high level of public dissatisfaction (67 percent) that autumn.
[71] *Irish Times*, 5 November 1982, p. 6.

Fianna Fail and Fine Gael both portray deflation as the grim but necessary price which the working – and non-working – class must pay for the fruits reaped through the single development course possible in a small open economy, and as a penalty for the unbridled competition of interest groups for favors from an "overloaded" state that borrowed recklessly to sate their greedy appetites.[72] Fine Gael is particularly fond of dubious "crisis of democracy" jeremiads but with some justice can point a finger at Fianna Fail's spending sprees as an aggravating factor in the debt crisis.[73] Nonetheless, in the "governability" critique, the boundaries of state interventionism, dependent industrialization, and of the ideology of market capitalism are all held constant and conveniently unquestionable. Since the Irish display a higher degree of "political socialization" or deference than is imputed by analysts to more advanced nations, Irish policymakers confronted the fiscal crisis with a large "legitimation surplus" to draw upon while performing the unpleasant task of restoring conditions for accumulation. After all, haven't the benefits justified past sacrifices?

But the Telesis report on industrial policy indicates that the most reliable legitimating trade-off in the state repertoire – that of swapping better pay for more jobs – was invalid:

Irish industrial policy aims to create jobs. As it is now designed, it expends too much energy creating job approvals. The two are not synonymous. Only 30% of the jobs approved in foreign-owned firms between 1972 and 1978 were actually on the ground in 1981. The total payments of [IDA] funds in the period 1973–80 was equal to 30% of grants approved.[74]

The most damaging critique of Irish strategies was composed in 1982 by this independent consulting agency. Pertinent to the waning consensual nature of the industrialization project Telesis observed:

An even greater discrepancy exists for indigenous industry. Sustainable jobs as a percentage of job approvals is only 14% while grant payments as a percentage of grant approvals has been 40% [or less than half of the foreign

---

[72] On the "overload" thesis and the "democratic distemper," see Michel Crozier, et al., *The Crisis of Democracy* (New York: New York University Press, 1975) and Ralf Dahrendorf, ed., *Europe's Economies in Crisis* (London: Weidenfeld and Nicolson, 1982). Also Mancur Olson, *The Rise and Decline of Nations: Economic Growth, Stagflation and Social Rigidities* (New Haven: Yale University Press, 1982). Lee favours this interpretation in his *Ireland: Politics and Society*.

[73] Edward Tufte, *The Political Control of The Economy* (Princeton: Princeton University Press, 1978).

[74] Telesis Report, *NESC: A Review of Industrial Policy* (Dublin: CSO, February 1982), p. 33. Report no. 64.

sector's disappointing performance]. The discrepancies are due mainly to company failures and employment losses in surviving companies.[75]

The good news for indigenous firms is that the "shake out" attending EEC entry was nearly over; the bad news was that few firms had adjusted to competitive conditions. Telesis criticized the state for encouraging a "businessman's dole mentality" among small firms and noted "most of the largest and strongest Irish companies are investing abroad in businesses only minimally related to Irish employment and export."[76] As to ambitions to create an integrated electronics industry (60 percent of job "approvals" in 1978–80 were electrical and mechanical engineering firms), Telesis found "manufacturing satellites performing partial steps in the manufacturing process" whose skill demands and linkages were "limited," as in Scotland, Puerto Rico, Singapore, and other cases.[77] Telesis laid the blame upon "timid" government which failed to press vigorously for creation of a "corporate base with sufficient resources and time horizon to undertake removal of obstacles" to more indigenously based export growth.[78] The report said the "ultimate limiting factor" on Irish strategy was the rival strategies of parent multinationals. But another comment hits the mark of structural constraints. Telesis found "private capital, both Irish and foreign, would find better opportunities in other countries if market forces alone were dictating their choices".[79] This constraint presumes a high "propensity to defer" during turbulent adjustments when elites call upon subordinate strata for sacrifices. But this high propensity is agreement to an *interest-based depiction of economic exigencies* at a time when alternative schemes of allocating the burdens of adjustment become possible. The need to adjust is distinct from the struggle to formulate an acceptable allocation of "austerities" among the population. A class does not exhibit a high "propensity to defer" when accepting the least bad of all policy choices, but rather when it accepts a narrowly defined set of options that serve the interests of another class or bloc. In this case the subordinate population accedes to a "surplus" burden in the adjustment process.

While approving of early efforts to attract foreign firms, Telesis emphasized the point that:

[75] *Ibid.*, p. 33.   [76] *Ibid.*, p. 14.   [77] *Ibid.*, p. 29.   [78] *Ibid.*, p. 136.
[79] *Ibid.*, p. 185.

No country has succeeded in developing high levels of industrial income without developing a strong indigenous sector. This is particularly true for small countries: Sweden, Denmark, Holland, Austria, Switzerland, and Finland all have strong home-based exporting companies. Even Belgium, which has relied more heavily on foreign-owned companies than these others, still has a group of strong indigenous companies ...[80]

Stressing the need to cultivate native industries, Telesis cites a list of internal barriers to expansion:

As Ireland's share of its traditional market erodes due to EEC competition, the factors which have protected some of its exports to the UK can often be barriers ... These barriers may be in production (retooling for different measurement standards, set-up cost between runs), design (cost of initial advertising campaigns and sampling programs), or distribution (meeting different standards of different user requirements). Not many Irish companies have been willing or able to make the high-risk investments and accept the long payback horizons for new technologies or product redesigns.

... most of the largest and strongest Irish companies are investing abroad in businesses only minimally related to Irish employment and export, and in local businesses at home which distribute imports or supply non-traded goods. From the national point of view this cannot be the best use of the managerial, financial and organizational capabilities of these companies.[81]

Irish entrepreneurs were chided for failing to exploit sub-supply opportunities: "In Belgium, a small country with a similar proportion of foreign-owned firms, indigenous firms are 3 times as successful in supplying the requirements of foreign-owned companies."[82] As a Labour critic pointed out, nowhere in the Telesis report are high wages or labor strife cited as significant causes of company failures.[83] The relatively low wages of Irish workers indeed may have induced firms to delay modernizing investments and thus hampered modernization. As a remedy Telesis advocated an essentially "Swedish strategy" peppered with a few French aspects:

exploit opportunities where natural raw material endowments can provide competitive advantage; ...

continually restructure industry to phase out businesses which are becoming subject to competition from low wage countries; ...

---

[80] *Ibid.*, p. 231.   [81] *Ibid.*, pp. 14–15, 111.   [82] *Ibid.*, p. 16.

[83] See John Throne, *Socialism or Catastrophe: 1980s* (Dublin: Militant Perspectives Pamphlet, 1982).

gain competitive productivity advantage in selected manufacturing businesses. (Wage rates or investment and tax subsidies can be used to gain advantage initially but they must be replaced by productivity advantage if incomes are to rise.[84]

Telesis uged the "building of fewer but larger companies with strong internal capability" through a holding company along the lines of the National Development Corporation sought by the Labour Party – though it recommended private consortium. A selective grant system for foreign firms should be balanced by high but conditional grants (including cost penalties) to indigenous exporters. Carrots *and* sticks. "We are not suggesting that government dictate investment decisions in large Irish companies," the consultants hasten to add:

Markets must dictate investment decisions. We are suggesting a more active dialogue between government policymakers (not only the development agencies) and large companies about investment plans, and mechanisms for the government to fiscally favor certain types of investments over others.

The form that this dialogue should take, whether it is called "planning agreements" as in the UK's unsuccessful attempts or "growth conventions" as in the more successful French experience, or "administrative guidance" as in the highly successful Japanese efforts is not crucial. What is required, however, is a non-biased exchange of information, and intentions in an atmosphere of trust, a scrupulous loyalty to commitments and the setting of realistic goals.[85]

But the form of dialogue *is* crucial to obtain the results Telesis advocates – trust, information exchange, etc. The political implications of the economic strategy are side-stepped. Carrots and sticks would threaten the prerogatives of management in industry or would if they were applied in an unbiased fashion. On the other hand, the labor force can acknowledge the devastating critique Telesis directs at current wisdoms, and welcomes the changes prescribed. But obviously any new and unproven strategy will initially

---

[84] *A Review of Industrial Policy*, p. 5.
[85] *Ibid.*, p. 235. For reactions to Telesis, see Sean Nolan, "The Telesis Report – A Review Essay," *Economic and Social Research Review* 14, 4 (July 1983) and Liam Connellen (Director General of the Confederation of Irish Industry), "Industrial Policy," in *The Irish Banking Review* (March 1983), pp. 15–28. Connellen registers the customary plea for "relatively lower real wages in Ireland" to overcome industrial handicaps.

demand substantial wage restraint and even more public expenditure cuts in the short-run.

The ironies of chasing progress are painfully evident. Elites inform job holders that in order to catch up with EEC living standards they must lag behind the rates of wage (and, by extension, social wage) growth among trading partners. The living standard gap between Ireland and the EEC average increased and only the admission of Greece buoyed Irish living standards, wages, and social services from the bottom of Common Market charts: a further one-fourth to one-third of the citizenry subsists in poverty.[86] In the absence of proof of "wage-led" losses of jobs or competitiveness elites incessantly admonish workers to restrain wages even as productivity gains are robust. These admonishments testify to the *exculpatory* and *extenuating* functions of a hegemonic ideology that portrays international economic conditions as omnipotent forces requiring invariant reactions from a blameless private sector. If this characterization is deemed credible, no decline in "propensity to defer" occurs.

Workers are instructed to invest – via wages foregone and rising taxation – in job-eroding productivity measures. The bulk of Irish-owned firms, reliant on internal demand, suffer more from ebbing demand than they can gain from wage "relief." As Elsenhans illustrates in historical perspective, investment must decline because demand is more vital to capitalist calculations than wage scales *per se*.[87] Still the message is continuously driven home that Irish workers are implicitly competing with *Asian* wage levels when the IDA is luring high-tech affiliates. The Central Statistics Office revealed that the average wage for "high-tech" employees in Ireland is slightly *less* than the average manufacturing wage. The state responds by raising aid and incentive levels through revenue extraction from fewer wage earners – until fiscal crisis erupts. External "shocks" hasten but do not by themselves cause crisis.

Rising demand elsewhere should stimulate export-oriented investment; but, the material basis for support of the state strategy is restored only if sustained trade growth occurs, *and* if the local economy is equipped to take advantage – both dubious assumptions. Belgium recorded productivity increases of 90 percent from 1970 to

[86] *Irish Times.*
[87] See Helmut Elsenhans, "Rising Mass Incomes As A Condition of Capitalist Growth," *International Organization* 37, 2 (Spring 1983).

1980 but, with fewer workers producing a roughly constant output due to demand conditions, it passed Ireland to top the EEC unemployment statistics in 1982.[88] Multiplier effects are weak, and the microchip's impact on tertiary employment should not encourage those interested in attaining politically tolerable levels of unemployment – and it is the *political* exhaustion of industrial strategies which is the analytic concern.

A second objection is that a "lump of labor" fallacy is being promulgated; that is, the analysis ignores the demand creation attending the cheapening of products. This is an open question. The least skeptical investigators foresee mismatches between the labor-shedding effect of process innovation and the timing of product innovations. An OECD study found that consumption "of information goods and services is still playing a fairly minor role in the budget of the average household."[89] Another disturbing factor was the mid-1980s "shake-out" in the electronics industry: Atari and Storage Technology closed shops – while Mostek "deferred" plans to locate a new plant in Ireland.

Export-oriented investment, in the absence of vigorous external demand, converts "peripheral post-industrialism" into a subset of dependent development (defined as excluding local consumers due to the export strategy). The process is regressive in a way akin to Frank's early notion of underdevelopment. Unlike Frank this analysis stresses the importance of *indigenous sources of support for this particular choice among possible responses to international forces and conditions*, the fragility of the dominant coalition, and the implications of this fragility, when under stress, for state autonomy in democracies where subordinate strata are mollified mostly through ideological means.

The "propensity to defer" remained high over three elections fought during 1981–82 as parties competed for the right to impose deflationary programs that differed from one another only marginally. Austerity packages were portrayed in the media as a secular pilgrimage, a repentance for sins that barefoot treaders of, as a Fine Gael minister colorfully put it, the "rough, stony path" may not recall having committed. They are induced anyway to feel guilty

[88] Giles Merritt, *World Out of Work* (London, Sphere Books, 1982), p. 111.
[89] Cited in Guenter Friedrichs and Adam Schaff, *Microelectronics and Society* (New York, Mentor, 1982), p. 210.

because the international market, like God, moves in mysterious ways that demand unquestioning obedience.

Deflationary policies feed the vicious circles and erode the sources of regime stability. (Borrowing rose precipitously in the 1973–76 period to offset energy prices and otherwise low consumer spending, which, when high, is import-oriented.) The "peripheral post-industrial" strategy does not arrest but aggravates the erosion. In 1983 the "average earner" paid 43 percent of income to taxes while hikes in indirect taxes depressed purchasing power – and the fortunes of local businesses. The real level of personal consumption was 15 percent lower in 1984 than in 1979 and total investment fell by a third in the same period as the foreign debt was rising five-fold. Irish economists found it "something of a paradox" that, despite a stricken domestic market, manufacturing output rose 5 percent in 1983 and 17 percent in 1984 so that economic recovery, such as it was, had been "all output, no jobs."[90]

Unemployment passed the 16 percent mark. By 1984 "leakages" into debt service and profit repatriation amounted to 10 percent of gross domestic spending, reducing a 4 percent GNP growth rate by half.[91] The beneficiaries of a 10 percent growth in trade certainly were high-tech firms, primarily US firms. US direct investment grew from £986 million in 1977 to £3.8 billion in 1983 – an annual reinvestment rate of 24 percent. In their most recent profitable EEC outlet US manufacturers recorded a 24 percent real rate of return compared to 5.6 percent elsewhere in 1984, although it is important to note this differential is due substantially to transfer price mechanisms channeling cash into the favorable Irish tax climate. Benefits which flow away cannot trickle down to consumers or job seekers.

The espoused solution was to do the same things, only somehow better. Thus a minister decried "unreal wage *demands*," and argued that future productivity gains would be rewarded not by vulgar wages (as opposed to refined profits) but, incredibly, in "the satisfaction and security of a long-term job."[92] This minister admitted that management efficiency, marketing expertise, and new product development were more crucial to Irish competitiveness than wage curbs, but paused for no thought on the implications of infringing

---

[90] *Sunday Tribune*, 6 September 1985, p. 1.   [91] *Irish Times*, 16 June 1983, p. 1.
[92] (John Bruton) *Irish Times*, 12 February 1983, p. 9.

upon private prerogatives in order to correct these deficiencies. The emphasis on wages diverts attention from serious questions regarding industrial strategy and state intervention. But this cannot be construed simply as an expression of base self-interest by "capital" if only because so many Irish businesses are harmed (and voters annoyed or alienated). Ideological "lag" better characterizes the problem; however, the "lag" is conditioned by an institutional environment that keeps "non-decisions" at bay. The dissident voice of the small Labour Party is, of course, muffled during periodic coalitions with Fine Gael. So, by itself, "lag" is an insufficient explanation. Certainly those who prosper through the current strategy know very well where at least their immediate interests lie.

CONCLUSION

It is only natural that economic elites in a "catalytic" state should single out wages as the sole culprit of competitive woes. The Irish cannot control the prices of imported input goods and there is no handy quantitative measure to determine the damage that poor management inflicts. There is no overarching organization to co-ordinate industries so as to maximize value-added and forge link-ages. So the option that is left is to blame "high" wages, whatever the evidence. If the populace swallow that story, "deference" remains high despite a breakdown in the material basis of consent to the economic strategy (what I call the "consensual satisfice").

But there are limits. The ICTU in 1982, for example, stated:

Congress (the ICTU) recognises the difficult economic circumstances confronting us and is prepared to make its contribution to the resolution of the problem but it cannot and will not acquiesce in any procedure or arrangement that would hamstring unions and result in the cost of economic difficulties being borne solely by workers.[93]

Irish workers are encouraged to invest – via wages and rising taxes and unemployment – in job-destroying measures. The bulk of Irish firms stand to suffer more from ebbing demand caused by austerity policies than they can gain in wage "relief". Investment will decline since demand is more important in capitalist calculations than wage levels *per se*.[94] In turn, the state must respond by hiking investment

---

[93] *ICTU Annual Report 1982*, p. 184.   [94] Elsenhans, "Rising Mass Incomes", p. 312.

incentive levels and drawing further revenues from fewer wage earners until fiscal crisis sets in. This crisis is staved off by borrowing until the state collides with the boundaries of this tactic. A struggle to control policy prescriptions resumes. In the 1980s the "crisis of democracy" model of Irish maladies held sway. Over 80 percent of those who cast votes did so for right-wing parties.

In the next chapter I examine the debt crisis, explore alternatives in industrial policy, and compare the Irish with other export-oriented cases.

CHAPTER 7

Getting it right: debt, taxes, and industrial strategy, 1984–1990

I couldn't believe it. "Oul wans" [elderly women] asking about
borrowing requirements – a canvasser in 1982.
    People don't like what's happening but they are convinced
that there is no alternative.
                    Dick Spring, Labour Party leader, 1988

In the 1980s Irish governments imposed austerity with remarkable
political ease and in a uniform fashion that culminated in 1987 with
Fine Gael's endorsement of the economic aims of the minority
Fianna Fail government – virtually a declaration of "a national
unity regime." The debt crisis was understandably the first priority;
it also obscured, if not eclipsed, debate over the shortcomings of
development policy. This chapter explains how consent was gained
for a particular diagnosis of crisis and for an extenuation of an
ebbing developmental orthodoxy.

The next section surveys the economic difficulties and political
liabilities of the industrial policy path which in effect was declared
void but not nullified. For want of an authoritative successor this
policy continued with minor modifications. Next I examine emergent alternatives within and outside the state's formal boundaries,
which all met political and conceptual barriers during the admin-
istrations of a Fine Gael–Labour coalition, a minority Fianna Fail
government, and since July 1989 a Fianna Fail–Progressive Democrat coalition. Fianna Fail would revive corporatist-style bargaining
via a program for national recovery signed, sealed, and delivered in
October 1987 despite the severe deflationary Budgets enacted at the
time. The state was searching for "policies that prevent the costs of
change from causing political disruption."[1] Fianna Fail resorted
to corporatist politicking to mediate the impact and responses to

[1] Katzenstein, *Small States in the World Economy*, p. 24.

159

international debt pressure and competition. This political "move" succeeded insofar as budget balancing was concerned.

The chapter next examines the response of the Irish state to the Single European Act and the attendant challenge of intensified competition in 1992. The latter at this juncture looks very much like a repeat performance of the accession to the European Economic Community.

ANATOMY OF A QUIET CRISIS

The 1982–87 Fine Gael–Labour Coalition government demonstrated anew that failure alone cannot kill an accepted economic strategy nor any other kind of policy orthodoxy. As in the Kuhnian account of scientific change, a major shift in policy requires a persuasive alternative that, moreover, is endorsed by key players in the decision-making arena.[2] Otherwise the prevailing policy paradigm lingers because there is no rival to which elites or the public can resort.

The presiding phrases of Irish political discourse in the 1980s have been the twin imperatives to "restore order to the public finances" and to create "the right climate for investment." The latter presumably proceeded from the former. No party seriously disputed these objectives and the three major parties – including the newly formed Progressive Democrats (essentially a Fianna Fail breakaway leavened by a few Fine Gael defectors) – differed marginally, if at all, over this policy prescription. In an increasingly rancorous coalition with Fitzgerald's Fine Gael the Labour Party could achieve little more than to restrain, rather than alter, the spending cuts campaign. Accordingly, no substantial challenge was mounted against the distribution of the burden of adjustment, which weighed heavily on the working and salaried middle classes and the poor.

Over four and a half years the coalition succeeded in cutting inflation from 17 percent to less than 4 percent, and lowered the borrowing requirement from 21 percent of GNP per annum to about 13 percent – although the debt was doubling to £26 billion

---

[2] Thomas Kuhn, *The Structure of Scientific Revolutions* (Chicago: University of Chicago, 1962). For an overview of debates over scientific paradigm change see J. K. Jacobsen and Roger Gilman, "The Dialectical Character of Paul Feyerabend's Philosophy of Science," *Nature, Society and Thought* 4, 1–2 (January–April 1991).

Irish (40 percent from foreign sources). Debt service payments consumed more than 25 percent of tax revenue versus 18 percent in 1980. But export volume rose 50 percent, manufacturing output 32 percent, and GDP by 9 percent (although after subtracting "black hole" debt service and other factor outflows GNP rises 3.5 percent).[3] Labor industrial productivity made remarkable strides ahead of the country's trading partners – rising 13.4 percent (1984), 4.7 percent (1985), 3.7 percent (1986) and 9.5 percent (1987).[4] The NESC states that over 1980–85 domestic demand fell 11 percent each year while investment (aggravated by public sector capital cutbacks) fell 2 percent per year.[5] Overall, gross investment as a percentage of GDP declined from 33.6 percent in 1979 (second only to Japan) to 27 percent in 1982 (far ahead of West Germany's 22 percent, Britain's 18 percent, and the US 16 percent) and to a still hefty 23 percent by 1984–85.[6]

Over 1980–84 real personal incomes increased 1.5 percent but, after taxes, amounted to a 7 percent fall in income, and a 12 percent fall over 1980–86 according to another source.[7] Emigration, after net inflows in the 1970s, averaged about 25,000 per year. But profits as a share of national income rose from 26 percent in 1982 to 30.6 percent in 1986.[8] Despite the heady performance registered in output, productivity, export growth and profits, jobs fell by 44,000 or 4 percent over 1983–87 – by 10 percent since 1980. "Whatever the explanation," a national newspaper's economic analyst observed, "the fact remains that the statistical relationship between output growth and employment growth has broken down in Ireland."[9]

An Economic and Social Research Institute report confirms this phenomenon which, as analysts in Britain, Australia, and the United States attest, is not unique to the Irish economy.[10] Over 1973–79 manufacturing output went up 5.1 percent and so did jobs by 0.7 percent; from 1979 to 1983 output rose 4.3 percent while jobs

[3] *Sunday Tribune*, 5 October 1986, p. 1; *Irish Times*, 8 March 1988, p. 6.
[4] *Sunday Tribune*, 21 August 1988, p. 1.
[5] NESC Report, no. 83 *A Strategy For Development* (Dublin: CSO, November 1986), p. 181.
[6] *Sunday Tribune*, 16 September 1984, p. 8.
[7] *A Strategy For Development*, p. 7; *Irish Times*, p. 2.
[8] *Sunday Tribune*, 21 August 1988, p. 6.
[9] Paul Tansey, *Sunday Tribune*, 14 August 1989, p. 14.
[10] ESRI Paper, no. 125 *Small Scale Manufacturing in Ireland* (November 1985) by Kieran Kennedy and Tom Healy, p. 158.

fell 3 percent; in 1984 alone output increased 13 percent while jobs
fell again. This trend, which confounds the core assumption legitimizing economic policy, stirred Irish business to promote "wealth
creation" over employment as the key goal of development. ESRI
members spotted the implication "in this view that a wealth creating strategy would probably be far more capital-intensive, with less
employment directly created in manufacturing."[11] More significant
is the implication that business associations were abandoning any
pretense of responsibility for job creation, which at least symbolic-
ally was the goal most coveted by trade unions in intermittent
semi-corporatist negotiations. The private sector therefore had
nothing to offer outside a narrow collective bargaining context.
So-called "wealth creation" made sense to labor only if a brokering
institution, which the private sector opposed, guaranteed the transfer and transformation of accumulated wealth into a satisfactory
blend of jobs, amenities and rising living standards. Otherwise, Irish
business, simply and starkly was admitting that the premises on
which prior bargains were based were false. Still, the 1984 *White
Paper on Industrial Policy* endorsed "wealth creation."[12]

The reasons unemployment had risen so alarmingly were: low
demand due to austerity policies and tax hikes, high interest rates
(discouraging small businesses), the massive export of capital via
profit repatriation which rose from 260 m in 1980 to 13. bn in 1986
(plus debt service), and cutbacks in IDA funding that reduced in
real terms the 1987 budget to half what it was in 1980.[13] This
lattermost trend was a policy response both to the Telesis critque
about grants and to a fall-off in available footloose projects. The
inflow of foreign direct investment dollars (at constant prices)
dropped from 260 m in 1981 to an average of about 170 m in the late
1980s.[14] The Irish share of American FDI in Europe slipped from
2.3 percent in 1979 to 1.5 percent in 1982 and remained at that level
while new EC entrants Greece, Spain, and Portugal gained. Here at
last was a potent motive to modify past policies: the environment
had changed, though not so drastically as to promote a major

[11] Kieran Kennedy and Denis Conniffe, eds., *Employment Policy in Ireland* (Dublin: ESRI, 1986), p. 17.
[12] *White Paper On Industrial Policy* (Dublin: Stationery Office, July 1984), Pl. 2491.
[13] *Irish Times*, 14 January 1988, p. 12.
[14] *Ibid.*

upheaval. By the mid-1980s the plight of Irish policy-makers *vis-à-vis* multinationals was reminiscent of the predicament of the dyspeptic diners in an old joke: the cuisine is terrible, and there's not enough of it.

The credibility of Irish developmental strategy waned insofar as job creation and living standard improvements were concerned. As early as 1981 a poll disclosed that a majority of the working class, half the civil service and 40 percent of professionals expressed little or no confidence in private companies as the "engine" of economic growth and/or social progress.[15] The notion had collapsed that, if only the state "got it right" creating an encouraging climate, private entrepreneurs would produce a cornucopia of benefits. These appraisals informed the reports of the ESRI and the NESC as well. The 1980s campaign by business, the IDA and the state (as expressed in the 1984 *White Paper on Industrial Policy* and the related government planning document *Building on Reality 1985–87*) to persuade the public and especially trade unions to accept a shift to the criterion of "wealth creation" was a thinly disguised confession of failure.

"The continuation of existing policies is not a viable option," a 1985 NESC study judged.[16] "It could give rise to continued emigration, further deterioration in public finances, and continual reduction in the flexibility of policy-makers." The report criticized the government, and particularly the aforementioned 1984 White Paper, for a lack of commitment, saying "if policy instruments capable of translating the changed orientations of stated industrial policy are not devised and implemented, nothing more than a transformation of the vocabulary of the bureaucracy will occur."[17] The ESRI criticized the White Paper for stopping "well short of the 'hands-on' approach by public agencies recommended by Telesis for the building of strong indigenous industry."[18] Another ESRI volume observed that expecting private industry to provide, under the most favorable circumstances imaginable, more than a third of the 23,000 new jobs required simply to hold the unemployment (18 percent in 1986) steady was to "go beyond the bounds of

[15] Cited in Wolfgang Weinz, "Economic Development and Interest Groups," in Brian Girvan and Roland Sturm, eds., *Politics and Society in Contemporary Ireland* (London: Gower Press, 1986), p. 91.

[16] *A Strategy For Development*, p. 320.   [17] *Ibid.*, p. 275.

[18] *Small Scale Manufacturing*, p. 161.

optimism."[19] In sum, an analyst judges: "it is difficult to avoid the conclusion that Irish economic performance has been the least impressive in Western Europe, perhaps in all Europe, in the twentieth century."[20] Hardly an unprecedented judgment. What is significant, though, is that appraisals formerly consigned to a marginal, mostly left-wing, political discourse flowed at last into the mainstream. It is equally significant that these critiques continued to exert very little influence. Why?

Policy-makers faced three broad alternatives. First, they could go on as before – stay the course despite the evidence. Second they could acknowledge "that the mere creation of wealth will not secure sufficient employment growth without an active government policy to ensure that this wealth is channelled into job creation; and that once we are out of the present financial difficulties, the policy must envisage employment growth in both the public and private sectors – and also probably in the combination of the two . . ."[21] This option involved a degree of direction that might antagonize key sectors of the incumbent government's support. Was the risk worthwhile? The third option circles back to the first alternative. "Given the repeated failures of private enterprise to respond to threat or opportunity, only the state, whether directly, or in partnership with the private sector, could supply the deficiency," says Lee, stating the plight of perfect despair. "The problem now was that the state itself had largely lost credibility . . . both sectors seemed to have failed."[22] This is the ideal outcome for a dominant coalition still prospering from the present policy course. Why devise new policies that prevent the costs of change from causing disruption when the disruptive potential is drained by emigration, the dole, and the demoralizing doctrine that there is no other, less punitive option? With four political parties (Fianna Fail, Fine Gael, the Progressive Democrats after 1986, coalition-bound Labour) and virtually all the media – with the intermittent exceptions of the *Irish Times* and *Sunday Tribune* – propagating the same dour message and prescribing the same harsh and unimaginative remedies, voters hardly could differ from the practitioners of the dismal science.[23]

[19] Kennedy and Conniffe, *Employment Policy in Ireland*, p. 288.
[20] Lee, *Ireland 1912–1985*, p. 521.
[21] Kennedy and Healy, *Small Scale Manufacturing*, p. 327.
[22] Lee, *Ireland 1912–1985*, p. 538.
[23] *Ibid.*, see Lee's acerbic comments on the economics profession, pp. 581–86.

THEORETICAL APPROACHES

An explanatory approach along "state-centric" lines, which tends to view the state as a more or less autonomous structure of actors and institutional networks, is not a very illuminating guide. It is accurate enough to say the Irish state was "monumentally unsuccessful either in ensuring sustained economic growth or in moderating unegalitarian tendencies in the class system" – except that the comment assumes the state genuinely *tried* to do the latter.[24] The evidence may be arranged as easily to show the state at all times was willing to aggravate, if necessary, class inequities in pursuit of growth goals.

It is broadly correct to comment that contemporary "state apparatus has indeed expanded, perhaps exchanging a growing capacity for diminished autonomy" if this means simply that the power to perform more tasks is permitted under circumscribed conditions,[25] except that we are entering an analytical twilight zone with regard to the definition of the state, and the relationship between state capacity and autonomy. Hence, the Irish state in the mid-1970s "was led to attempt to retain its capacity to act via recourse to borrowing" which predictably resulted in "dramatically diminished autonomy."[26] Yet why would states which, according to the "state-centric" approach, tend to develop and promote their independent purposes, deliberately sacrifice discretionary latitude in any policy arena?

If the concept "capacity" refers both to resources and to "the authority and organizational means" to deploy resources, then analysis becomes inevitably confused. It makes no sense to say that a state can swap a degree of autonomy for enhanced capacity *in the same policy area*, as if one can meaningfully exercise power without retaining control. That would be illusory.

Here the state is viewed as an organizational matrix profoundly interlinked with civil society, especially key producer groups, shaping private preferences and in turn is influenced in a wide variety of sites within and outside the formal structure, according to the material resources and wits deployed by actors. The state is neither a creature of special interests nor a particular class. The impact on policy of public and private actors competing within the

---

[24] Breen, et al., eds., *Understanding Contemporary Ireland*, p. 209.   [25] *Ibid.*, p. 43.
[26] *Ibid.*, p. 212.

matrix is of course a matter to be settled in each instance by empirical inquiry.

Certainly, the "organizational context alters the calculations of rational actors" promoting – or brokering – policies.[27] This is a vital analytical point if one recognizes that the "organizational context" itself can become the object of political contest, especially in times of economic crisis. Organized interests know very well how institutional structures and "policy legacies" help or hinder advancement of their diagnostic definitions and policy preferences, and will seek whenever possible to change the "organizational context" (e.g., introduce or dismantle policy instruments) in advantageous ways. Those initiatives may be blocked or else materialize in weak forms (as in the case of the Labour Party–ICTU support for a National Development Corporation). Yet these efforts require attention because cumulatively they can alter the political context and they guide attention to sources and strategies of resistance.

Explaining policy choice requires that we draw back from the organizational context to the level of the international arena and, as Gourevitch urges, examine how it can "strengthen or weaken certain arguments and the resources of those advancing them" in the course of a policy debate.[28] Yet even this is too passive a conceptualization which must be complemented by a proposition reversing the usual implied causal relationship. That is, domestic groups deploy resources to propagate their interpretations of the causes, consequences and by extension proper responses to international economic events. Those arguments incorporate both a hegemonic policy strategy for solving the crisis and a *tactical* concern for retaining (or gaining) power in the process. Fault-finding is not enough. A hegemonic policy "candidate" portrays the desired action not only as necessary but wise and beneficial for groups whose consent is needed. This is not to imply that a group cannot promote policies which a disinterested observer would approve as practical and equitable. A hegemonic policy is indeed self-regarding for the core members but is designed to appeal to the pockets, if necessary, and the intellects, if possible, of other players. The best outcome for core members is if other players agree to the proposed distribution of benefits and burdens. Second-best is if the core members persuade

---

[27] Hall, *Governing The Economy*, p. 119.
[28] Gourevitch, "Keynesian Politics," in Hall, ed., *The Political Power of Economic Ideas*, p. 102.

other players, without concessions, that they face a Hobson's choice – this course, or nothing. Second-best is the mode under which 1980s Irish politics was successfully conducted. However, as alternatives emerge, and hard-pressed groups perceive that the logic of growth no longer works as advertised, this second-best outcome becomes a wasting asset.

The Irish state inflicted an IMF-style austerity program with all predictable consequences but one – no significant discontent arises.[29] This high "deference" derived from a united front among right-wing parties, and a media which reflected conservative diagnoses. In Ireland, even more than in Britain, there seemed "no alternative." So, we next review alternatives that government or government-related bodies considered during the 1980s. Second, we examine counter-proposals by Left and independent parties.

ENTERTAINING ALTERNATIVES

As late as 1981 an Irish economics study confidently claimed that, unlike agriculture, "increases in manufacturing output are associated with increased productivity and increased employment."[30] The next year an NESC response to the Telesis report reaffirmed the objective of "an internationally competitive base in Ireland which will support increased employment and higher living standards," observing that to do so required, however, "more finely tuned policy instruments to remove main barriers to entry" for an "internationally competitive *indigenous* industry."[31] But by the end of the decade Irish newspaper headlines and banner lines regularly proclaimed confounding results: "Export Boom But No Jobs Spin-Off" (*Irish Independent*, 1 July 1988), "Why Growth Is Up But Jobs Are Down" (*Sunday Tribune*, 21 July 1988), "Multinationals Thriving Here Despite Recession" (*Irish Times*, 14 January 1988), "Baby Boom Jobs Crux has International Dimension" (*Irish Times*, 21 July 1990), "Growing Economy Can Mean Less Jobs" (*Irish Times*, 4 August 1990) and, getting the point, "New Industrial Policy Is Needed To

[29] By contrast, see Thomas Biersteker, "The Relationship Between Economic and Political Reforms: Structural Adjustment and The Political Transition in Nigeria." (Mimeo 1990)

[30] John W. O'Hagan and Kevin P. McStay, *The Evolution of Manufacturing Industry in Ireland* (Dublin: Helicon Books, 1980), p. 5.

[31] NESC Report, no. 66 *Policies For Industrial Development: Conclusions and Recommendations* (Dublin: Stationery Office, September 1982), p. 50.

Cut Dole Queues" (*Sunday Tribune*, 14 August 1988). Something was amiss.

Initial official responses to the Telesis critique were the National Planning Board's *Proposals For Plan, 1984–87* and the *White Paper on Industrial Policy*. The Board endorsed Telesis and urged formation of a new NIEC-style council "so as to achieve a wider consensus" and also so that the government take the lead in creating a "climate for consent."[32] In the framework of a medium-term program the Board recommended that the state give priority aid to firms providing backward linkages, expansion of an Employment Incentive Scheme, advocated investment in infrastructure, and rejected the view that capital-intensive investment would diminish jobs (which technically is correct but not under Irish circumstances of recession-restricted output growth).[33] The Board invoked the ritualistic refrain about pay restraint, pointing out, however, that beneficial effects will ensue "only if the rising retained profits are invested in Ireland."[34]

The Board daringly suggested "requiring firms to place increases in retained profits, which had not been invested in Ireland over the years, in Irish government securities" which then would be channeled into public sector projects or into promoting further private sector investment.[35] However, the Board averred that this forceful course might prove "counter-productive"; foreign investors must not be made nervous. The Board repeated an earlier NESC critique of the lack of a manpower policy and stated that the appropriate minister, not the IDA, ought to direct industrial policy. But in a most concise and despairing comment the Board, perhaps conscious of political obstacles to and costs of policy change, recommended the creation of a minister in charge of unemployment and emigration.

The White Paper acknowledged that "industrial policies which had clearly served Ireland well in the 1960s and 1970s are now having less success."[36] In new circumstances (more competition, less footloose industry) the Paper stated that the following goals were desirable – though did not suggest how they would be best achieved. Irish policy should:

(i)   create and maintain the maximum number of sustainable jobs, as many as possible of them high-skilled . . .

---

[32] NPB, *Proposals For Planning* (Dublin: Stationery Office, April 1984), p. 248.
[33] *Ibid.*, p. 210.
[34] *Ibid.*, p. 244.   [35] *Ibid.*, p. 245.   [36] *White Paper On Industrial Policy*, p. 3.

(ii) maximize value-added ... and to capture the wealth thus created for further investment and employment ...

(iii) develop a strong and internationally competitive industrial sector in Ireland ...

(iv) promote the more rapid development of our natural resources ...

(v) promote the integration of foreign industry into the Irish economy through greater linkages ...

(vi) improve the rate of return on the government's investment in the commercial state companies.[37]

The White Paper announced a "Company Development Approach" which involved "picking winners," identifying promising and cooperative private companies with the objective of building up Irish based companies with strong export market positions. A National Development Corporation was charged with supplying equity investment – hardly what Labour had in mind. "The NDC should aim to become self-financing in 6–8 years," the Paper stipulated, "It should therefore be able to sell off its investments profitably in order to replenish its capital."[38]

The White Paper endorsed "wealth creation" over "job creation" on the grounds that greater domestic value-added augmented the capacity to create jobs elsewhere in the economy – and it mentioned no administrative mechanism to assure that this happened. The Paper drew criticism for declining to come to grips with the need for new and/or differently deployed policy instruments to attain objectives, and it did not attempt to link industrial policy considerations to a wider realm of taxation and social policy. The Paper reflected, foremost, Fine Gael's reluctance to tamper with the market, or rather with an approved pattern of market intervention.

In this climate, Lee observes that the authors were "confident that public perception of trade union exploitation of the state sector had already deeply discredited the idea of an expanded state role."[39] Whence this "public perception" came from is a matter skipped over quite lightly. The White Paper views were re-capitulated in *Building On Reality 1984–87*, which was criticized by the NESC for "a failure on the part of Government, and more

---

[37] *Ibid.*, pp. 5–6.

[38] Cited in Jim Fitzpatrick and John Kelly, eds., *Perspectives On Irish Industry* (Dublin: Irish Management Institute, 1986), pp. xxxii–xxxiii.

[39] Lee, *Ireland 1912–1985*, p. 537.

particularly the Department of Trade, Commerce, and Tourism to convert the expression of broad strategic sentiments into an operational decision-making framework ... The Department has not grasped the opportunity to take control of industrial policy."[40] The NESC emphasized the crucial need for productive capital expenditure even in the reviled public sector and asked that cuts in expenditure be done, where necessary, with an eye on "distributive implications." The NESC recognized that "a fundamental dualism has become apparent" between foreign and indigenous industry and that resources must shift to technology acquisition and export market development."[41]

A 1985 sectoral report noted that indigenous Irish firms still "are highly dependent on UK machinery suppliers for ideas in developing new products and processes" and that these were few enough.[42] An ESRI study of small-scale manufacturing (defined at 0–50 employees) argued that technological upgrading and enhancement of crucial "sub-supply skills will not happen by unaided growth of market forces."[43] The Institute recognized that the output–employment relationship "is likely to be less favorable in future" and suggested a strongly interventionist strategy aiming at creating a proliferation of import-displacing subsuppliers for large firms. Although a small industries program presents a "relatively cheap method of creating jobs," the majority nonetheless must come from private sources and publicly funded employment. In an experimental spirit alien to the White Paper, the ESRI encouraged public authorities to explore "the scope for new forms of enterprise, such as workers' and producers' co-operatives, and even the possibility of establishing direct state manufacturing enterprise in selected areas were major avenues "that should be considered."[44]

A 1986 NESC report viewed the economic scene as "almost unremittingly grim" with no prospect of recovery "unless there is a radical change in policy." The authors called for (1) an integrated macro-economic policy to correct fiscal imbalances while promoting targeted sectors; (2) a fundamental reform of the tax system; (3) the

---

[40] NESC Report, no. 79 *Economic and Social Policy Assessment* (Dublin: Stationery Office, January 1985), p. 39.

[41] *Ibid.*, p. 29.

[42] Sectoral Development Committee Report, no. 8 *Report and Recommendations On The Technological Capacity of Indigenous Irish Industry* (Dublin: Stationery Office, June 1985), p. 9.

[43] Kennedy and Conniffe, *Small Scale Manufacturing*, p. 162.   [44] *Ibid.*, p. 148.

promotion of active micro-interventionist policies; and (4) the removal of major inequities.[45] The report otherwise foresaw growing public "disaffection," a concern ignored in other official literature. On the revenue front the NESC notes that Ireland has the highest consumption taxes, lowest corporate taxes, and employer social insurance contributions at half the EEC average. From an inequitable structure tax revenue as a percentage of GNP rose from 29 percent in 1980 to 36.7 percent in 1985 (and over 40 percent in 1989). The share of capital taxation was one-fifth that of Thatcher's "enterprise culture" Britain (0.23 versus 1.2 percent). Property taxes accounted for less than 4 percent versus 8 percent in 1979 and 10 percent in 1970. Meanwhile, the state inflicted "high marginal tax rates on low levels of income," which amounted for a single person to a combined tax (plus social insurance and levies) of 55.5 percent at two-thirds the level of the average wage (£11,100 Irish in industry in 1985–86). The NESC laid what in official circles was an unusual stress on linking revenue reform to industrial policy, implying that the former conditioned the options open to the latter.[46] This report approved of Telesis, chided the overemphasis on electronics industry and pointed out that chemical and office equipment industries over 1980–85 ceased to generate jobs.

Finally, an NESC study published in 1987 presented a detailed plan for doubling manufacturing employment in two decades at a cost of £200 million per year.[47] This study sets out in copious detail a "phased entry/development strategy" geared to indigenous engineering industries, and designed to overcome barriers to entry (scale, technology, finance, marketing, product differentiation) so as to create an integrated industrial structure. The author alludes to successful directive approaches to industrialization in Japan, Taiwan, and South Korea, and contends that "it still makes sense to borrow for productive investment" which yields good returns in revenue, lower outlays for unemployment, and state equity profits. On the delicate question of control, the study suggests it might be "more costly for the state to aim for private sector involvement than to operate through state enterprise" but that it was in practice a matter for "case by case" consideration.[48]

[45] *A Strategy For Development*, p. 309.   [46] *Ibid.*, p. 3.
[47] NESC Report, *Engineering Industries in Ireland* (Dublin: Stationery Office, September 1987). Authored by Eoin O'Malley, p. 156.
[48] *Ibid.*, p. 182.

In sum, policy alternatives were indeed devised and circulated at least in the realms of academe and public administration. This alternative "package" comprised selective industrial policy, tax reform with equity as the key criterion and a reinvigorated corporatism to foster consultation and consent. Implementing these policies involved political risk and economic cost but these had to be weighed against the hazards of "staying the course," which every Irish government judged negligible until the advent of Charles Haughey's minority Fianna Fail administration in 1987. Fianna Fail fastened on the aforementioned 1986 NESC report, entitled A Strategy for Development, as a framework for devising policies and for securing consent for adjustment prescriptions. This experience will be evaluated below, after examining alternatives advocated on the political fringes.

ADVOCATING ALTERNATIVES

After bringing down the Coalition in January 1987 over health cuts, Labour vowed to abstain ten to fifteen years from another governing venture. "We need to establish a hard core, left-wing section of the electorate," said party leader Dick Spring, responding to pressures to move in a more radical direction.[49] The Labour Party, rife with internal feuding, fell from 9.4 percent of the vote and 16 seats in 1982 to 6.4 percent and 12 seats in February 1987. Meanwhile, the Workers Party edged up to 3.8 percent (from 3.3 percent) and 4 (from 2) seats and overtook Labour in Dublin (11.4 percent to 9.5 percent).

In the summer of 1988 Spring unveiled "Labour's Alternative – Job Creation and Fair Tax in Tomorrow's Ireland," a document encompassing many NESC and ESRI recommendations. The National Development Corporation (NDC), it said, should fund projects according to "a framework of clear objectives" with "high-quality management adequately rewarded," and penalties assessed for failure. The commercial semi-state sector was to be run along commercial lines and "social goals, if any, should be clearly distinguished and costed." The IDA role regarding foreign investment would be assumed by the reformed NDC, applying tighter conditions and criteria. Labour also approved borrowing for select productive projects.

---

[49] *Sunday Tribune*, 6 September 1987, p. 6.

Unlike Fianna Fail, Fine Gael, and especially the tax cut crusading Progressive Democrats, Labour rejected tax reduction *per se*, opting for a revenue neutral tax reform which included new corporate and capital taxes, a farm tax, a new property tax, and abolition of mortgage tax relief and of the £16,000 ceiling on social insurance.[50] Top income tax rates were left at 45 percent (53 percent given the PRSI ceiling abolition), stirring internal party protest that "the proposals come dangerously close to falling into the trap of debating the economy in terms of the Right."[51] Nonetheless, Labour linked in systematic fashion revenue reform to an active industrial program.

The Workers Party was particularly caustic: "Contrary to the daily stream of prejudice and propaganda," wrote Workers Party president Proinsias De Rossa,

about "white elephants" and "bottomless pits" ... our 17 main public enterprises had trading profits of £447 million and net profits, after financial charges, of £85 million. This is despite the policies of successive Coalition and Fianna Fail governments which meant that state companies were starved of capital, forced to borrow from private banks at exorbitant rates of interest, and prohibited from competing with private enterprise or revealing their potential for growth and job creation ... We believe that public enterprise can be the power-house of economic recovery and industrial growth.[52]

Over 1988–89 Labour, the Workers Party, the Democratic Socialist Party (with one TD, Jim Kemmy), independent deputies and senators and pressure groups met in forums to work out common approaches on economic and social issues "to the greatest possible extent."[53] The formerly tense relationship between Labour and the Workers Party became "cordial and constructive."[54] This new cordiality arose in a year when, in June, one headline announced "Quarter of Population Live in Poverty, Says Agency," followed in September by "One Third of Population is now Living in Poverty."[55] (Both reports, respectively by the Combat Poverty

---

[50] Maev-Ann Wren, "How Labour Differs in Tax Cut Stakes," *Irish Times*, 20 June 1988, p. 13.
[51] Emmet Stagg, quoted in *Irish Times*, 22 July 1988, p. 1.
[52] *Irish Times*, 26 July 1988, p. 12.
[53] *Irish Times*, "Left Wing TDs Draft Common Economic Policy," 21 January 1988, p. 7.
[54] *Irish Times*, "Labour and Workers Party Agree On Tactics For New Dail," 28 June 1989, p. 1.
[55] *Irish Times*, 28 June 1988, p. 3 and 28 September 1988, p. 1.

Agency and the ESRI, repudiated the "growth solves all" view). The Irish Left resisted the lure of monetarist socialism as applied in Spain, Australia and New Zealand. The key tasks were to demonstrate that the prevailing diagnosis was flawed and that the Right's definition of crisis owed more to a skewed distribution of power than to the intrinsic validity of argument. The TUC endorsed this attack, and in 1990 the Manufacturing, Science and Financial Union (a 1989 merger of ASTMS and TASS) contributed an ambitious plan for melding Telesis, NESC, and Labour aims into a scheme of job creation.[56] In the short term, however, these programmatic challenges exerted little appeal beyond trade union circles, and, in any case, were drowned out by the "fiscal rectitude" chorus. But the cumulative force of 1980s policy reviews, plus austerity, did result in a change in the role of the IDA.

THE IDA'S ADJUSTMENT

From the mid-1980s the IDA was relieved of its tacit role of national saviour. Agency goals became modest but stringent: 37,000 jobs over the period 1987–90. The IDA henceforth would publish data on "actual," not "projected" jobs, focus on indigenous industry, foster substitution via a National Linkage Programme, promote local sourcing, more R & D and expansion of existing foreign plants in Ireland.[57] These measures stemmed from a recognition that the IDA must form part of a coordinated state approach.

The IDA cut staff by 100 (to 670), separated overseas and domestic industry divisions, and closed offices in Houston, Cleveland, Paris, Milan, and Copenhagen.[58] It expanded Tokyo staff and opened an office in Seoul. The focus on the Far East paid off with twenty-six Japanese firms locating in Ireland (fifteen between 1987 and 1990) and commitments from Taiwanese and Korean firms.[59] The IDA imposed tough grant criteria, and established conditions for repayment in certain cases. An Irish industry division was charged with selecting and cultivating competitive local firms. The key IDA target was software companies. Nonetheless, a 1987 editorial profile of the IDA chief maintained:

---

[56] *Irish Times*, 28 June 1990, p. 14.   [57] *Irish Times*, 18 December 1987, p. 17.
[58] *Irish Times*, 18 September 1989, p. 1.
[59] *Irish Times*, 24 July 1990, p. 3.

the case for reform of our costly industrial policy is building up. The IDA spent £185 million last year, but that was only part of an estimated £400 million spent on industrial supports by it and another 19 agencies. Tax breaks for industry could be costing another £650 million a year in lost revenue, according to government figures. Yet the manufacturing work-force has tumbled by around 30,000 in the last four years.[60]

In 1988 and 1989 the IDA announced that 60 percent of actual jobs created were in Irish firms (15,000 of a total 25,000). Overseas firms were buying more Irish raw materials and services, 131 percent more in 1987 alone.[61] The IDA refurbished the Ferenka site, dividing it into 16 units employing, in 1987, 150 people with 400 more jobs in the pipeline. (Still, this amounted to a third of the original Ferenka work force.) The rub here is that the IDA remained *de facto* the major job creation agency. However expertly, and even ingeniously, the IDA carried out its tasks, the full employment "mission" was clearly beyond credible reach. It was no longer so valuable a political asset.

THE TRIUMPH OF RETRENCHMENT POLITICS

When the Left mentioned "so-called realities" propagated by the Right, there were limits to how far the inverted commas extended. "The issue for socialists," said Dick Spring, "is not whether [the debt] should be controlled – but how it should be done."[62] In coalition the Labour Party helped promote the 1985 Anglo-Irish Agreement, a liberal contraception bill, and a National Develop-ment Corporation while incurring defeats on a divorce referendum and an abortion amendment (which were as much part of Premier Garret Fitzgerald's "constitutional crusade" for a pluralistic society as they were Labour issues). By 1986, however, two-thirds of Labour's membership expressed dissatisfaction with the coalition's "hairshirt economics."[63] Nothing but a major oil strike would have saved the Coalition.[64] On January 20, 1987 the party pulled out of

---

[60] Damien Kiberd, "Profile: Padraigh White," *Sunday Tribune*, 2 August 1987, p. 11.
[61] *Irish Times*, 8 January 1989, p. 7.
[62] *Irish Times*, 28 September 1987, p. 1.
[63] Michael Lavers, Peter Mair, Richard Sinnott, *How Ireland Voted: The Irish General Election of 1987* (Dublin: Poolbeg, 1987), p. 12.
[64] There were tantalising indications. Several oil and another gas (besides Kinsale) strikes occurred in the 1980s though all were judged either too small in volume or too deep to recover.

coalition over proposed health cuts. A majority (53 percent) of Fine Gael members were quite relieved that the partnership ended. Pundits viewed the Coalition as a vehicle with the accelerator floored (Fine Gael) and the safety brake on (Labour) – in, of course, reverse gear.

In opposition Fianna Fail promised "prudent fiscal management" but chided the Coalition for lacking assertive programs, and in the election state investment figures of £200 to £500 million were mentioned by various spokespersons.[65] A key event, according to *Magill* editor Brian Trench, was the publication in November 1986 of NESC report *Strategy For Development* (cited earlier), "which offered a way of talking in the same breath about controlling finances and stimulating growth."

Almost uniquely for an NESC report, it was sold out in three months. Its method and approach were absorbed into the Fianna Fail election manifesto. It has since been referred to directly in both the Fianna Fail budget of March 1987 and [later] the Programme For National Recovery, as negotiated with the "social partners" during the summer and autumn of 1987. "It was nice to see someone out there was listening at last," comments Garry Danaher, secretary of the NESC.[66]

What Fianna Fail fastened upon in a document brimming with interventionist prescriptions was the plea to cut £60 million. (Fine Gael proposed £40 million.) The Fianna Fail slogan, "There is a better way," film buffs recognized, aped that of the protagonist in Michael Ritchie's satire *The Candidate* (1972), who undergoes a U-turn personally and politically. The slogan was extremely apt.

In the 1987 election Fianna Fail lost 1 percent of the vote but due to the vagaries of proportional representation gained 6 seats for a total of 81, two shy of a majority; 12 percent of Fine Gael and 20 percent of Labour switched to Fianna Fail. However, 18 percent of Fine Gael and 8 percent of Fianna Fail defected to the neo-liberal Progressive Democrats, who became the third largest party with 14 seats. Fine Gael fell from 70 to 51 seats, and Labour from 16 to 12 with its lowest poll since 1933.

Fianna Fail formed a minority government and, after sustained attacks on Fine Gael's "indiscriminate cuts" while in opposition, commenced to cut £485 million. Health expenditure was sliced

---

65 *Irish Times*, 9 June 1981, p. 1.
66 Brian Trench, "Where Others Fear To Tread," *Magill*, January 1988, p. 6.

6 percent, education 7 percent, agricultural spending fell 18 percent, roads and housing were down 11 percent, social welfare rose 1 percent, and allocation to the IDA, the Marketing Board and Tourist Board was reduced.[67] The military budget was reduced 7 percent. The National Board for Science and Technology and the Institute for Industrial Research and Standards were merged. An Foras Forbatha, an environmental watchdog, was abolished at a time when half the streams and lakes were threatened with toxic materials.[68]

"The policies which we have adopted are dictated entirely by the fiscal and economic realities," Haughey claimed. "I wish to state categorically that they are not being undertaken for any ideological reason or political motives" but because they are "dictated by the sheer necessity of economic survival."[69] Haughey stated on another occasion that public expenditure cuts would mean "there would be more for private investment" – when invariably deflationary measures reduced the incentive to invest.[70] In September Fine Gael's new leader Alan Dukes renounced, conditionally, the role of opposition, saying: "When the Government is moving in the right overall direction, I will not oppose the central thrust of its policy."[71] The two major parties had reached an economic accord at last until, as they said, order was restored to public finances.

But Fianna Fail revived tripartite bargaining as well. "My colleagues and I have always favoured direct negotiations between trade unions, Government and the employers for a plan for national recovery," Haughey announced, unfurling a Programme for National Recovery hammered out among the state, the Irish Congress of Trade Unions, the Federated Union of Employers, the Confederation of Irish Industries, and the Irish Farmers Association (the Irish Creamery and Milk Suppliers withdrew earlier).[72] Haughey credited the NESC report *A Strategy For Development* with providing "the first elements of a consensus between the social partners, in terms of an analysis of the problem."[73]

[67] *Irish Times*, 14 October 1987, p. 1.
[68] Tales of silage spills and toxic waste hazards filled the news reports throughout the summer of 1987. There were frequent significant "fish kills" especially in the West. The Fisheries Board authorities reported that they lacked the adequate allocation of petrol to patrol the rivers due to state cutbacks.
[69] *Irish Times*, 21 October 1987, p. 1.   [70] *Irish Times*, 14 October 1987, p. 7.
[71] *Irish Times*, 13 September 1987, p. 13.
[72] *Irish Times*, 10 October 1987, p. 16.   [73] *Ibid.*

The PNR essentially was a wage agreement in which particularly the public sector unions consented to 2.5 percent pay raises in exchange for tax relief (a promise to bring two-thirds of taxpayers into the standard 35 percent band), keeping welfare in line with inflation, a shorter work week (prospectively), and job creation targets that were obviously "aspirational." The premier concern was to halt the growth of the debt to GNP ratio by 1990. The program offered the unions little other than a regular consultative mechanism, which trade union leaders, fearful of being marginalized as were their UK counterparts, deemed important enough.[74] Nonetheless, the deal worked because inflation remained low at 2.1 percent over 1988. Although inflation doubled in 1989, tax concessions, the ESRI estimated, gave wage earners real if modest income gains.[75] The Programme for National Recovery, which trade unionists narrowly approved, promised reviews of capital and corporate tax treatment, and imposed social insurance contributions on farmers and the self-employed. But the PNR did not interfere with health cuts, education cuts, reduction in public sector employment (8,000–10,000 by voluntary means) or the abolition of the National Social Services Board, the Health Education Bureau, the Regional Development Organisations, or – though talks ceased briefly in protest – An Foras Forbartha. In three more months Fianna Fail introduced another £300 m in public expenditure cutbacks. This evidently was what *The Economist* termed Fianna Fail's "vaguely formulated socialism" in action.[76]

There was little reason to doubt that Fianna Fail, after restoring order to the public finances, would eventually resort to what Haughey termed "prudent reflation." After all, Fianna Fail attracted a plurality – nearly 40 percent of the working-class vote. The government was preparing the basis for a National Development Plan for submission to the EEC for Structural Funds, seeking £3.7 billion in subsidies for a £9 billion five-year infrastructural modernization scheme. Meanwhile, the public expenditure cuts bit deeply and an analyst might easily make the case that Fianna Fail's response to unemployment consisted of subtle encouragement of emigration. Deputy leader Brian Lenihen embarrassed the admin-

---

[74] Brian Donaghy, "What The Plan Gives The Unions," *Irish Times*, 10 October 1987, p. 9.
[75] Cliff Taylor and Pat Nolan, "Programme Gave Industry An Edge," *Irish Times*, 9 January 1990, p. 8.
[76] *The Economist*, 16 January 1988, "A Survey of The Republic of Ireland," p. 6.

istration when he spoke with approval of emigration in a *Newsweek* interview. (Emigration rose from 27,000 in 1987 to 32,000 in 1988, and 46,000 in 1989.) The government and much of the media portrayed the "new migrants" as relatively well-educated people, not the navvies and house servants of yesteryear. The Dublin Institute of Technology had sent 60 percent of its graduates abroad since 1980.[77] (Only 11 percent returned, contrary to claims that many do so after gathering experience elsewhere.) But surveys indicate that the majority of migrants go involuntarily and to less glamorous or remunerative work. In London the Irish chaplaincy reported 77 percent of men worked in construction (often "on the lump," non-unionized and uninsured) while 54 percent of women worked in "child care or elderly care," 28 percent as waitresses, and 14 percent in offices.[78] In 1989 the Irish state forked out a token £500,000 to fund welfare emigrant services in the United Kingdom and United States.

"In Ireland, emigration is not an alternative," a newspaper columnist argued: "it is part of the natural order of things."[79] Certainly, it is part of the *political* order of things, and it is only natural that free market economists and conservative groups portray politically contingent phenomena as forces of nature with which it is unwise to tamper. What is not so "natural" in an industrialized democracy is that such propositions go unchallenged in mainstream debate. There is, of course, a valid argument that groups promoting new policies and allocations of the burden of adjustment suffer less from neglect than from paltry resources and small followings which is reflected in media disinterest. Whatever the reason, the terms of policy discourse are narrowly defined.

The *Sunday Tribune*, regarded as the most left-of-center national publication, editorialized over 1987–88 that in order to alleviate scandalous poverty, senior public servants earning over £15,000 should sacrifice a percentage of their salaries.[80] At the same time the ESRI reported that multinational firms profit repatriations "represents 32 to 37 per cent of the sales of the firms in the last six months of 1987," stressing that "any crude attempt" to interfere would "most

---

[77] *Irish Times*, 1 September 1989, p. 7.
[78] *Irish Times*, 15 August 1988, p. 8. See Fintan O'Toole, "Highway Robbery," *Magill*, April 1988, pp. 22–26.
[79] Paul Tansey, "Emigration Is Part Of What We Are," *Sunday Tribune*, 17 July 1988, p. 12.
[80] *Sunday Tribune*, 2 August 1987, p. 6, and 17 July 1988, p. 11.

certainly cause an abrupt cessation of foreign investment in Ireland together with the closure of many existing enterprises."[81] The ICTU pointed out that the corporate tax take was 3 percent of total revenue in 1988 compared with 9 percent in 1965 and an OECD average of 7 percent.[82] Property taxes had fallen over twenty years from 15 percent to 4 percent – though the ICTU was less in favor of rises here because many members were homeowners and mortgage holders. The ICTU broadly agreed with ESRI urging that the state pursue value-added strategies in industry and undertake reforms to extend the tax base. Yet the only option the editors of a progressive newspaper promoted in the short term was what was tantamount to a "job security" tax on civil servants. This recommendation coincided perfectly with the Right's campaign to denigrate (and ultimately to privatize the more profitable portions of) the public sector.

The second example of the confined ideological space for debate concerned a controversy that broke out in July 1988 when a report on Ireland by The Economist Intelligence Unit (EIU) produced more pessimistic unemployment projections than the IDA issued: a rise to 23 percent (or 306,000) by 1992.[83] The EIU assumed that unemployment stood at 18.9 percent (247,000) at its 1987 starting point; the IDA cited Central Statistics Office data indicating the figure really was 17.7 percent (or 232,000) and that therefore the projection was inaccurate. Unemployment was levelling off, the IDA claimed. The EIU conceded making a minor error but argued the trend of unemployment was upward. Yet neither set of figures provided reason for believing that a resumption of economic growth would increase net job creation or enhance prosperity. If so, as an ESRI researcher pointed out with a political candor and acumen rare among economists: "the present fragile social consensus is likely to come under strain if workers, and indeed the community at large, feel the income and other constraints which they have endured have resulted, not in enhanced job opportunities, but in increased profits, a sizeable proportion of which are expatriated."[84] Profits indeed rose. An analysis of publicly quoted companies – an unrepresentative sample likely to err on the low side – found pre-tax profits in

---

[81] *Irish Times*, 12 December 1987, p. 1.   [82] *Irish Times*, 15 June 1989, p. 2.

[83] See *Irish Times* editorial 29 July 1988 and Jim Dunne, "Shooting The Messenger," *Irish Times*, 30 July 1988, p. 12.

[84] Jerry Sexton, "Ray of Hope," *Irish Times*, 1 August 1988, p. 14.

1989 "increasing on average by over 25 per cent over 1988, or 15 per cent if banks are included."[85] At the 1990 ICTU annual conference an MSF union spokesperson claimed that profits overall had risen 25 percent in each of the previous two years.[86] The government had "gotten it right." Where were the jobs?

By embracing the NESC report as a plan for policy action, Fianna Fail astutely averted attacks from the "social partners" whose consent was needed for a wage agreement. Thereafter, the government traded tax relief for adherence to wage norms, and gained the freedom to impose austerity. The agencies dealing with "job search programmes, training, and social employment schemes" removed approximately 10,000 off the dole figures under Fianna Fail's reign.[87] The minority government granted oil exploration companies more favorable terms (including abolition of state participation in profits and exemption of oil and gas production from royalty payments) because, as Minister for Energy Ray Burke explained, "concessions of a radical nature are necessary."[88]

The policy strategy must be judged effective with regard to the government's short-term goals. The Programme for National Recovery was the most vital element in the ensuing upturn: an employers association survey found 95 percent adherence to wage guidelines.[89] External sources of inflation luckily remained in check. Consumer spending rose 3.1 percent in 1988 and 4.7 percent in 1989. (Union spokespersons observed, however, that in 1989 particularly, "real" wage rises were negated by indirect tax hikes and mortgage payment increases.)[90] Wage restraint plus job losses, a conservative economics writer noted, "meant that the output and productivity gains in industry have been appropriated by capital rather than labour."[91] The economy experienced a resumption of GDP growth of 4 percent by 1989. A once-off tax amnesty, the unexpectedly high economic growth, and the variety of additional tax bites brought in surprisingly high revenue levels. The exchequer borrowing dropped to 6.1 percent of GNP.

[85] *Irish Times*, 9 January 1990, p. 13.
[86] Patrick Nolan, "National Forum Sought To Discuss Employment," *Irish Times*, 5 July 1990, p. 1.
[87] *Evening Press*, 7 August 1987, p. 5.   [88] *Irish Times*, 1 October 1987, p. 11.
[89] Reported in Nolan and Taylor, "Programme Gave Industry An Edge," in *ibid*.
[90] Patrick Nolan, "Main Unions Likely To Support New Pact," *Irish Times*, 9 January 1990, p. 14.
[91] Paul Tansey, "Irish Industry's Profits Boom, and Rise Is Set To Continue," *Sunday Tribune*, 21 August 1988, p. 17.

Accordingly, the 1989 budget reduced the standard income tax rate from 35 to 32 percent (and top rate from 58 to 56 percent), kept welfare payments in line with inflation (12 percent for the long-term unemployed), and availed of EEC Structural Funds to arrest the protracted decline in public capital spending. The Finance minister predicted job growth and resorted to electioneering rhetoric "rekindled spirit of the nation") while denying government interest in an early general election.[92] One month later an *Irish Times/MRBI* poll found Fianna Fail garnered 54 percent, a 3 percent rise in support over Fine Gael and Labour since December.[93] In May, Prime Minister Haughey dissolved the Dail and sought a Fianna Fail majority result.

The Irish electorate had not returned a government to office since 1969. The streak continued. The 15 June 1989 election produced: Fianna Fail 77 seats (down 3), Fine Gael 55 (up 5), Labour 15 (up 4), Workers Party 7 (up 3), Progressive Democrats 6 (down a devastating 8) and 6 independents (up a seat as the Green Party captured its first in Dublin). The swing was arguably just that – a swing to the Right and, more so, to the Left. A Fine Gael strategy of out-flanking the upstart Progressive Democrats to their Right paid off with regained seats. But the Left, broadly defined, improved even more with 7 new seats between Labour and the Workers Party plus Democratic Socialist Party member Jimmy Kemmy and independent Tony Gregory (the latter reelected) for a total of 24: a cheering, if far from powerful, performance. After a long and fitful series of negotiations Haughey and Progressive Democrat leader (and ex-Fianna Fail minister) Desmond O'Malley worked out an agreement to form a coalition government which was formally approved 12 July in the Dail, 83–76.[94]

In the election Haughey had not reckoned, pollsters said, with the enormous public concern and anger over the cuts especially in the health services (86 percent) and over emigration levels (78 percent cited it as a major issue) that matched the 1950s exodus rate which in turn had stimulated the shift to the "Whitaker–Lemass" strategy now viewed even in *Strategy for Development* as part of the problem.[95] The minority Fianna Fail government had misconstrued a wide-

---

[92] *Irish Times*, 26 January 1990, p. 11.   [93] *Irish Times*, 25, 26, 27 December 1989, p. 7.
[94] For a chronicle of the rise of the Progressive Democrats, see Raymond Smith, *The Quest For Power: Haughey and O'Malley* (Dublin: Aherlow, 1986).
[95] *Irish Times*, 12 June 1988, p. 7.

spread "deference" grudgingly given to the adjustment recipe as enthusiastic support for the impact of retrenchment. As the NESC had urged, Haughey approached stabilization of the debt-to-GNP ratio, reduced income tax levels and curbed public expenditure. But the NESC warned too that "getting these macroeconomic policies right might not be sufficient to get industrial expansion fast enough" to generate the material benefits of jobs and living standard improvements.[96] The state required microeconomic instruments with which to promote an industrial policy "involvement of a more direct character." The government launched reviews of industrial policy in accordance with NESC recommendations. Fianna Fail did not contemplate a reform of the tax system.[97]

Fianna Fail offered nothing of a positive nature that voters could rally around. The recovery was experienced as a restricted affair. As an opposition Deputy observed, "impressive-sounding economic indicators do not necessarily result in improved prospects for the people of the country." The realm of economics and "what appeared to be happening in the real world were two separate things."[98]

The June 1989 election drove home the point that "wealth creation" was not a winner at the ballot box, not the means for recreating what I termed in chapter 2 a consensual bargain over development policy. Fianna Fail paid for the Coalition with a pair of cabinet posts for Progressive Democrats and a promise to reduce the standard income tax rate to 25 percent by 1993. Health spending rose. But Fianna Fail quashed the Progressive Democrat plea for Thatcher-style privatization of the public sector. (Irish Steel and Irish Life Assurance later were considered, the government stressed, as individual cases for privatization.) With another installment of the Program for National Recovery in the offing, Haughey would not risk stirring ICTU opposition on an issue he evaluated strictly on pragmatic grounds. The ICTU was improving its stature as a corporatist partner. The ITGWU and the FWUI, the two largest unions, announced their merger as of 1 January 1990. From that point fifteen unions would represent 80 percent of total membership,

---

[96] *A Strategy For Development*, p. 253.
[97] A Commission On Taxation was appointed in April 1980 and met from then until October 1985. The chief recommendations – fewer deductions and lower rates – were noted, but shelved.
[98] Eamon Gilmore (Workers Party TD), *Irish Times*, 24 August 1989, p. 9.

and further consolidations were likely. The newly amalgamated union would be called the Services, Industrial, Professional and Technical Union (SIPTU).

General Secretary Bill Attley of the FWUI, who became a president of SIPTU in 1990, was credited with exerting decisive influence in favor of accepting Haughey's proposal of wage restraint for tax relief.[99] "Our role," Attley argued, "is to bargain about the whole range of areas which have been traditionally regarded as management prerogative."[100] The logic of bargaining under severe retrenchment pressures within an open economy encourages this trend. Over the 1980s decentralized bargaining favored employers. The share of profits over wages rose. Even the stronger trade unions made meager, if any, gains because of inflation. As Lange observes elsewhere in Western Europe, the importance of "non-economic factors" in conditioning the "likelihood of worker co-operation with wage regulation rises sharply" with the onset and acknowledgment of "structurally bleak economic prospects."[101]

But it is clear that, in the absence of a brokering institution to assure positive-sum gains are allocated fairly, trade union peak organizations cannot get what they want in the wider realm of the political economy (jobs, social wage gains, input into investment decisions) if they give the employer organizations what they want. In the Irish context, and increasingly in global impact, the customary relationships between investment or output to job creation or *local* appropriation of benefits no longer hold reliably.[102] The basis for bargaining – the basis of economic policy reasoning – requires reappraisal. The trade unions want to "bring the state back" into the bargaining nexus to restore the credibility of corporatist ventures via the power of current and *prospective* policy instruments. The ICTU prizes the potential power it may wield through "mechanisms of consultation." The employers associations reap satisfactory gains but are wary of the direction the "mechanism of

---

[99] Aileen O'Meara, "Profile: Bill Attley, The Most Powerful Trade Union Leader In The Country," *Sunday Tribune*, 26 January 1989, p. 11.

[100] *Ibid.*

[101] Lange, "Unions, Workers, and Wage Regulation," in Goldthorpe, ed., *Order and Conflict in Contemporary Capitalism*, p. 116.

[102] On a global scale, see Christopher Freeman, John Clarke, and Luc Soete, *Unemployment and Technical Innovation* (London: Frances Pinter Press, 1982).

consultation" may take.[103] For a social bargain or "pact" to work the state must act as guarantor and as initiator of the process of negotiation. It is increasingly apparent that a government must intervene microeconomically if the aggregate growth of the economy is to have more than an abstract impact on the population. So there is an opportunity, an opening of room for maneuver by pragmatic policy entrepreneurs intent on devising a strategy around which the current coalition can rally or else a different coalition can form. While an opportunity is there, necessity is not. The Fianna Fail–PD government could try to side-step reappraisals and policy changes because of the appearance of the Single European Act (SEA).

The passage of the SEA was a foregone conclusion. Even the Parliamentary Labour Party leadership, who resisted the EEC in 1972, supported it. A constitutional challenge resulted in a 1987 referendum in which 70 percent (of a 44 percent turnout) endorsed acceptance. Raymond Crotty, a key figure in the anti-SEA campaign, complained that:

The Tanaiste, Mr. Lenihan, admitted in the Dail that the government had spent from taxpayers' money £1,700,000 on leaflets and £16,000 on media advertisement to influence in the best banana republic fashion, the people's choice. That was about fifty times more money than the entire anti-SEA movement was able to mobilise by voluntary subscription. In addition, the Government Information Service was used to issue a constant stress of propaganda in favour of the SEA.[104]

The "sweetener" for accepting the SEA was the doubling of Structural Fund payments. In March 1989 the minority Fianna Fail government submitted a £9.1 billion National Development Plan to Brussels, seeking a £4.7 billion EEC contribution. (The EEC contribution was adjusted the next year to approximately £3.35 billion.) This five-year program of infrastructural, industrial, and tourism development was expected to generate 30–35,000 jobs each year.[105] So, by expanding resources available, Community support relieved pressures upon the state to reassess policy.

[103] "FUE Says Recovery Is Working," *Irish Times*, 27 August 1988, p. 8. The Federated Union of Employers argued earlier that any attempt to impose statutory machinery "would greatly reduce Ireland's attractiveness as an industrial location." *Irish Times*, 12 January, 1988, p. 11.

[104] Raymond Crotty, *A Radical's Response* (Dublin: Poolbeg, 1988), p. 156.

[105] Aileen O'Meara, "Spending The Euro-Billion Bonanza," *Sunday Tribune*, 26 March 1989, p. 1.

The objective of the Structural Fund is to upgrade under-developed regions of the European Community to a competitive standard. The NESC noted that the largest EC member states with "industries with economies of scale and highly innovative sectors," benefit most and that Ireland is not such a place.[106] Even income transfers of the order of 2 to 3 percent of Irish GNP per annum over five years are hardly going to make Irish industry the equal of what used to be termed West German firms.[107] In short, there is no reason to expect Structural Fund spending to bring about a sustained improvement in Irish employment, living standards, and emigration patterns in the absence of enactment of new development policies (which, of course, may fail too). As of mid-1990 the Finance Minis-ter attested to the *Financial Times* that "the national morale was never higher."[108] *The Guardian* of London editorialized approvingly of the success of the "Irish model."[109] In the late summer of 1990 economic analysts in the mainstream media continued characteriz-ing the troubling relationship between high aggregate growth and low job creation as "ironic."[110]

COUNTER HEGEMONIC PRESCRIPTIONS AND IRISH POLITICS

Recall that the Telesis report, the avowed basis for Fianna Fail action on industrial policy, urged a vigorous alternative strategy of development. A "national enterprise agency" should serve as a "corporate shell" for firms because "the industrial infrastructure does not exist in Ireland and the network of subsuppliers has to be created in a more planned and organized way."[111] The state must emphasize competitive advantage by exploiting native raw mater-ials – food processing, fisheries development, processing of mineral finds – and by expanding research capacities in selected industries. A "carrots-and-stick" approach is needed *vis-à-vis* private industry, and new coordinating mechanisms and forums are required.

The Telesis report provides a programmatic core around which a consensual developmental bargain could be reconstructed. Yet there is scant reason to expect that the *degree* and *kinds* of interven-

106 Cited in *Irish Times*, 14 September 1989, p. 9.
107 A point made by many Irish economic commentators.
108 *Financial Times*, 19 February 1990, section iv, p. 1.
109 "The Irish Model," *The Guardian*, editorial, 26 September 1990, p. 11.
110 *Irish Times*, 4 August 1990, p. 1.   111 *NESC Report* (Telesis), no. 64, pp. 232–33.

tion Telesis advocates would suffice to meet social goals. If the adverse effects of "peripheral post-industrialization" continue, one may anticipate splits inside the dominant coalition over policy strategy, enabling another coalitional configuration to arise (perhaps trade unions, local non-supplier firms, authentic pragmatists in either major party and "technobureaucrats" who can swing either way). Pertinent here is the Stephens' observation on Jamaican politics that where popular loyalties are "clientelistic," the "party leadership is allowed a greater flexibility to change its ideological stance without alienating (or educating) its supporters."[112] But the ideological premises of development policy can be altered to support an alternative course, so it really is important to inquire why "people in that situation are likely to think that way."[113] A left-wing Pollyanna might envision the rise of a "democratic-entrepreneurial state," which goes by other, more emotive names. Most likely, a moderate Fianna Fail-led government would seek to strike a balance between export industries' requirements and domestic welfare needs that is politically tolerable.[114]

The potential resistance is powerful. The dominant export coalition is justifiably apprehensive that the pragmatic path Telesis advocated is "the camel's nose beneath the tent." A weak Irish bourgeoisie needs the state but fears the state "acting for itself," or, less metaphysically, "acting for other interests." A "recurring dependent development syndrome" can come into play as growth resumes in conjunction with increase in retained benefits. The anti-statist chorus then would grow. In the short term, social pressure on elites is "populist" in form, centred on no specific agenda, and so is easily diffused.

[112] Evelyn and John Stephens, "Democratic Socialism in Dependent Capitalism: An Analysis of The Manley Government in Jamaica," *Politics and Society* 12, 3 (1983).

[113] Gourevitch, "Breaking With Orthodoxy," p. 128.

[114] In 1989 Merrill Dow pulled out of a prospective industrial site in East Cork in the midst of a local controversy over environmental controls stirred by local residents. Although one Fianna Fail TD depicted protesters as "a shower roaring and shouting like Balubas," the response of the government was on the whole to side with resident concerns, and negotiate promptly a stringent agreement with Sandoz pharmaceutical company over pollution safety. The response contrasts sharply with the Ferenka episode a decade earlier when virtually all blame was heaped upon the locals. Also see Susan Baker, "Dependent Industrialisation and Political Protest: Raybestos Manhattan in Ireland," *Government and Opposition* 22, 3 (Summer 1987); and Robert Allen and Tara Jones, *Guests of The Nation: The People of Ireland versus The Multinationals* (London: Earthscan Publications, 1990).

CONCLUSION

Political ideas and economic theories are not neutral.[115] There are "implicit value positions embedded in any analysis of how social institutions operate," and which condition the choices made in particular situations.[116] Contemporary critics argue that the "master concepts" of neo-classical economics are increasingly divergent from reality: citing, for example, erosion in the relevance of standard trade theory or the severing of the customary relation of growth to job creation.[117] These are becoming important debates and have enormous policy implications. But the immediate point is that "economic necessity does not predict the society's actual social arrangements" nor does it determine an "optimal" policy choice.[118]

Is there an optimal choice? Do actors always depart from economic efficiency when including "political" factors? An observer makes the allegedly axiomatic case that "greater politicization will reduce the coherence of policy and the speed with which adjustments can be taken" because it "reduces the flexibility of both the private sector and the state."[119] But is this actually so? Przeworski compiles data attesting that neo-liberal nostrums have not worked well, if at all: "Argentina and Brazil, where several attempts at stabilization occurred, but also Poland and Bolivia, where stabilization was successful, show that the pursuit of the elusive criterion of 'efficiency' can be counter-productive politically and even economically."[120] The political factors in the economic policy equation – democratic participation and state guarantees – may be absolutely essential for a recovery and for efficiency.[121]

---

[115] Fred Block, *Postindustrial Possibilities: A Critique of Economic Discourse* (Berkeley: University of California, 1990), p. 2.

[116] Ibid. p. 12. Block criticizes the definitions and role of GNP, capital, the market and labor; decrying, for example, "a methodology that assumes that increases in output are inherent in the equipment itself and divert attention from the centrality of organization factors."

[117] On trade see Zysman, *Governments, Markets and Growth*, and Kuttner, *The End of Laissez-faire*. On the impact of automation on neo-classical theory, see Giovanni Dosi et al., eds., *Technical Change and Economic Theory* (London Frances Pinter, 1990).

[118] Block, *Postindustrial Possibilities*, p. 22.

[119] Haggard, *Pathways From The Periphery*, pp. 160, 234.

[120] Adam Przeworski, "Economic Reform in New Democracies: A Social Democratic Approach" (mimeo, University of Chicago, May 1992), p. 1.

[121] Ibid. pp. 2–3, 18. His arguments are: "that (1) reforms that constitute the current standard recommendation – stabilization and liberalization – are necessary but they are not sufficient to restore the capacity to grow unless they are accompanied by active state

Sweeney suggests guidelines for building a vibrant public sector. O'Malley examines new approaches to exploit the employment and the potential of indigenous high tech industries.[122] The Industrial Policy Review Group (Culliton Report) urged the state to allot less energy and expense on overseas firms and to promote a "cluster of firms" strategy aimed at exploiting sophisticated niche markets. The group also criticized training schemes for failing to link up with employment. The Central Bank, like the Industrial Review Group, noted that a requisite "radical reform of the tax system is not inconsistent with fiscal consolidation."[123] There are indeed many vexing connections to be made of tax and fiscal policies to industrial policy and to social welfare. But there are no lack of alternatives on the table for consideration.

The charge that there is a lack of "coherent alternatives" is a common retort to critics. Even if true, it would be irrelevant. In the 1980s, the Irish state could afford to "view industrial policy and wage bargaining as analytically distinct" because interests and economic ideology coincided nicely behind a desired political purpose.[124] The industrial schemes and adjustment packages enacted over the decades hardly exhibit the coherence that authorities demand from challengers. The entire structure was *ad hoc*. A new set of solutions will emerge as circumstances change, and parties are spurred by economic straits to elevate alternatives into the realm of possibility. Then, as political opportunities arise, the Irish can apply whatever options fit a credible policy framework. Such a possibility arose in the aftermath of the December 1992 election, to which we turn next.

coordination of the allocation process. (2) Since any reform package must consist of discrete steps taken over an extended period of time, without a social policy which protects at least those whose subsistence is threatened by the reforms, political conditions for their continuation become eroded. (3) Unless the representative institutions play a real role in shaping and implementing the reform policies, the consolidation of democracy may be undermined.

[122] O'Malley, *The Irish Engineering Industry*.
[123] *Irish Times*, 9 December 1991, p. 18.
[124] Hardiman, *Pay, Politics and Performance*, p. 243.

Afterword: 1991–1993

And here I sit so patiently waiting to find out what price you
have to pay to get out of going through all these things twice.
Bob Dylan

In January 1991 a *Guardian* editorial lauded "the continuing Irish
economic miracle."[1] Because of prudent economic management
and an incomes bargain with trade unions (which the Irish
government, unlike British Tories, acknowledges) Ireland in 1989
and 1990 boasted the fastest growing economy in the European
Community. Exports were booming, borrowing was down, and
inflation was low. All seemed civil and sane. Across the frontiers,
however, Irish citizens were experiencing events differently than
British editors imagined. If rapid economic growth without prosperity is miraculous then that was indeed what was happening. As
one scans the economic situation an intense sensation of *déjà vu*
grows.

A noteworthy volume taking a cultural inventory on the Irish
miracle has as its theme for the 1990s a "state of aimlessness"
stemming from a widespread and, for many citizens, realistic sense
that Ireland "does not have a future."[2] The editor cited the
persistent problems: unemployment, emigration, poverty, indebt-
edness, right-wing triumphalism, and the deceptively distant
sounds of fury in the North of the island (and, lately, on the British
mainland).

Unemployment broke the 20 percent mark in 1991 (official statistics a little later were juggled to lower the rate several points) and
was twice the EC average. At least 1 million citizens – and

[1] *The Guardian*, 31 January 1991, p. 14.
[2] Richard Kearney, "Introduction: Thinking Otherwise," in Kearney, ed., *Across The Frontiers: Ireland in the 1990s* (Dublin: Wolfhound Press, 1989), p. 7.

40 percent of children – were living in poverty. Emigration was discouraged by the British economic doldrums, and disconsolate emigrants were returning to Ireland. An ESRI study foresaw no prospect of a halt in rising Irish joblessness before 1996.[3] In a hauntingly symbolic act postal workers during a strike in 1991 made a charitable exception for people mailing applications for "Morrison visas" in order to emigrate to (or remain legally in) the United States. So the bleak opening lines in Whitaker's *Economic Development* echoed across three decades.

The solutions of the 1950s became, as critics warned, the problems of the 1990s.[4] In the early 1990s several investigative bodies (the Industrial Policy Review Group, the Oireachtas Joint Committee on Employment, the Task Force of the social partners) discerned again that the state had no coherent industrial policy: "what exists is a hotch potch of various unconnected schemes."[5] The key "paradox" or "irony," as commentators delicately put it, is that the Republic contrives to get high aggregate growth while suffering from rising unemployment, a hemorrhage rate of a tenth of GNP and a chronic deflationary environment. Why not try more wage restraint? "Wage demands have been moderated since 1987," an Irish analyst tartly observed, "we now have the highest unemployment in the history of the state."[6]

In March 1957, at the low ebb of the autarky, Professor C. F. Carter complained that the "coexistence of high unemployment and high emigration with undeveloped resources is nonsense, and nonsense *which can very well be put right.*"[7] Few in Ireland took much issue with the "Doheny & Nesbitt School of Economics" (a synonym for a band of neo-liberal economists). But Chubb and Lynch shrewdly observe regarding economists that "their art consisted in knowing how far it was possible to go, or even how much it was possible to say."[8] So what is it possible to say, and why? Until the December 1992 elections, very little.

---

[3] *Irish Times*, 29 November 1990 on growth rates; and 26 June 1991 on ESRI report.
[4] See, for example, Bew, Hazelkorn, Patterson, *Dynamic of Irish Politics*, p. 161.
[5] *Irish Times*, 3 January 1992, pp. 1, 13.
[6] Dick Walsh "Look Forward To A New Europe But Keep Your Eyes on Home Ground," *Irish Times*, 7 December 1991, p. 12.
[7] Chubb and Lynch, *Economic Development and Planning*, p. 3.
[8] *Ibid.*, p. 4. Although one may wonder with Joseph Lee whether restraint was ever needed except by a very exceptional and unheeded few.

PRAGMATISM, ORTHODOXY, AND CRISIS

Putting finances in order required cooperative relations with trade unions and so Fianna Fail continued quasi-corporatist bargaining, forging a successor to the PNR pay agreements, called the Programme for Economic and Social Progress (PESP). The PESP in January 1992 agreed to a three-year pay rise of 14.5 percent in exchange for more aid for health and secondary schools, more third level places, a crackdown on tax evasion, and job promotion. On the other hand, Fianna Fail, to the unions' dismay, pursued privatization which, critics argued, followed a pattern of rescuing failed public firms while denying funds to public enterprises that were prospering and had expansive potential – a "perverse investment policy."[9]

The coalition did respond to PESP demands to close tax loopholes, and between 1990 and 1992 company tax revenue tripled. The government also moved to increase taxes on bonds and dividends. The Finance Minister reported numerous protests in business and the ranks of upper incomes over an intensification in revenue-collection enforcement, taxes on the "perk" of company cars and the removal of tax shelter status from co-ops. In December 1991, however, the government reacted to a crunch of rising costs and falling revenues by taxing some social welfare benefits and trying to retract a public sector pay increase agreed in the PESP. The Progressive Democrats, staunch in foisting high ethical standards on their coalition partner, had no problem whatever urging that the pay guidelines of the PESP bargain be reneged (though three of four citizens polled opposed breaking the agreement).

The Finance Minister evaded queries as to whether the government was depressing demand and feeding a downward cycle.[10] As public capital expenditure fell from a half to a third of total investment, gross investment dropped from 28.4 percent of GNP in 1982 to just 18 percent in 1987 and was three-quarters of 1982 levels in 1990.[11] Kieran McGowan, the IDA chairman, attributed a decline in Irish firm start-ups (and net industrial job losses in 1991 and

---

[9] Paul Sweeney, *The Politics of Public Enterprise and Privatisation* (Dublin: Tomar Press, 1990), pp. 62–63. He continues: "Thus money was poured into Irish Steel, B&I, Great Southern Hotels and NET when on the brink, but was not given to the profitable companies such as GSH (later), Aer Lingus, Irish Sugar and Irish Life."

[10] *Irish Times*, 16 December 1991, p. 8.   [11] *Sunday Tribune*, 19 April 1992.

1992) to falls in domestic demand.[12] The deflationary bind was obvious. The government reported that net pay went up slightly (1 to 1½ percent) in 1990 and 1991 while other reports found these gains were gobbled up by VAT taxes on phone bills, footwear, and clothing. A rash of lay-offs composed almost equally of "downsizing" multinationals and local companies dependent on local demand followed in the summer of 1992 and added to the national sense of emergency.[13] The continuing core problem has been the insistence by politicians, dependent on narrow economic formulations, on treating the debt problem in isolation from reforms of industrial policy and of the tax system.

WHERE THE BEEF IS

Fianna Fail ratings dropped from 60 percent in January 1991 to 39 percent by year's end, suffering setbacks in local elections. Haughey's popularity plummeted as he became the target for a host of accusations of corruption over 1992–92. These seamy matters involved the purchase by University College Dublin of Carysfort College, Greencore, the purchase of a site by Telecom Eireann, an Irish Helicopter company report slipping into the hands of the Prime Minister's son who happened to work for a rival firm, the installation by the state of an expensive wind power device on Haughey's privately owned island and, above all, a beef processing scandal.

Although a bid to oust Haughey in November 1991 flopped, the last straw came shortly afterward when a former minister of state implicated Haughey again in the wiretapping of two journalists in 1982. Under the cumulative weight of accusations, and the pressure of Progressive Democrats, Haughey finally resigned. In January 1992 Albert Reynolds became Prime Minister.

It is not necessary to delve here into all the devious details of the cavalcade of scandals afflicting Fianna Fail, but the Goodman International beef high jinks, exposed by British television, deserves attention as an instructive glimpse at entrepreneurs at work. In 1987

---

[12] *Irish Times*, 19 December 1991, p. 16.
[13] These included Waterford Wedgwood, AT Cross, The State Forestry Company, Pulse Engineering, Wang, Don Bluth Entertainment, Airmotive (an Aer Lingus subsidiary), Smith & Nephew, Master Pork Packers, and "doubts" about Apple Computers in Cork. *Irish Times*, 21 August 1992, p. 1.

Goodman International, the largest Irish cattle export firm, wanted to export beef to Iraq, then at war with Iran and so a risky market. In the Spring of 1987 the chief Larry Goodman, a friend of Prime Minister Haughey and contributor to Fianna Fail, obtained state export insurance to cover beef exports so that if Iraq defaulted Irish taxpayers were stuck with the tab. This insurance was granted even though other state officials had discouraged it and despite the fact that Goodman was under investigation for fraud (and subsequently found guilty). Goodman then shipped to Iraq £150 million worth of beef; much of it reportedly "old." The Iraqis defaulted. But the Irish government canceled the insurance when officials discovered 40 percent of the beef was not even Irish in origin. Goodman International went bankrupt and sued the state for £180 billion.

A second strand of the Goodman web of scandal were the negotiatons with the IDA that same year. "We were talking about picking winners," a former civil servant in Industry and Commerce pleaded.[14] The policy goal was to concentrate the cattle export industry in the hands of Goodman (with virtual monopoly power over native farmers) and one other firm. This objective invoked the Telesis Report recommendations though in a cursory and opportunistic fashion. To this ill-considered end the state was to pitch in £90 million drawn from IDA, European, and other sources. Prime Minister Haughey freely admitted that he "pressurized the IDA to bring forward this scheme."[15] Haughey, who also supported the blanket export credit insurance, pressed the IDA in May 1987 to drop a jobs performance clause it wanted inserted into the contract.[16] Was this a sound economic initiative or "blatant favoritism"? As of this writing, the inquiry continues.

The IDA scheme never got under way but the Goodman inquiry eventually brought down the government. Premier Albert Reynolds was Minister of Industry and Commerce at the time and so was involved in the Goodman deal. Reynolds at beef tribunal hearings accused Coalition partner Desmond O'Malley, who had persistently attacked Fianna Fail, of being "reckless, irresponsible and dishonest." The internal furor led to a rupture in the Coalition and a declaration of an election three days later.

---

[14] *Sunday Tribune*, 12 April 1992, p. 6.   [15] *Sunday Tribune* (Ireland) 22 March 1992.
[16] *Irish Times*, 11 October 1992.

SCANDALS AND SYSTEM

The unraveling of the Fianna Fail–Progressive Democrat coalition owed more to iniquities than inequities, to tales of juicy financial scams rather than ideologically charged conflict. Nonetheless, the scandals made visible an underlying systemic problem of collusion. In the 1990 presidential election Labour's Mary Robinson won a stunning victory over Fianna Fail. By the eve of the 1992 election the leaders of the three small parties (Labour, the Workers Party, and the Progressive Democrats) – two left-wing, one right-wing – led Fianna Fail and Fine Gael in popularity. Overall, support for leftist and independent candidates rose from under a fifth to a quarter of the population.

Were systemic remedies in the offing? Not directly. Hardiman pinpoints the lack of incentives in the Irish system for parties to produce coherent class-oriented policy options, and suggests that "the government must facilitate the articulation of class-oriented interests, within parliament and without."[17] The problem is that this development is one which neither Fianna Fail nor Fine Gael desire.[18] What the major parties ideally want is a highly centralized trade union movement (not to mention, a centralized employer association which came about in January 1992 when the FIE and CII merged into the Irish Business and Employers Confederation) that can deliver wage restraint yet is bereft of the strong class identity and interests that challenge employers' prerogatives or may become the basis for forming a majority party under another banner.

Claiming trade unions "no longer enjoyed the bargaining advantage they had previously possessed" is possibly true if this "advantage" is construed as the capacity to compel employers to negotiate in good faith.[19] But the complaints by employers associations that unions have too much power were always largely rhetoric, apart from the truism that *any* degree of union power is by definition too much.[20] Certainly, the 1992 attempt to claw back public sector pay

[17] Hardiman, *Pay, Politics and Economic Performance*, p. 198.
[18] Bew, et al., *The Dynamic of Irish Politics*, p. 123.
[19] Hardiman, *Pay, Politics and Economic Performance*, p. 217.
[20] *Ibid.*, p. 178. The FUE in the 1970s thought that the "advantage in industrial relations rested to an excessive degree with the unions and that legislative action was needed to correct the imbalance." This is because "concerted agreements gave the trade unions

hardly was the behavior of a state that was inclined to knuckle under, or to favor, labor. As the ICTU general secretary protested, the public pay in question was "more accurately described as overdue payments or monies which the government has borrowed from its staff as interest-free four-year loans," and amounted to less than uncollected capital gains taxes.[21] However, despite mutual frustrations, neither the government nor the unions are inclined to end the institutional bargaining process.[22]

After the December 1992 election a jilted Fine Gael Party chided Labour for proceeding to consort with sleazy Fianna Fail, and ritualistically rued both parties for their "over-optimistic belief in state intervention." But nothing could be more optimistic than to expect unbridled private enterprise to save the economy. Even Fine Gael leader John Bruton earlier had pronounced the state-subsidized private enterprise policy a failure.[23]

In the decade since the Telesis Report the Irish spent £4.5 bn to net 7,000 industrial jobs. The corporate sector also enjoyed an explosion in tax relief amounting to another £3 bn over the 1980s, and perhaps several times that amount.[24] The IDA estimated the cost per job at £14,300 but another study found the Irish paid £228,000 per job. On adding tax relief, European Social Fund money and all other aids one got a figure of £500,000 per job.[25] A wag in the Green Party figured on a calculator that at 4.5 bn one could divide the sum into £18,000 per unemployed person.[26]

Despite emigration, cutbacks, and massive aid to industry there were 35,000 fewer people working in Ireland than a decade previously. Economic remedies were spectacularly ineffective and so

---

direct access to government and some would say, an unprecedented input to policy" (p. 247). On the other hand, Hardiman notes that governments threatened to impose statutory controls upon unions to "hasten" collective wage bargains in 1970, 1975, 1976 and 1979 – which is not ordinarily deemed an indicator of the awesome power of, or a sign of favor for, the group so threatened (p. 215). My interviews with trade unionists indicate they had a very sober – some would say too sober – sense of their limits both in the spheres of industrial relations and in political concertative bargaining.

[21] *Irish Times*, 18 December 1991, p. 1.
[22] Saying that "class or sectional politics would be economic suicide," new Prime Minister Albert Reynolds restated old party themes. "Fianna Fail stands for the co-operative and humane working of the economy and of society for the good of all and not the chosen few. This is a vital and ever more important role as society becomes more fragmented and less cohesive." *Irish Times*, 30 December 1991, p. 1.
[23] *Irish Times*, 4 October 1992.   [24] *Irish Times*, 5 April 1992.
[25] *Sunday Tribune*, 29 March 1992.
[26] *Sunday Tribune*, 5 April 1992, p. 41.

the political stance that there was no choice was wearing thin. "Adjustment fatigue," the Irish Central Bank came to call it. Even Garret Fitzgerald made a case for "relaxation of budget constraints" for spending because the gap between economic and social performance is "increasingly intolerable."[27]

EUROPEAN CHOICES?

Might European Community funds revive Ireland? An expensive government propaganda campaign was mounted in 1992 to stave off a seconding of Denmark's nay vote to the Maastricht Treaty on a common monetary and defense policy. Prime Minister Reynolds denied a correctly attributed remark by a government official that the government must "strike terror into the hearts" of the Irish public to win consent for the Maastricht treaty.[28] There were implied threats that CAP funding – already down due to reforms of price supports of cereals, beef, and milk – would be removed entirely to punish recalcitrant voters.[29] In June the Irish endorsed the treaty by a 69.1 percent vote despite many citizens saying they still didn't know what to make of it. One editor regretted the "chorus of consensus that shut out critical perspectives" on the Maastricht vote.[30]

Prime Minister Reynolds wangled an EC commitment of £8 bn in total Structural and Cohesion funds for infrastructure spending over seven years. But there was certainly room for skepticism about the EC as a pure economic boon. The Irish GNP per capita was 59.2 percent of the EC average in 1973 and, on paper, reached 69 percent in 1992. But this gain was illusory because, after adjusting for repatriated profits and debt payments, the figure falls to 61.4 percent,[31] which was lower than the 1960 figure of 62.3 percent. Unemployment was five times higher than at entry, and critics wondered what influence 15 representatives can possibly wield among 550 European parliament members.[32] Clearly, prosperity

---

[27] *Irish Times*, 1 August 1992. [28] *Sunday Tribune*, 26 April 1992.

[29] *Irish Times*, 26 January 1992.

[30] Vincent Browne, "Media guilty of Supporting EC Consensus," *Sunday Tribune*, 21 June 1992, p. A15.

[31] *Irish Times*, 8 March 1992.

[32] Raymond Crotty, "Treaty Not Good For the Plain People of Ireland," *Irish Times*, 3 December 1991.

has more to do with distributional policies – at the domestic and EC levels – than with simply setting the country adrift on a rising tide.[33]

The stress of keeping up with German interest rates came to the fore in the winter of 1992–93. When Britain and Italy left the Exchange Rate Mechanism in September the Irish currency appreciated by 20 percent against the British pound and about 10 percent versus continental trading partners over six months. This hurt exporters while also hitting mortgage-holders and investment because of interest rate hikes to preserve currency value. Under speculative pressure (including, it was charged, speculation by some Irish banks) the Irish punt finally devalued in the Spring. The formula of high interest rates and overvalued currency added up to the dead end of deflation and unemployment.

That adverse experience underscores another latent aspect of EC monetary rules, which is that the "only competitive leverage left to the states to reduce their manpower costs and improve competitiveness is a dismantling of social service systems. Already in Spain and Ireland, but also in Belgium and the Netherlands, the EMU [European Monetary Union] is cited as a reason for reducing social services."[34] Nonetheless, the two Left parties are committed to work within the EC wherein Labour leader Spring, for example, said the concern should be for developing "new instruments to ensure a fair share for all the regions, and not simply those at the center."

THE 1992 ELECTION

In negotiations after the December 1992 election Labour rejected Fine Gael as a coalition partner (together with the Democratic Left and/or possibly the Progressive Democrats) because the latter was too "condescending and patronizing." The two Left parties, however, underwent internal change – drastic in one case – and a *rapprochement*. Labour, like its British counterpart, softened its stances on nationalization, mortgage relief, and property taxes in order to appeal to middle-class voters. Meanwhile the Workers Party underwent a split, partly because of the end of the cold war. In March 1992 six of seven Workers Party Deputies bolted to form

---

[33] For a social Democratic appraisal of the EC see George Ross, "After Maastricht: Hard Choices for Europe," *World Policy Journal* 9, 3 (Summer 1992).

[34] *Irish Times*, 31 December 1992, Supplement, p. 3.

the Democratic Left Party. The rumor that the Official IRA sup-
plemented party funds through illegal activities was an embarrass-
ment to parliamentary members, as were aspects of the party's
economic strategy which smacked of a bygone East European socialism and which were already being shed. The objective was to break
with a "closed disciplinary organizational style," promote an open
internal structure, and generate feasible alternatives.

There was already a wider latitude for left cooperation in earlier
inter-party contacts when the Workers Party was intact. The Democratic Left held talks with the Labour Party and worked out accords
on mutually desired policies, which were used in a joint election
document in 1992 though the parties also published separate
manifestoes. (One sign of Left *rapprochement* was a Democratic Left
Party campaign advertisement pairing Fianna Fail with "No
change," themslves with "Real change," and a conciliating identifi-
cation of Labour with "Some change.")

Labour was certain to improve its count (and in the election
exceeded the 27 or 28 seats predicted). So although party leader
Albert Reynolds denounced Labour's plan for a once-off 50 percent
rise in borrowing to fund job-creating projects as "indefensible and
irresponsible," Fianna Fail's Brian Lenihan pleaded with supporters
to transfer votes to Labour which he said, like Fianna Fail, had "its
root in social radicalism"and was "not hung up on" a fetish for
"unfettered private enterprise."[35] Here the end of the cold war had a
salutary effect because "playing the red card" *vis-à-vis* Labour was no
longer a credible or advantageous tactic. In the December election
the Labour Party doubled its parliamentary seats from 16 to an historic high of 33 and, after lengthy and suspenseful negotiations,
formed a government with Fianna Fail on 12 January. The new coalition's program promised to be the most progressive ever attempted.

Under EC strictures borrowing is not to exceed 3 percent and
Labour agreed to observe this limit although a rise remained possible. Fianna Fail agreed to halt privatization and to use funds from
past privatization for spending and to provide more equity to state
companies such as Aer Lingus and Bord na Mona and thus alter the
"perverse investment policy" cited earlier.

Labour also won Fianna Fail's assent to create a state bank for
investment. County Enterprise Development Boards were initiated

---

[35] *Irish Times*, 22 November 1992.

to stir local initiatives and fit schemes regionally. The new government would proceed to split the IDA into a domestic branch (called "Forbairt," incorporating the Trade Board and Eolas) and a foreign branch. The Department of Industry and Commerce already was undergoing changes in order to focus on policy. The coalition favored the Culliton report which recommended against extending the 10 percent corporate tax rate beyond 2010 or extending it to other sectors, toward a shift of repayable grants in form of equity, and concentrating more resources on fewer firms to develop a niche sector market.

The EC Cohesion Funds will go to an employment creation fund of £250 million which will triple over time and be applied to public works such as port, waste treatment, road, and rail. The coalition partners agreed on mortgage relief to ease pressure from recent rate hikes. Child care payments are up and there is a pledge to intensify tax-collection and enforcement procedures so as to "ensure equality between those on PAYE, the self-employed, and those with substantial investment incomes."

The new government would establish special savings accounts with 10 percent tax to encourage investment in equities. Labour pressed for a doubling of housing starts to 3,500, and an injection of cash to reduce hospital waiting lists and to help HIV/AIDS sufferers. There would be structures for safeguarding the rights of consumers and helping the homeless.

A National Economic and Social Forum was to be established as a new corporatist center – a candidate as the key brokering mechanism – for devising initiatives in job creation and was to include not only the usual social partners but representatives for women, the unemployed, and the disabled. The government created three new ministries: Enterprise and Employment, Tourism and Foreign Trade, and Equality. The gamble undertaken is that a surge of non-inflationary demand and employment can be generated through infrastructure spending, training, and wage subsidy schemes and minor tax reform while the government and the interest groups confer in corporatist settings to devise an equitable scheme of adjustment. There is genuine evidence here of a breakthrough by groups carrying forward social democratic alternatives. Though the 2–1 seat advantage of Fianna Fail in coalition militates against implementing a Labour "wish list," the left wing within the larger party is sympathetic to many Labour stances.

CONCLUSION

I have argued that international economic forces do not determine the precise policy response of a given state or the definition of interest by internal actors as to policy preferences. This presupposes some degree of choice and the presence of resources that make choice possible. Global economic shifts and shocks are "interpreted" by dominant coalitions in ways congruent with upholding their power against challengers who can gain from altered patterns of state activity. Powerful actors may deliberately exacerbate national economic sensitivity (that is, reliance on external agents) when the means for diminishing it are present. External forces and agents are (far from tame) pieces on the domestic political game board in the pursuit of domestic advantages. Economic adversity, when acute and protracted, can erode the propensity of subordinate strata (and components of the dominant coalition) to defer to the development policy and adjustment schemes, thus triggering a "situation of indeterminacy" over policy content and outcome within policy networks, within the dominant coalition, and between the latter and non-elites.

The politics of debt offers examples of state responses to declining "deference." The International Monetary Fund supplies particular domestic actors with internal leverage in their struggles over policy content, and the IMF, in turn, requires a "stabilizing cadre" within the state to promote its standard structural adjustment formula.[36] The IMF is not the only agent invoked for purposes of exerting local leverage nor is the function invariably malign. For example, when Washington pressured Israel, an exceptional sort of debtor, to put its finances in some semblance of order: "the message that Israeli leaders tacitly convey is that they welcome Washington's discipline," an analyst shrewdly noted. "It helps them make a case for austerity in their bids for consensus at home."[37]

But when arcane economic forces become embodied in

---

[36] Stephen Haggard, "The Politics of Adjustment: Lessons From The IMF's Extended Fund Facility," in Miles Kahler, ed., *The Politics of International Debt* (Ithaca: Cornell University Press, 1986), p. 186. Also, on the IMFs "profoundly ideological role," see Robert Wood, "The International Monetary Fund and The World Bank in a Changing World Economy," in Arthur MacEwan and William K. Tabb, eds., *Instability and Changes in The World Economy* (New York: Monthly Review Press, 1989), pp. 298–315.
[37] Milton Viorst, "Israel Faces its Economic Woes," *The Nation*, 16 March 1985, p. 304.

institutional agents, the market begins to appear in popular perceptions as a coterie of affluent aliens who determine over tax-deductible lunches how long the locals tighten their belts. The market no longer is an inexorable and intangible power. Accordingly, in the mid-1980s restive publics in Argentina, Brazil, Venezuela, and the Dominican Republic compelled their governments to tread warily toward fiscal rectitude. Mexico counted on ruling party ties to trade unions to enforce severe austerity measures. In Nigeria a military government imposed IMF-approved structural adjustment on a resistant population; it took bayonets to prove that there was no "alternative."[38]

Although social disturbances do not distress bankers, institutional instability does. When the capacity of states to enforce rules diminishes, international banks and lending agencies consider conciliatory measures. "It's not a case that we ignored the deadline," a bank negotiator said of Bolivia, "there was no one to talk to," because the country was undergoing its ninth cabinet change in two years, not to mention five general strikes.[39] Declining deference by subordinate strata allows governments a breathing space –whether they want it or not – when dealing with international lenders but not, of course, a reprieve. These situations may stir policy entrepreneurs lodged in the state to search for adjustment packages that broaden the scope of "orthodox" options available in the international lending regime.

A widespread decline in deference provides local elites with opportunities as well as dangers. Even where their own misfiring strategies are to blame, a dominant domestic coalition can co-opt populist pressures into a more "nationalist" course to restore their authority. Though this is an unlikely Irish scenario, the Latin American Debt Commission in the 1980s noted: "In every Latin American and Caribbean country there are major pressures to turn inward, to reject cooperation with the IMF, to turn their backs on existing obligations and to look for solutions which stress a higher degree of protectionism and states control."[40]

Popular attention may be diverted from local shortcomings by pointing fingers at foreign villains. But any act repudiating international market forces or agencies is a hazardous precedent for local

---

[38] Biersteker, "Structural Adjustment" (mimeo, 1990).
[39] *New York Times*, 5 February 1985.
[40] *New York Times*, 11 March 1984.

elites to set. Although local capital and foreign banks may prefer Pinochets, the military option and Chicago-style economics are at least temporarily discredited in the larger debtors.[41] Even the Nigerian military government feels compelled to promise repeatedly that it will return to civilian rule.[42] This configuration of circumstances enhances the importance of studying how "situations of indeterminacy" regarding state strategy, coalition formation, and debt negotiation are contained or exploited by domestic contestants for political power.

This volume has focused on a democratic dependent state pursuing, and coping with the consequences of, a "peripheral post-industrial" development. The term denotes (1) a policy-induced diffusion of high tech affiliates with the objective of installing them as the leading sector (or, as the IDA puts it, "fermentation ground"), (2) a truncated form of development (low linkages, meager R & D, less sophisticated elements), and (3) an ideological expression of prevailing export-led policy designed to counteract the political exhaustion of a development phase. The latter was a strong motive of Irish elites, given that a state-capitalist alternative were ruled out. The adverse effects of "peripheral post-industrialism" are most acute in states deploying a few weak policy instruments (the "catalytic" mode). But the problems cited here are manifested across the spectrum of regime types, developmental levels, modes of intervention, and state–society configuration.

South Korea and Taiwan use statist approaches for promoting their electronic sectors within an integrated development scheme. Still they rely, despite some gains, primarily on Japan for technology generation. Apart from Northern protectionism, the NICs and LDCs face formidable internal obstacles to the creation of autonomous R & D systems. But advanced industrial nations also confront problems regarding the formulation or adaptation of institutional policy mechanisms for promoting competitive efficiency while moderating the costs and distributing the benefits.[43]

The interaction of high tech development with market patterns exerts pressures on states to resort to subtle protectionist measures,

---

[41] See R. Kaufman, "Democratic and Authoritarian Responses to the Debt Issue," in Kahler, *The Politics of International Debt*.

[42] Biersteker, "Structural Adjustment."

[43] Gosta Esping-Anderson, *The Three Worlds of Welfare Capitalism* (Princeton: Princeton University Press, 1990), pp. 9–35 and 221–29.

domestic deflationary schemes, or perhaps even creative adjustment policies and the exploration of new cooperative arrangement of costs and benefits of economic growth. In the absence of a persuasive alternative program wedded to a potent social coalition, a panoply of policy instruments and a wealth of organizational resources will make little impact. Even Scandinavian polities, noted for sophisticated concertation and conciliation mechanisms, have difficulties in the 1990s navigating through a changing international division of labor and patterns of trade.[44] In this sense, harking back to the *Ulysses* quote, the Irish truly have arrived in Europe.

Markets and high technology both offer indispensable rewards. But, as the scramble for advantageous niches continues globally, political pressures will mount for leaders to devise means to avert the negative effects. "Perhaps the profoundest problem that faces society," Paul Goodman observed decades ago, "is to decide in what functions the computer style is not relevant – and therefore to curtail and forget it."[45] The same may be said for the role of markets, and when deference to what John Kenneth Galbraith terms the "conventional wisdom" is declining, this social task begins.

For, as many scholars have observed, it is the contradictions in capitalism, and particularly the deviations from textbook dictums, that have enabled Western societies not only to chase progress but to achieve their degrees of democracy and prosperity.[46]

[44] J. Faberberg, A. Cappelen, L. Mjoset, R. Skarstein, "The Decline of Social Democratic State Capitalism in Norway," *New Left Review* 181 (1990), pp.60–94.

[45] P. Goodman, *People or Personnel and Like a Conquered Province* (New York: Random House, 1986), p. 76.

[46] Dietrich Rueschemeyer, Evelyn H. Stephens, and John Stephens, *Capitalist Development and Democracy* (Oxford: Polity Press, 1992), p. 302, and Block, *Postindustrial Possibilities*, "The successes of capitalist development are a product of limitations on market freedom" (p. 46).

Bibliography

Adler, Emanuel. "Ideological 'Guerrillas' and The Quest for Technological Autonomy: Brazil's Domestic Computer Industry," *International Organization* 40, 3 (Summer 1986).

Allen, Robert and Tara Jones. *Guests of The Nation: The People of Ireland versus The Multinationals* (London: Earthscape Publications, 1990).

Almond, Gabriel. "The Return To The State," *American Political Science Review* 82, 3 (September 1988).

Anderson, Charles. "Public Policy and The Complex Organization: The Problem of Governance and The Further Evolution of Advanced Industrial Society," in Leon Lindberg, *Politics and The Future of Industrial Society* (New York: David McKay, 1976).

Arnold, Bruce. *What Kind of Country? Modern Irish Politics 1968–1983* (London: Jonathan Cape, 1984).

Baker, Susan. "Nationalist Ideology and The Industrial Policy of Fianna Fail: The Evidence of The Irish Press," *Irish Political Studies* 1, 1 (1986).

"Dependent Industrialisation and Political Protest: Raybestos Manhattan in Ireland," *Government and Opposition* 22, 3 (Summer 1987).

Baran, Paul. *The Political Economy of Growth* (New York: Monthly Review Press, 1957).

Baran, Paul and Paul Sweezy. *Monopoly Capital: An Essay On The American Economic and Social Order* (London: Pelican, 1968).

Becker, David. *The New Bourgeoisie and The Limits of Dependency* (Princeton: Princeton University Press, 1983).

Becker, David, Jeff Frieden, Sayre P. Schatz, and Richard Sklar, eds. *Postimperialism: International Capitalism and Development in The Twentieth Century* (Boulder: Lynn Rienner, 1987).

Beckett, J. C. *The Making of Modern Ireland, 1603–1923* (New York: Knopf, 1966).

Beer, Samuel. *British Politics In The Collectivist Age* (New York: Vintage, 1969).

Bell, Daniel. *The Coming of Post-Industrial Society* (London: Penguin, 1973).

Bell, J. Bowyer. *The Secret Army: A History of The IRA 1916–70* (London: Sphere Books, 1972).

Bendix, Reinhard. *Nation-Building and Citizenship: Studies of Our Changing Social Order* (Berkeley: University of California Press, 1977).

Bergsten, C. Fred, Thomas Horst, and Theodore H. Moran. *American Multinationals and American Interests* (New York: Brookings Institution, 1978).

Bernstein, Henry and Howard Nichols. "Pessimism of The Intellect, Pessimism of The Will: A Response To Gunder Frank," *Development and Change* 14, 4 (October 1983).

Bew, Paul and Henry Patterson. *Sean Lemass and The Making of Modern Ireland* (Dublin: Gill and Macmillan, 1982).

Bew, Paul, Ellen Hazelkorn and Henry Patterson. *The Dynamics of Irish Politics* (London: Lawrence and Wishart, 1989).

Biersteker, Thomas. "Structural Adjustment and the Political Transition in Nigeria" (Mimeo, 1990).

    Multinationals, The State, and Control of The Nigerian Economy (Princeton: Princeton University Press, 1987).

    Distortion or Development? Contending Perspectives on The Multinational Corporation (Cambridge: MIT Press, 1979).

Block, Fred. *Post-Industrial Possibilities: A Critique of Economic Discourse* (Berkeley: University of California Press, 1990).

    The Origins of International Economic Disorder (Berkeley: University of California Press, 1977).

Bluestone, Barry and Bennett Harrison. *The Great U-Turn: The Restructuring of Industry and The Polarizing of America* (New York: Basic Books, 1989).

Breen, Richard, Damian F. Hannan, David B. Rottman, and Christopher T. Whelan. *Understanding Contemporary Ireland: State, Class and Development in The Republic of Ireland* (Dublin: Gill and Macmillan, 1990).

Brewer, Anthony. *Marxist Theories of Imperialism* (London: Routledge and Kegan Paul, 1982).

Bristow, John. "State Sponsored Bodies," in Frank Litton, ed., *Unequal Achievement: The Irish Experience 1957–1982* (Dublin: Institute of Public Administration, 1982).

Brown, Terence. *Ireland: A Social and Cultural History* (London: Fontana, 1985, 2nd ed.).

Browne, Noel C. *Against The Tide* (Dublin: Gill and Macmillan, 1986).

Browne, Vincent, John Feeney, John Howard. "Don't Cry Just Yet for Ferenka," *Magill 6*, 1 (December 1977).

Burk, Kathleen and Alec Cairncross. *Goodbye Great Britain: The 1976 IMF Crisis* (New Haven: Yale University Press, 1992).

Burnham, Walter Dean. *The Current Crisis in American Politics* (New York: Oxford University Press, 1984).

Cameron, David R. "Does Government Cause Inflation? Taxes, Spending and Deficits," in Leon Lindberg and Charles Maier, eds., *The Politics of Inflation and Economic Stagnation* (Washington: Brookings Institution, 1985).

Cammack, Paul. "Bringing The State Back In?" *British Journal of Political Science* 19, 2 (April 1989).

Cardoso, Fernando. "Associated Dependent Development: Theoretical and Practical Implications," in Alfred Stepan, ed., *Authoritarian Brazil* (New Haven: Yale University Press, 1973).

Cardoso, Fernando and Enzo Faletto. *Dependency and Development in Latin America* (Berkeley: University of California Press, 1979).

Carey, N. S., ed. *Politics, Public Enterprise and The Industrial Development Agency: Industrialization Policies and Practices* (London: Croom Helm, 1974).

Carnoy, Martin. *The State and Political Theory* (Princeton: Princeton University Press, 1984).

Carr, Raymond. *Puerto Rico: A Colonial Experiment* (New York: Vintage, 1984).

Chomsky, Noam. "Objectivity and Liberal Scholarship," in James Peck, ed., *The Chomsky Reader* (New York: Pantheon, 1987).

Chubb, Basil. *The Government and Politics of Ireland* (Oxford: OUP, 1970; Stanford: Stanford University Press, 1982, 2nd ed.).

Cabinet Government in Ireland (Dublin: Institute of Public Administration, 1974).

Chubb, Basil and Patrick K. Lynch, eds. *Economic Development and Planning* (Dublin: Institute of Public Administration, 1969).

Clarke, Jeremy and Vincent Gable. "The Asian Electronics Industry," *IDS Bulletin, Institute of Development Studies* 13, 2 (1982).

Coates, David *Labour In Power?* (New York: Longman, 1980).

The Labour Party and The Struggle for Socialism (Cambridge: Cambridge University Press, 1975).

Cohan, Al. *The Irish Political Elite* (Dublin: Gill and Macmillan, 1973).

Cohen, Stephen S. *Modern Capitalist Planning: The French Model* (Berkeley: University of California Press, 1977).

Collier, David, ed. *The New Authoritarianism in Latin America* (Princeton: Princeton University Press, 1979).

Connelen, Liam. "Industrial Policy," *Irish Banking Review*, March 1983.

Coogan, Tim Pat. *Disillusioned Decades: Ireland 1966–87* (Dublin: Gill and Macmillan, 1987).

Cooper, Charles. "Science, Technology and Development," *Economic and Social Review* 2, 2 (January 1971).

Cooper, Charles and Noel Whelan. *Science Technology and Industry in Ireland* (Dublin: National Science Council, 1973).

Cooper, Richard N. *The Economics of Interdependence* (New York: McGraw-Hill, 1966).

Corrigan, Josephine. *Business and Sales Taxation in The Republic of Ireland* (New York: Praeger, 1971).

Coughlin, Anthony. *The Common Market: Why Ireland Should Not Join* (Dublin: Common Market Study Group, 1970).

"The Economics of Independence," *The Ripening of Time* 5, 1 (November 1976).

Cranley, Martin. "The National Resources of Ireland," *Administration* 8, 1 (1976).

Crotty, Raymond. *A Radical's Response* (Dublin: Poolbeg, 1988).

Ireland In Crisis: A Study in Capitalist Colonial Development (Dingle: Brandon Press, 1986).

"Capitalist Colonialism and Peripheralisation: The Irish Case," in Dudley Seers, ed., *Underdeveloped Europe* (Atlantic Highlands, NJ: Humanities Press, 1979).

Irish Agricultural Production: Its Structure and Output (Cork: Cork University Press, 1966).

Crozier, Michel, Samuel Huntington, and J. Watanuki. *The Crisis of Democracy* (New York: New York University, 1975).

Cullen, L. M. *An Economic History of Ireland Since 1660* (London: B.T. Batsford, 1972).

Cullen, L. M., ed. *The Formation Of The Irish Economy* (Cork: Mercier Press, 1968).

Cumings, Bruce. "The Origins of The North-East Asian Political Economy: Industrial Sectors, Product Cycles and Political Consequences," *International Organization* 38, 1 (Winter 1984).

Curtis, L. Perry. *Apes and Angels: The Irishman in Victorian Caricature* (Washington DC: Smithsonian Institution, 1971).

Dahl, Robert. *Dilemmas of Pluralist Democracy* (New Haven: Yale University Press, 1982).

"On Removing Certain Impediments to Democracy in the United States," *Dissent* 25, 3 (Summer 1978).

Dahrendorf, Ralf, ed. *Europe's Economies in Crisis* (London: Weidenfeld and Nicolson, 1982).

Derwin, Des. "Talk Bread, and The Bakery," *Left Perspectives* 2, 2 (Summer 1982).

Dickson, Tony, ed. *Scottish Capitalism* (London: Lawrence and Wishart, 1980).

Donaldson, Lorraine. *Development Planning in Ireland* (New York: Praeger, 1966).

Dos Santos, Theotonio. "The Crisis of Development Theory and the Problem of Dependence in Latin America," in Henry Bernstein, ed., *Underdevelopment and Development in The Third World* (London: Penguin, 1973).

Dosi, Giovanni, et al. eds. *Technical Change and Economic Theory* (London: Frances Pinter Press, 1990).

Durkan, Joe. "The Irish Economy: The Recent Experience and Prospective Future Performance," in Brendan R. Dowling and Joe Durkan, eds., *The Irish Economy* (Dublin: Economic and Social Research Institute, 1978).

Duvall, Raymond and John Freeman. "International Economic Relations and The Entrepreneurial State," *Economic Development and Cultural Change* 32, 2 (1984).

"The Technobureaucratic Elite and The Entrepreneurial State in Dependent Industrialization," *American Political Science Review* 77, 3 (1983).

Edwards, Owen Dudley, ed. *Conor Cruise O'Brien Introduces Ireland* (Dublin: Gill and Macmillan, 1969).

Edwards, Owen Dudley and T. Desmond Williams, eds. *The Great Hunger* (New York: New York University Press, 1973).

Ellis, P. Beresford. *A History of The Irish Working Class* (London: Gollancz, 1972).

Elsenhans, Hartmut. "Rising Mass Incomes as a Condition of Capitalist Growth: Implications for the World Economy," *International Organization* 37, 2 (Spring 1983).

Esping-Andersen, Gosta. *The Three Worlds of Welfare Capitalism* (Princeton: Princeton University Press, 1990).

Esping-Anderson, Gosta, Roger Friedland, and Erik Olin Wright. "Modes of Class Struggle and The Capitalist State," *Kapitalistate* (Summer 1973).

Evans, Peter. "Declining Hegemony and Assertive Industrialization: U.S.–Brazil Conflicts in The Computer Industry," *International Organization* 43, 2 (Spring 1989).

Dependent Development (Princeton: Princeton University Press, 1979).

Evans, Peter, Dietrich Rueschemeyer, and Theda Skocpol, eds. *Bringing The State Back In* (Cambridge: Cambridge University Press, 1985).

Fagerberg, Jan, Adne Cappelen, Lars Mjoset, and Rune Skarstein. "The Decline of Social-Democratic State Capitalism in Norway," *New Left Review* 181 (May–June 1990).

Fanning, Ronan. "The Great Enchantment: Uses and Abuses of Modern Irish History," in James A. Dooge, ed., *Ireland in The Contemporary World: Essays in Honour of Garret Fitzgerald* (Dublin: Gill and Macmillan, 1986).

The Irish Department of Finance 1922–1958 (Dublin: Institute of Public Management, 1978).

Farrell, Brian. *Sean Lemass* (Dublin: Gill and Macmillan, 1983).

The Founding of Dail Eireann: Parliament and Nation-Building (Dublin: Gill and Macmillan, 1973).

Fitzgerald, Garret. *Toward A New Ireland* (Dublin: Torc Books, 1973).

Planning in Ireland (Dublin: Institute of Public Administration, 1968).

State Sponsored Bodies (Dublin: Institute of Public Administration, 1963).

Fitzpatrick, David. *Politics in Irish Life 1914–1921* (Dublin: Gill and Macmillan, 1977).

Foster, Roy F. "Ascendency and Union," in Roy F. Foster, ed., *The Oxford History of Ireland* (Oxford: Oxford University Press, 1992).

Modern Ireland 1600–1972 (London: Penguin, 1989).

Foster-Carter, Aidan, "From Rostow To Gunder Frank: Conflicting Paradigms in The Analysis of Underdevelopment," *World Development* 4, 3 (March 1976).

Frank, Andre Gunder. "What Is To Be Done With Straw Men?" *Development and Change* 14, 4 (October 1983).

Capitalism and Underdevelopment in Latin America (New York: Monthly Review Press, 1969).

Freeman, Christopher, John Clark, and Luc Soete, *Unemployment and Technical Innovation* (London: Frances Pinter Press, 1982).

Freeman, John R. *Democracy and Markets: The Politics of Mixed Economies* (Ithaca: Cornell University Press, 1989).

"State Entrepreneurship and Dependent Development," *American Journal of Political Science* 26, 2 (1983).

Freiden, Jeff. "The Indebted Emerald Isle" (mimeo, 1984).

Friedrichs, Guenter and Adam Schaff. *Microelectronics and Society* (New York: Mentor, 1982).

Galbraith, John Kenneth. *Economics and The Public Purpose* (New York: Houghton Mifflin, 1973).

Gallagher, Michael. *The Irish Labour Party in Transition 1957–82* (Manchester: Manchester University Press, 1982).

Garvin, Tom. *The Evolution of Irish Nationalism* (Dublin: Gill and Macmillan, 1981).

Gereffi, Gary. *The Pharmaceutical Industry and Dependency in The Third World* (Princeton: Princeton University Press, 1983).

Gerschenkron, Alexander. *Economic Backwardness in Historical Perspective* (Cambridge, Mass: Harvard University Press, 1962).

Gibson, Norman and John Spencer, eds. *Economic Activity in Ireland: A Study of Two Open Economies* (Dublin: Gill and Macmillan, 1977).

Gilmore, George. "The Failure of Republicanism," *The Ripening of Time* 5, 1 (November 1976).

Gilpin, Robert. *The Political Economy of International Relations* (Princeton: Princeton University Press, 1987).

Goodman, Geoffrey. *The Miners Strike* (London: Pluto Press, 1985).

Goodman, Paul. *People or Personnel and Like A Conquered Province* (New York: Random House, 1968).

Gouldner, Alvin W. *The Dialectic of Ideology and Technology* (New York: Seabury Books, 1976).

Gourevitch, Peter. "Keynesian Politics: The Political Sources of Economic Policy Choices," in Peter Hall, ed., *The Political Power of Economic Ideas* (Princeton: Princeton University Press, 1990).

Politics In Hard Times (Ithaca: Cornell University Press, 1986).

"Breaking With Orthodoxy: The Politics of Economic Responses To The Depression of The 1930s," *International Organization* 38, 1 (1984).

Gramsci, Antonio. *Prison Notebooks* (New York: International Publishers, 1971).

Greaves, Desmond. *The Irish Transport and General Workers Union: The Formative Years 1909–1923* (Dublin: Gill and Macmillan, 1982).
The Irish Crisis (New York: International Publishers, 1974).
Grieco, Joseph. *Between Dependency and Autonomy: India's Experience with the International Computer Industry* (Berkeley: University of California Press, 1984).
Hadjimichalis, Costis. *Uneven Development and Regionalism: State, Territory and Class in Southern Europe* (London: Croom Helm, 1987).
Haggard, Stephen. *Pathways From The Periphery: The Politics of Growth in Newly Industrializing Countries* (Ithaca: Cornell University Press, 1990).
"The Politics of Adjustment: Lessons From The IMF's Extended Fund Facility," in Miles Kahler, ed., *The Politics of International Debt* (Ithaca: Cornell University Press, 1986).
Hall, Peter. *Governing The Economy* (New York: Oxford University Press, 1986).
"Patterns of Economic Policy: An Organizational Approach," in Stephen Bornstein, David Held, and Joel Krieger, eds., *The State in Capitalist Europe: A Casebook* (Cambridge: Harvard University Press, 1984).
Hall, Peter, ed. *The Political Power of Economic Ideas: Keynesianism Across Nations* (Princeton: Princeton University Press, 1989).
Hardiman, Niamh. *Pay, Politics and Economic Performance in Ireland, 1970–1987* (Oxford: Oxford University Press, 1988).
Hardiman, Niamh and Stephen Lalor. "Corporatism in Ireland: An Exchange of Views," *Administration* 32, 2 (1984).
Hargrave, Brian. *Cosgrave's Coalition" Irish Politics in The 1970s* (London: Select Editions: 1980).
Harris, Lorelei. "Class, Community and Sexual Divisions in North Mayo," in Chris Curtin, Mary Kelly, and Liam O'Dowd, eds., *Culture & Ideology in Ireland* (Galway: Galway University Press, 1984).
Hayward, Jack. "The Politics of Planning in Britain and France," *Comparative Politics* 7, 2 (January 1975).
Hayward, Jack and Michael Watson, eds. *Planning, Politics and Public Policy: The British, French and Italian Experiences* (London: Cambridge University Press, 1975).
Hechter, Michael. *Internal Colonialism: The Celtic Fringe in British National Development* (Berkeley: University of California Press, 1977).
Hirschman, Albert O. "The Turn to Authoritarianism in Latin America and The Search For Its Determinants," in David Collier, ed., *The New Authoritarianism in Latin America* (Princeton: Princeton University Press, 1979).
Exit, Voice and Loyalty (Cambridge, MA: Harvard University Press, 1970).
The Strategy of Economic Development (New Haven: Yale University Press, 1958).
Hobsbawm, Eric J. *Industry and Empire* (London: Penguin, 1971).

Hofheinz, Roy and Kent Calder. *The East Asia Edge* (New York: Basic Books, 1983).

Holland, Stuart. *Uncommon Market: Capital, Class and Power in The European Community* (London: Macmillan, 1980).

Hollingsworth, Mark. *The Press and Political Dissent* (London: Pluto Press, 1986).

Hood, Norman and Stephen Young. *Multinationals in Retreat: The Scottish Experience* (Edinburgh: Edinburgh University Press, 1982).

Hoppen, K. Theodore. *Ireland Since 1800* (New York: Longman, 1989).

Horowitz, Irving Louis. *Three Worlds of Development* (New York: Oxford University Press, 1972).

Hudson, Roy and Jim Lewis, eds. *Uneven Development in Southern Europe* (London: Methuen, 1985).

Hull, C. H., ed. *Economic Writings of Sir William Petty* (Cambridge: Cambridge University Press, 1899).

Hymer, Stephen. "The Multinational Corporation and The Law of Uneven Development," in Hugo Radice, ed., *International Firms and Modern Imperialism* (London: Penguin, 1972).

Ikenberry, John. "The Irony of State Strength: Comparative Responses To The Oil Shocks in the 1970s," *International Organization* 40, 2 (Spring 1986).

Inglehart, Ronald. *The Silent Revolution* (Princeton: Princeton University Press, 1977).

Jacobsen, J. K. "The Politics of Austerity in Ireland," *New Politics* 4, 3 (Summer 1993).

"Microchips and Public Policy: The Political Economy of High Technology," *British Journal of Political Science* 22, 4 (October 1992).

"Peripheral Postindustrialism: Ideology, High Technology and Development," in James A. Caporaso, ed., *A Changing International Division of Labor* (London: Frances Pinter Press, 1987).

"Ireland's Right Wing Rut," *The New Leader* 15 June 1987.

"Chasing Progress: The Politics of Industrial Development in Ireland" (Ph.D. diss. University of Chicago, 1982).

"Stalemate in Northern Ireland," *Dissent* 29, 1 (Winter 1982).

"The Republic of Ireland: Perils of Pragmatism," *Dissent* 27, 3 (Summer 1980).

"Irish Politics and Post-Industrial Prospects," *Third Degree* 2, 1 (Spring 1979).

"Changing Utterly?: Irish Development and The Problem of Dependence," *Studies: An Irish Quarterly Review* 268, 67 (Winter 1978).

Jacobsen, J. K. and Roger Gilman. "The Dialectical Character of Paul Feyerabend's Philosophy of Science," *Nature, Society and Thought* 4, 1–2 (Jan.–Apr. 1991).

Jacobsen, J. K. and Claus Hofhansel. "Safeguards and Profits: Civilian Nuclear Exports, Neo-Marxism and The Statist Approach," *International Studies Quarterly* 28, 2 (June 1984).

James, Jeffrey. *The Economics of New Technology in Developing Countries* (London: Frances Pinter, 1982).

Jenkins, Barbara. "Reexamining The Obsolescing Bargain: A Case Study of Canada's National Energy Policy," *International Organization* 40, 1 (Summer 1986).

Jessop, Bob. *State Theory: Putting Capitalist States in Their Place* (Oxford: Polity Press, 1990).

"Corporatism, Parliamentarianism and Social Democracy," in Philippe Schmitter and Gerhard Lehmbruch, eds., *Trends Toward Corporatist Intermediation* (New York: Sage, 1984).

Johnson, David and Liam Kennedy. "Nationalist Historiography and the Decline of the Irish Economy: George O'Brien Revisited," in Sean Hutton and Paul Stewart, eds., *Ireland's Histories: Aspects of State, Society, and Ideology* (London: Routledge, 1991).

Jonas, Susanne. "Dependency and Imperialism: The Roots of Latin American Underdevelopment," in Ira Katznelson, David Gordon, and Philip Brenner, eds. *The Politics and Society Reader* (David McKay, 1976).

Kaim-Caudle, P. R. *Social Policy in the Irish Republic* (London: Weidenfeld and Nicolson, 1967).

Katsiaouni, Olympios. "Administrative Arrangements For Planning: Some Aspects of The Irish Experience," *Administration* 26, 1 (Spring 1978).

Katzenstein, Peter. *Small States in The World Economy* (Ithaca: Cornell University Press, 1986).

Kaufman, Robert R. "Democratic and Authoritarian Responses To The Debt Issue: Argentina, Brazil, Mexico," in Miles Kahler, ed., *The Politics of International Debt* (Ithaca: Cornell University Press, 1986).

Kaufman, Robert R., Daniel S. Geller, and Harry I. Chernotsky. "A Preliminary Test of The Theory of Dependence," *Comparative Politics* 7, 3 (April 1975).

Kearney, Richard, ed. *Across The Frontiers: Ireland in the 1990s* (Dublin: Wolfhound Press, 1989).

Keatinge, Patrick. *A Place Among The Nations* (Dublin: Gill and Macmillan, 1977).

Kennedy, Kieran, ed. *Ireland in Transition: Economic and Social Change since 1960* (Cork and Dublin: Mercier Press, 1986).

Kennedy, Kieran and Denis Conniffe, eds. *Employment Policy in Ireland* (Dublin: Economic and Social Research Institute, 1986).

Kennedy, Kieran, T. Giblin, and D. McHugh. *The Economic Development of Ireland in The Twentieth Century* (London: Routledge, 1988).

Kennedy, Liam. "The Rural Economy," in Liam Kennedy and Philip Ollerenshaw, eds., *An Economic History of Ulster* (Manchester: University of Manchester Press, 1985).

Keohane, Robert. *After Hegemony* (Princeton: Princeton University Press, 1984).

Keohane, Robert, and Joseph Nye. *Power and Interdependence* (Boston: Little Brown, 1977).

Keynes, John Maynard. "National Self-Sufficiency," *Studies: An Irish Quarterly Review* 86, 2 (June 1933).

Kidron, Michael. *Western Capitalism Since The War* (London: Penguin, 1971).

Killeen, Michael J. *Industrial Development and Full Employment*, published by Industrial Development Authority, Dublin 1976.

Kolko, Joyce. *Restructuring The World Economy* (New York: Pantheon, 1988).

Krasner, Stephen. "Approaches To The State: Alternative Conceptions and Historical Dynamics," *Comparative Politics* 16, 2 (January 1984).

   Defending The National Interest (Princeton: Princeton University Press, 1978).

Krieger, Joel. *Reagan, Thatcher and the Politics of Decline* (New York: Oxford University Press, 1986).

Kumar, Krishan. *Prophecy and Progress* (London: Penguin, 1978).

Kurth, James R. "The Political Consequences of The Product Cycle: Industrial History and Political Outcomes," *International Organization* 33, 1 (Winter 1979).

Landes, David S. *The Unbound Prometheus: Technological Change and Industrial Development In Western Europe From 1750 to The Present* (London: Cambridge University Press, 1969).

Lange, Peter. "Unions, Workers and Wage Regulation," in John Goldthorpe, ed., *Order and Conflict in Contemporary Capitalism: Studies in The Political Economy of Western European Nations* (Oxford: Oxford University Press, 1984).

LaPalombara, Joseph and Stephen Blank. *Multinational Corporations in Comparative Perspective* (New York: McGraw Hill, 1977).

Lavers, Michael, Peter Mair, and Richard Sinnott. *How Ireland Voted: The Irish General Election of 1987* (Dublin: Poolbeg, 1987).

Lebow, Richard Ned. *White Britain and Black Ireland: The Influence of Stereotypes on Colonial Policy* (Philadelphia: The Institute For The Study of Human Issues, 1971).

Lee, Joseph J. *Ireland 1912–1985: Politics and Society* (Cambridge: Cambridge University Press, 1989).

   "Worker and Society Since 1945," in Donal Nevin, ed., *Trade Unions and Change in Irish Society* (Cork: Mercier Press, 1980).

   The Modernisation Of Irish Society, 1848–1918 (Dublin: Gill and Macmillan, 1973).

Lemass, Sean. "The Role of State Sponsored Bodies in the Economy," in Basil Chubb and Patrick K. Lynch, eds., *Economic Development and Plnning* (Dublin: Institute of Public Administration, 1972).

Lewis, John P. and Valeriana Kalleb, eds. *U.S. Foreign Policy and The Third World: Agenda 1983* (New York: Praeger, 1983).

Lindberg, Leon. "Energy Policy and The Politics of Economic Development," *Comparative Political Studies* 10, 3 (October 1977).

Lindberg, Leon, Claus Offe, Robert Alford, eds. *Stress and Contradiction in Modern Capitalism* (Lexington, MA: D. C. Heath, 1975).

Lindblom, Charles. *Politics and Markets* (New York: Basic Books, 1977).

Lipset, Seymour Martin and Stein Rokkan. *Party Systems and Voter Alignments* (New York: Free Press, 1967).

Lipson, Charles H. *Standing Guard: The Protection of U.S. Foreign Investment* (Berkeley: University of California, 1985).

Logan, Bruce. "The Irish Parliamentry Tradition" (Ph.D. diss. University of Chicago, 1975).

Lynch, Patrick K. "The Economic Scene," in Owen Dudley Edwards, ed., *Conor Cruise O'Brien Introduces Ireland* (Dublin: Gill and Macmillan, 1969).

"The Irish Economy Since The War," in Kevin T. Nowland and T. Desmond Williams, eds., *Ireland In The War Years and After* (Dublin: Gill and Macmillan, 1969).

"The Economics of Independence: Some Unsettled Questions of Irish Economics," *Administration* 7, 2 (1959).

Lyons, F. S. L. *Ireland Since The Famine* (London: Fontana Books, 1973).

MacAleese, Dermot. "Ireland In The Common Market," in John Vaizey, ed., *Economic Sovereignty and Regional Policy* (Dublin: Gill and Macmillan, 1978).

A Profile of Grant-Aided Industry in Ireland (Dublin: Industrial Development Authority, 1978).

"Capital Inflow and Foreign Direct Investment in Ireland 1952–70," *Journal of The Statistical and Social Inquiry Society* 22, 4 (1970–71).

McCarthy, Charles. *The Decade of Upheaval: Irish Trade Unions in The 1960s* (Dublin: Institute of Public Administration, 1973).

McDermott, Philip. "Multinational Manufacturing and Regional Development: External Control in the Scottish Electronics Industry," *Scottish Journal of Political Economy* 26, 2 (1979).

MacDonough, Oliver. *Ireland: The Union and Its Aftermath* (London: Allen and Unwin, 1977).

MacEwan, Arthur and William K. Tabb, eds. *Instability and Change in the World Economy* (New York: Monthly Review Press, 1989).

McKeon, John. "Economic Appraisal of Industrial Projects in Ireland" (mimeo, IDA 1980).

McLelland, David. *The Achieving Society* (Princeton: Von Norstrand, 1961).

McMenamin, P. S. "The Industrial Development Process in the Republic of Ireland, 1953–72," in John Vaizey, ed., *Economic Sovereignty and Regional Policy* (Dublin: Gill and Macmillan, 1976).

Mair, Peter. *The Changing Irish Party System: Organisation, Ideology and Electoral Competition* (London: Frances Pinter Press, 1987).

Manning, Maurice. *The Blueshirts* (Dublin: Gill and Macmillan, 1972).

Irish Political Parties (Dublin: Gill and Macmillan, 1972).

Martin, Andrew. "Political Constraints on Economic Strategies in Advanced Industrial Societies," *Comparative Political Studies* 7, 4 (1977).

Marx, Karl. *Capital*, vol. 1 (New York: International Publishers, 1958).

Matthews, Alan. "The Economic Consequences of EC Membership for Ireland," in David Coombes, ed., *Ireland and The Economic Community: Ten Years of Membership* (Dublin: Gill and Macmillan, 1983).

Meenan, James. *The Irish Economy Since 1922* (Liverpool: Liverpool University Press, 1972).

Merritt, Giles. *World Out of Work* (London: Collins, 1982).

Migdal, Joel. *Strong Societies and Weak States: State-Society Relations and State Capabilities in The Third World* (Princeton: Princeton University Press, 1983).

Mollenkopf, John. *The Contested City* (Princeton: Princeton University Press, 1983).

Mooney, Peter J. "Incomes Policy," in Joe Dowling and John R. Durkan, eds., *Irish Economic Policy* (Dublin: Economic and Social Research Institute, 1978).

Moore, Barrington Jr. *Reflections On The Causes of Human Misery* (Boston: Beacon Press, 1972).

Moran, Michael. "The Politics of International Business," *British Journal of Political Science* 8, 2 (April 1978).

Moran, Theodore H. "Multinational Corporations and Dependency: A Dialogue for Dependistas and Nondependentistas," *International Organization* 32, 1 (Winter 1978).

Multinational Corporations and The Politics of Dependence: Copper in Chile (Princeton: Princeton University Press, 1974).

Munck, Ronaldo. *Politics and Dependence in The Third World* (London: Zed Press, 1984).

Munger, Frank. *The Legitimacy of Opposition* (New York: Sage, 1974).

Murphy, John A. *Ireland in The Twentieth Century* (Dublin: Gill and Macmillan, 1975).

Murray, Jim and Jim Wickham. "Technocratic Ideology and The Reproduction of Inequality: The Case of the Electronics Industry in The Republic of Ireland," in G. Day, ed., *Diversity and Decomposition in the Labour Market* (Aldershot: Gower Press, 1982).

Murray, Robin. "The Internationalization of Capital and the Nation-State," *New Left Review* 67 (May–June 1971).

Mytelka, Lynn K. "Knowledge-Intensive Production and the Changing Internationalization Strategies of Multinational Firms," in James A. Caporaso, ed., *A Changing International Division of Labor* (London: Frances Pinter, 1987).

Nisbet, Robert. *Social Change and History* (London: Oxford University Press, 1969).

Nolan, Sean. "The Telesis Report – A Review Essay," *Economic and Social Research Review* 14, 4 (July 1983).

O'Carroll, J. P. "Strokes, Cute Hoors and Sneaking Regarders: The Influence of Local Culture on Irish Political Style," *Irish Political Studies* 2, 1 (1987).

O'Connor Lysaght, D. R. "British Imperialism in Ireland," in Austen Morgan and Bob Purdie, eds., *Ireland: Divided Nation, Divided Class* (London: Ink Links Press, 1980).

O'Connor, Robert and Philip Kelly. "Agriculture: Medium-Term Review and Outlook," in Brendan R. Dowling and Joe Durkan, eds., *Irish Economic Policy: A Review of The Issues* (Dublin: Economic and Social Research Institute, 1978).

Odell, John. *U.S. International Monetary Policy* (Princeton: Princeton University Press, 1982).

O'Donnell, Guillermo. "Reflections on the Patterns of Change in The Bureaucratic-Authoritarian State," *Latin American Research Review* 12, 2 (Winter 1978).

Modernization and Bureaucratic Authoritarianism: Studies in South American Politics (Berkeley: Institute of International Studies, University of California, 1973).

O'Hagan, John W. and Kevin P. McStay. *The Evolution of Manufacturing Industry in Ireland* (Dublin: Helicon Books, 1986).

O'Malley, Eoin. *The Irish Engineering Industry: Strategic Analysis and Policy Recommendations* (Dublin: Economic and Social Research Institute, September 1987).

"The Decline of Irish Industry in The Nineteenth Century," *Economic and Social Review* 12, 1 (October 1981).

Industrial Policy and Development: A Survey of The Literature From the Early 1960s (Dublin: Stationery Office, NESC Report No. 56, December 1980).

Organization for Economic Cooperation and Development *Interfutures: Facing The Future* (Paris: OECD, 1979).

O'Rourke, Desmond. "An Unofficial Appraisal of The Irish Economy," *Studies: An Irish Quarterly Review* 267, 2 (Autumn 1978).

Orridge, Anthony W. "The Blueshirts and The 'Economic War': A Study of Ireland in The Context of Dependency Theory," *Political Studies* 31, 3 (September 1983).

O'Toole, Fintan. "Highway Robbery," *Magill*, April 1988.

Olson, Mancur. *The Rise and Decline of Nations: Economic Growth Stagflation, and Social Rigidities* (New Haven: Yale University Press, 1982).

Panitch, Leo. "The Development of Corporatism in Liberal Democracies," *Comparative Political Studies* 10, 1 (April 1977).

Peillon, Michel. *Contemporary Irish Society* (Dublin: Gill and Macmillan, 1982).

Polanyi, Karl. *The Great Transformation* (Boston: Beacon Press, 1957).

Pollard, Sidney. *The Idea of Progress* (London: Pelican, 1968).

Ponting, Clive. *Breach of Promise: Labour in Power 1964–1970* (London: Penguin, 1990).

Poulantzas, Nicos. *State, Power, Socialism* (London: New Left Books, 1979).

The Crisis of The Dictatorships (London: New Left Books, 1976).

Prager, Jeffrey. *Building Democracy in Ireland: Political Order and Cultural Integration in A Newly Independent Nation* (Cambridge: Cambridge University Press, 1986).

Probert, Belinda. *Beyond Orange and Green: The Political Economy of The Northern Ireland Crisis* (London: Zed Press, 1978).

Przeworski, Adam. "Economic Reform in New Democracies: A Social Democratic Approach" (mimeo, 1992).

  Capitalism and Social Democracy (Cambridge: Cambridge University Press, 1985).

Przeworski, Adam, and Michael Wallerstein. "Democratic Capitalism At The Crossroads," *Democracy* 2 (July 1982).

Ross, George. "After Maastricht: Hard Choices in Europe," *World Policy Journal* 9, 3 (Summer 1992).

Rostow, W. W. *Politics and The Stages of Economic Growth* (London: Cambridge University Press, 1971).

  The Stages of Economic Growth: A Non-Communist Manifesto (London: Cambridge University Press, 1960).

Rudolph, Lloyd I. and Susanne H. *The Modernity of Tradition: Political Development in India* (Chicago: University of Chicago Press, 1967).

Rueschemeyer, Dietrich, Evelyn Huber Stephens, and John Stephens. *Capitalist Development and Democracy* (Oxford: Polity Press, 1992).

Ruggie, John Gerard, ed. *The Antinomies of Interdependence* (New York: Columbia University Press, 1983).

Rumpf, Erhard and A. C. Hepburn, *Nationalism and Socialism in Twentieth Century Ireland* (New York: Barnes and Noble, 1977).

Ryan, Louden. "Investment Criteria in Ireland," *Journal of The Statistical and Social Inquiry Society of Ireland* 11 (1961–62).

Sacks, Paul. *The Donegal Mafia: Machine Politics in The Irish Republic* (New Haven: Yale University Press, 1976).

Schmitt, David E. *The Irony of Irish Democracy* (Lexington, Mass: D. C. Heath, 1973).

Schmitter, Philippe C. "Still The Century of Corporatism?" in P. C. Schmitter and Gerhart Lehmbruch, eds., *Trends Toward Corporatist Intermediation* (Beverley Hills: Sage, 1979).

  Interest Conflict and Political Change in Brazil (Stanford: Stanford University Press, 1971).

Schumpeter, Joseph. *Capitalism, Socialism and Democracy* (New York: Harper and Row, 1975, 3rd ed.).

Scibberas, Edmund. *Multinational Electronic Companies and National Economic Policies* (Greenwich, Conn: JAI Press, 1977).

Shanks, Michael. *Planning and Politics: The British Experience 1960–76* (London: Allen and Unwin, 1977).

Shonfield, Andrew. *Modern Capitalism* (London: Oxford University Press, 1965).

Sinn Fein – The Workers Party. *The Irish Industrial Revolution* (Dublin: Repsol Publications, 1977).

Sinnott, Richard. "The Electorate," in Howard Penniman, ed., *Ireland At The Polls: The Dail Election of 1977* (Washington: American Enterprise Institute, 1978).

Sklar, Richard. *Corporate Power In An African State: The Political Impact of Multinational Mining Companies in Zambia* (Berkeley: University of California, 1975).

Smith, Raymond. *The Quest For Power: Haughey and O'Malley* (Dublin: Aherlow Press, 1986).

Smith, Tony. *The Pattern of Imperialism* (Cambridge: Cambridge University Press, 1981).

Stepan, Alfred. *The State and Society: Peru in Comparative Perspective* (Princeton: Princeton University Press, 1978).

Stephens, Evelyn and John Stephens. "Democratic Socialism in Dependent Capitalism: An Analysis of The Manley Government in Jamaica," *Politics and Society* 12, 3 (1983).

Stewart, James. "Aspects of The Financial Behaviour of Multinational Companies in Ireland," in Jim Fitzpatrick and John Kelly, eds., *Perspectives on Irish Industry* (Dublin: Irish Management Institute, 1986).

Strauss, Eric. *Irish Nationalism and British Democracy* (London: Methuen, 1953).

Sweeney, Paul. *The Politics of Public Enterprise and Privatisation* (Dublin: Tomar Press, 1990).

Sweeny, John. "Foreign Companies in Ireland," *Studies: An Irish Quarterly Review* 247/248, 62 (Autumn/Winter 1973).

Teeling, John. "The Evolution of Offshore Investment" (Ph.D. diss., Harvard Business School, 1975).

Trench, Brian. "Where Others Fear To Tread," *Magill*, January 1988.

Tufte, Edward. *The Political Control of The Economy* (Princeton: Princeton University Press, 1978).

Turner, Louis. *Multinationals and The Third World* (London: Croom Helm, 1974).

Vernon, Raymond. *Sovereignty At Bay* (New York: Basic Books, 1971).

Vilamil, Jose J. "Puerto Rico 1948–1976: The Limits of Dependent Growth," in J. J. Vilamil, ed., *Transnational Capitalism and National Development* (Atlantic Highlands, NJ: Humanities Press, 1978).

Vogel, David. "The Corporation as Government: Challenges and Dilemmas," *Polity* 8, 1 (Fall 1975).

Walsh, Dick. *The Party: Inside Fianna Fail* (Dublin: Gill and Macmillan, 1986).

Warren, Bill. *Imperialism: Pioneer of Capitalism* (London: New Left Books, 1982).

Weinz, Wolfgang. "Economic Development and Interest Groups," in Brian Girvan and Roland Sturm, eds., *Politics and Society in Contemporary Ireland* (London: Gower Press, 1986).

Whitaker, T. K. "From Protection To Free Trade," *Administration*, 25, 2 (1976).

White, Padraigh. "Industry in Ireland Today," in *Ireland in The Year 2000* (Dublin: An Foras Forbatha, 1980).

Whyte, John. *Church and State in Modern Ireland* (Dublin: Gill and Macmillan, 1982, 2nd ed.).

Wickham, Jim. "The Politics of Dependent Capitalism: International Capital and the Nation-State," in Austen Morgan and Bob Purdie, *Ireland: Divided Nation, Divided Class* (London: Ink Links, 1980).

Winner, Langdon. *Autonomous Technology: Technics out of Control As A Theme in Political Thought* (Cambridge, Mass: MIT Press, 1977).

Woodham-Smith, Cecil. *The Great Hunger* (New York: Signet, 1962).

Zolberg, Aristide. "Moments of Madness," in Ira Katznelson, Philip Brenner, and David Gordon, eds., *The Politics and Society Reader* (New York: David McKay, 1976).

Zysman, John. *Governments, Markets and Growth: Financial Systems and The Politics of Industrial Change* (Ithaca: Cornell University Press, 1983).

OFFICIAL PUBLICATIONS

Dail Eireann, Parliamentary Debates
Seanad Debates

Economic Development, 1958
Programme For Economic Expansion, 1958
Second Programme For Economic Expansion, 1964
Third Programme For Economic Expansion, 1969
Programme for National Recovery, 1987

National Industrial Economic Council (NIEC) Reports
National Economic and Social Council (NESC) Reports
Economic and Social Research Institute (ESRI) Reports

International Labor Organization (ILO) Reports
Organization for Economic Cooperation and Development (OECD) Reports
Irish Congress of Trade Unions, Annual Reports
US Chamber of Commerce Reports
US Department of Commerce Reports

Newspapers and periodicals
Irish Times
Irish Press
Irish Independent
Hibernia

Sunday Tribune
Trade Union Information
The Guardian (UK)
Magill

Index